THE WORTH OF PERSONS

THE WORTH OF PERSONS

The Foundation of Ethics

❖

James Franklin

BOOKS

NEW YORK · LONDON

First American edition published in 2022 by Encounter Books, an activity of
Encounter for Culture and Education, Inc., a nonprofit, tax-exempt corporation.
Encounter Books website address: www.encounterbooks.com

Manufactured in the United States and printed on acid-free paper.
The paper used in this publication meets the minimum requirements of
ANSI/NISO Z39.48–1992 (R 1997) (*Permanence of Paper*).

FIRST AMERICAN EDITION

LIBRARY OF CONGRESS CATALOGING-IN-PUBLICATION DATA

Names: Franklin, James, 1953– author.
Title: The worth of persons: the foundation of ethics / James Franklin.
Description: New York : Encounter Books, 2022. |
Includes bibliographical references and index. |
Identifiers: LCCN 2022002505 (print) | LCCN 2022002506 (ebook) |
ISBN 9781641772785 (hardcover) | ISBN 9781641772792 (ebook)
Subjects: LCSH: Ethics--Anthropological aspects. |
Philosophical anthropology. | Human beings.
Classification: LCC BJ52.F73 2022 (print) | LCC BJ52 (ebook) |
DDC 170 – dc23/eng/20220223
LC record available at https://lccn.loc.gov/2022002505
LC ebook record available at https://lccn.loc.gov/2022002506

1 2 3 4 5 6 7 8 9   20 22

CONTENTS

❖

INTRODUCTION

❖

"W<small>HAT A PIECE</small> of work is man," says Hamlet. "How noble in reason, how infinite in faculty, In form and moving how express and admirable, In action how like an Angel, In apprehension how like a god ..." Hamlet is right that possession of such properties as reason, apprehension, and the capacity to act confer on humans a moral weight, a nobility, dignity, or worth that makes it important what happens to humans and what they do.

What happens to humans can be a tragedy. What happens to rocks cannot. When we see pictures of atrocities, we understand that the victims were people like us, people who until their end possessed reason, apprehensions, personal unity, hopes, loves, and individuality as we do. That is what makes their death a tragedy and not, like the explosion of a lifeless galaxy, a firework. Gross metaphysical differences like that between humans and rocks imply gross moral differences.

If we turn to philosophical works on the foundations of ethics, the array of concepts is very different from talk of nobility, perfections, dignity, and tragedy. Those are found in classic literary texts, but in ethical works, discussion is all about right and wrong actions, consequences and rules, rights and duties, virtues and dilemmas. Those are all respectable ethical topics, but they are only central to ethics on a view of it as fundamentally about what to do (how to live, what actions are right and wrong). That is a very partial view of ethics. It skates over the surface, by disconnecting what humans ought to do from what sort of entities they are. Its superficiality often leads to painting ethics in pastel shades, as if it were a polite and reasoned discourse about subtle questions, infused with little sense of urgency.

The present work is philosophy, not literature. But it aims to reconnect ethical theory with the nature of the entities, mainly humans, to which ethics applies. It argues that the central foundational notion in ethics is the worth or dignity of persons. Chapter 1 explains how the "what to do" aspect of ethics depends on the worth of persons – for example, that the fundamental reason why murder is wrong is that it is the (deliberate) destruction of something of great worth (rather than its violating a rule, instantiating a vice, or subtracting from the greatest good of the greatest number). Rights, duties, virtues, harms, consequences are shown in Chapter 2 to be meaningful only because of the worth of the humans involved. The equality of persons, which is widely agreed to be crucial for the justice of social arrangements, itself needs a robust notion of worth so as to explain what it is about persons that is equal.

Chapter 3 contrasts the worth-of-persons approach to ethical foundations with other classical theories of ethics, such as evolutionary, divine command, Humean and Aristotelian views. That allows the nature and distinctiveness of the present approach to become clear.

It is then argued that human worth is a metaphysically strong notion, but one that is not freestanding. Worth supervenes on a number of properties which are not themselves explicitly ethical but which distinguish humans from other entities in the world – rationality, consciousness, the rational will, the unity and diversity of the self, emotional structure and love, individuality.

This, the central argument of the book, is distributed over several chapters. Chapter 4 argues, against the metaphysics-phobia of Rawls and others, that it is correct to search for properties of persons that will ground worth, and that the primary bearers of worth are substances (persons), rather than properties or activities of them such as knowledge, happiness, or life courses. Chapter 5 develops the notion of supervenience (or grounding), the relation between non-moral properties of humans such as rationality and the moral property of worth that arises from them. Supervenience is the usual notion found in metaphysics, an asymmetric, necessary relation by which some properties stand as a basis that necessarily gives rise to others – an example outside ethics is the way in which the evidence in a legal case grounds the rationality of a judgment that guilt has been proved beyond reasonable doubt. It is explained how supervenience deals with Hume's is-ought gap and Mackie's argument that moral properties are too "queer" to fit into a scientific world picture. Chapter 6 identifies what properties of humans do ground worth – not only rationality and consciousness but the ability to decide on the basis of reasons, the unified and diversified self, the emotional structure of persons and love, and individuality.

Chapter 7 considers the worth of the non-human parts of reality: both of animals that share a trace of properties such as rationality, and the non-animal environment, which has a quite different, "aesthetic," kind of intrinsic value. Chapter 8 then gives some explanation of how obligation arises from worth. But rules of conduct and guidance for action are not the aim of the project. The point of foundations is not to determine what to do; this is a book about the foundations of ethics, not about casuistry. It does not aim to produce exceptionless principles to resolve moral dilemmas, but to explain why they are dilemmas in the first place – why the two sides of dilemmas both have moral force. Foundational work should explain why killing in self-defense poses a moral dilemma – either choice leads to the death of a human – but should not resolve the question.

Finally, epistemology is addressed in Chapter 9. Knowing the bases of worth like rationality and consciousness is possible because we are rational and conscious. We also have some access to other people's consciousness and emotional structure by empathy and love. Knowing the supervenience of worth on those bases is possible because supervenience is such an intimate relation – although it can happen that some cause such as early deprivation results in an error like self-hate.

The Epilogue lays out briefly the problem of the compatibility or otherwise of the present realist theory of ethical foundations with various views of the cosmos, such as materialist atheism, pantheism, and personal theism. A metaphysics-heavy account of ethics is not fully complete without some explanation of how it fits into cosmology (since, for example, a strictly materialist view of the universe might be thought to undermine any robust notion of worth). But that is a project that will have to be pursued separately.

The ethical foundational theory developed here is loosely Kantian. But that means the realist Kant who defends human dignity and absolute inner worth, not the Kant who attempts to develop maxims on the basis of universalizability and to lay down exceptionless rules of conduct. The theory also has some Thomist elements, especially in taking seriously the Aristotelian notion of a perfection or excellence. The fact that worth supervenes on (inter alia) rationality means that the development of rationality is a perfection of humans, which explains why everyone has a right to education. While not utilitarian or consequentialist, the theory does take consequences seriously, since consequences are effects on beings of worth, so what happens to such beings matters absolutely.

The leading ideas of the theory of ethics developed here are:

- Ethics in the sense of what to do follows from something much more basic, the worth of persons.

- The foundations of ethics should not be approached with a phobia about metaphysics; beings that matter ethically, like humans, are inherently different from ones that don't, like stones.

- Worth belongs primarily to substances (full-blown entities), like humans, not to properties or activities of them like knowledge or life histories.

- The point of foundations is not to produce principles to decide difficult questions of what to do, but to explain why difficulties arise.

- Essential to ethics is the Aristotelian notion of a perfection or excellence.

- Humans are in contact with and subject to an ethical realm in the same way they are in contact with and subject to a realm of logic and evidence.

- The worth of persons is doubtfully compatible with a purely materialist view of the universe, but what alternative cosmology is sufficient is not easy to say.

Each of these is a minority position in ethical theory. The combination is unique.

CHAPTER ONE

Absolute Ethics and the Worth of Persons

ETHICS IS NOT fundamentally about what to do.[1]

Of course, questions of right and wrong, good and bad actions, rights and duties, virtues and vices, are an important part of ethics. But they are not *fundamentally* what ethics is about. That is for two reasons. First, what we are most disturbed by ethically – what most violently forces itself on us as ethically objective – is not anything to do with actions, but the terribleness of suffering. Second, whenever we ask *why* some action is right or wrong, we find we are led back to reasons that are not themselves about action but concern the good or evil of those affected by the action. For example, what makes the act of killing wrong is in the first place the evil of the death of the victim.

Let us take these two reasons in turn, in order to understand what is most central to ethics.

EVIL AND ABSOLUTENESS

When we are confronted with pictures of genocide victims dug up, those of Srebrenica, for example, we know, "Those were people like us, and something terrible happened to them." Our emotional reaction gives us an immediate insight into the violation and destruction of something of immense value, a human life. It is gross violations of the right to life that most immediately impose on us a sense of the objective inviolability of human worth. That is where we first understand how it is that ethics is objective – that good and evil matter in some absolute sense and that right and wrong cannot all be a matter of mere opinion or personal choice.

If we then see pictures of victims of a natural evil as at Pompeii, we again think, "Those were people like us, and something terrible happened to them," even though no rights were violated as no actions caused their deaths. The notion of an evil happening, in the sense of a human tragedy, is separate from that of an evil deed. Both are ethically significant, but in different ways. No one is to be blamed for natural tragedies, but we have duties to prevent or mitigate natural evils, if we can.

To be skeptical about something as ethically basic as the terribleness of the evil suffered by victims of genocide (or natural evil) would be not only a mistake but an evil act against the victims. Raimond Gaita writes in *Good and Evil: An Absolute Conception*:

> The person who says that we must consider the argument that morality may be an illusion says that we must in intellectual conscience question, and if the argument goes a certain way have the courage to deny, the reality of the evil which at other times we think it our duty to remember. Of course no one is really serious about it. But who would confidently say that such frivolity is without consequence?[2]

No doubt, objectivity can be found also in the demandingness of ethical commands, or in the absoluteness of rights and the nobility of virtues. But those do not have the same immediacy or urgency. It might be almost conceivable to suspect that absoluteness claims for commands or rights are a production of self-righteous fanatics certain of their own rectitude. But not evils. As Roy Holland puts the question, "When you learned of those monstrosities were you not horrified and did you not absolutely condemn them?"[3]

Horror is an emotional as well as a rational reaction. To lack the emotions necessary to understand what the suffering of victims is like would be to miss out on a crucial source of ethical understanding. It is indeed possible to lack those emotions, as can happen with severe autistics.[4] It is possible to override them, as with suicide bombers and soldiers under orders to commit atrocities. But doing so is either a symptom or a cause of serious damage to one's humanity. Ethical theory, too, can lack humanity if it does not give a central place to direct recognition of the worth and suffering of people.

"Direct" and "emotional" does not mean either "infallible" or "contrary to reason." There must be some rational explanation as to why worth gives rise where appropriate to those emotional reactions and an account of when they can be trusted. It must be explained, too, how such emotional reactions are cognitive – for one thing, understanding suffering is a form of *understanding*. It is part of the aim of this book to provide such explanations. At the same time it would be overthinking the case to require that we interpose such reasons between our awareness of human suffering and our recognition of its evil. Our direct awareness of evil is the phenomenon to be explained (and not explained away) by any philosophical account.

The close relation of right and wrong to a direct awareness of evil is one of the points of Jesus's parable of the Good Samaritan, a favorite story of both believers and non-believers. In response to the question "Who is my neighbor?" Jesus tells the story of a Jew attacked by robbers and left half-dead beside the road. Two strict religious officials pass by on the other side, but a Samaritan, a member of a normally hostile group, "feels compassion for him" (or "takes pity on him") and stops to help and to take care that he is nursed back to health.[5] To avoid responding to a victim left for dead beside the road is to fail in our common humanity, what Jesus calls "being a neighbor." What makes the Samaritan's action a good or right one is not a rule or a virtue but the ethical significance of the victim who is in urgent need of assistance.

It is especially in such extreme cases of evil that we are forced to admit our sense of the worth of persons, but we can equally become aware of it in more positive and ordinary circumstances. Indeed the normal daily experience of low-key mutual positive affirmation among friends, family, and colleagues has the purpose of affirming human worth. In normal life, we assure people of their worth because we believe in that worth.

The recognition of human worth immediately raises difficult questions such as: What is it about humans that gives them this worth? Do they have equal worth? Do other entities such as animals, gods, and rainforests have it to some degree? How do we know about worth? Surely pure emotional reactions – perhaps culturally shaped – are not reliable guides to ethical reality, so how can they be calibrated? Is worth a natural property or something mysterious? Is all of ethics reducible to (or deducible from) facts about worth, or is there more to it? Does an approach based on worth favor utilitarianism, deontology, natural law, virtue theory, or something else? Those are fair questions. Direct emotional reactions to sufferers will not answer them. They will be addressed in due course. But compared to the objectivity of the worth of persons, they are matters of fine detail. Just now, let us deepen our appreciation of how many of the central concerns of ethics are very direct outcomes of human worth.

MORAL PROGRESS AND REGRESS
ON THE WORTH OF PERSONS

The twentieth century saw both progress and regress on the worth of persons. It was a century of widespread horrors, but in countries where those were contained, the life of ordinary citizens came to be protected by assumptions of their rights and worth. A brief review will show how the concept of human worth either did or did not have purchase in what happened, and the difference it made.

The human-induced tragedies of the Holocaust and the Gulag are within living memory, and repeated in this century in the Middle East and North Korea. Hannah Arendt explains how the systems that caused those events were assaults on humanity in a way that went beyond just the sum of the individual deaths. "Suffering, of which there has been always too much on earth, is not the issue, nor is the number of victims. Human nature as such is at stake."[6] What happened was different in a way that exceeded earlier practices:

> The Western world has hitherto, even in its darkest periods, granted the slain enemy the right to be remembered as a self-evident acknowledgment of the fact that we are all men (and only men). It is only because even Achilles set out for Hector's funeral, only because the most despotic governments honored the slain enemy, only because the Romans allowed the Christians to write their martyrologies, only because the Church kept its heretics alive in the memory of men, that all was not lost and never could be lost. The concentration camps, by making death itself anonymous (making it impossible to find out whether a prisoner is dead or alive) robbed death of its meaning as the end of a fulfilled life. In a sense they took away the individual's own death, proving that henceforth nothing belonged to him and he belonged to no one.[7]

The aim is depersonalization, to treat a human person as having none of the dignity that belongs to humans:

> The first essential step on the road to total domination is to kill the juridical person in man. This was done, on the one hand, by putting certain categories of people outside the protection of the law and forcing at the same time, through the instrument of denationalization, the nontotalitarian world into recognition of lawlessness; it was done, on the other, by

placing the concentration camp outside the normal penal system, and by selecting its inmates outside the normal judicial procedure in which a definite crime entails a predictable penalty....The next decisive step in the preparation of living corpses is the murder of the moral person in man. This is done in the main by making martyrdom, for the first time in history, impossible[8] [as the deaths were anonymous and there were no surviving witnesses].

In consequence, "the human masses sealed off in [the camps] are treated as if they no longer existed, as if what happened to them were no longer of interest to anybody, as if they were already dead."[9] The purpose of cattle trucks was symbolic as well as logistic. The aims were not purely utilitarian. "Among the keenest pleasures of power is to violate human dignity."[10]

We hope, whether confidently or not, that the community of states in which such things do not happen will continue to make the running in world history.

Arendt's remark that the Western tradition always took notice of the individual is partly true, and certainly true in comparison with modern totalitarianism. But absolutely speaking, it is not entirely accurate as history. "Life is cheap" assumptions of earlier times mark a difference from the present. Such events as the Romans' crucifying six thousand followers of Spartacus's slave revolt along the Appian Way, or the huge toll of Chinese coolies to push through the British Columbia section of the Canadian Pacific Railway,[11] or the massive casualties taken for granted by commanders in World War I, are recognized as contrary to current moral understandings. In well-run countries, everyone has benefited from the translation of these ideals into legal terms, with such advances as the abolition of slavery, the Universal Declaration of Human Rights, and the extension of basic health and rescue services to cover everyone. The history of the containment of industrial accidents by legal means is one among many success stories of gradual protective measures for life and limb extending to all.[12] Expendability of people is no longer taken for granted. (There is, of course, some way to go for those outside the boundaries of the First World, and for some inside.)

Western thought and practice has in recent decades also become more sensitive to those moral faults that directly attack victims' sense of personal worth, such as racism, discrimination against persons of lesser power in society, intolerance, and bullying. It is clear how those assaults on the dignity of persons are directly related to the worth of persons. Their failure to respect that worth is exactly what is wrong with them.

(In this work we will not attempt to distinguish between "dignity" and "worth." The word "dignity" has some tendency to be associated with the more symbolic aspects of humanity, so that an offense to one's dignity, or "an indignity," is usually an insult or humiliation rather than a physical assault.[13] But in more common usage, "worth" and "dignity" are interchangeable.)

We have achieved, too, a better understanding of the evils of those health conditions and events that undermine persons' sense of self-worth, such as depression and abuse. It is a tragedy when a person – necessarily of great worth – believes otherwise and comes to lack care for their own survival. Or indeed if a whole class or race takes on servility, believing that its only value is to build Pharaoh's pyramid.[14] We understand, too, how a sense of self-worth is necessary for a sense of moral agency, a sense that can be fragile and might be undermined by a belief such as that one has hysteria.[15]

All those developments, positive and negative, show how ingrained in our cultural assumptions the worth of persons has become. Any work on the foundations of ethics should give a central place to those assumptions.

WHAT MAKES ACTIONS RIGHT OR WRONG?

The worth of persons is not the usual place to start in ethics. The range of topics commonly spoken of in ethics includes rules of right and wrong action, virtues, values, consequences, rights, obligations, dilemmas, and so on. But when we look below the surface of each of them, we find that they lead back to the worth of persons, and that they are unintelligible without that concept.

The aim at present is not to deduce moral rules, virtues, and so on, from the worth of persons. How possible that is will be considered later. For now the aim is to show that the worth of persons is necessary for rules and virtues, rather than sufficient. Rules, rights, and virtues, it is argued, make no sense without reference to worth.[16]

Often ethics is taken to be primarily about deciding what actions are right and wrong, and what rules we should follow in so deciding. Is taking a bribe ever right? Are "Thou shalt not kill" and "Do to others as you would have them do to you" correct rules of action, always or often? What ought I do and not do?

Of course, how we should act is ethically important. But action is *for* something (whether external or internal to the actor), and the rightness of the action depends heavily on the rightness of the purpose and the value of the outcome. The value of an outcome is not itself a property of an action.

One way to recognize that there must be something ethically more basic than action is to consider how we think about whether rules should have exceptions. A list of rules cannot be the ultimate answer to basic ethical questions. We can always ask whether a rule is right – or not right, or right generally but with exceptions. We often do ask that question, and we have resources to answer it. For example, we ask about the rule "Thou shalt not kill," could killing in self-defense be allowed? Surely protecting myself is good, since my being killed is bad. The *reason* for the rule "Thou shalt not kill" is that being killed is bad, and that is not about rules of action, it is about the evil of being dead. The very reason for the rule implies that it could have an exception in the case of self-defense. Whatever we decide in the end about the allowability of self-defense, the debate about it forces us to think about the reasons that lie behind the rules. Those reasons must be more ethically basic than the rules themselves.

The same reasoning applies to the dilemmas that are a staple of teaching in school and undergraduate ethics: such as "If a lifeboat can't hold everyone, who should go first?" or "Should we push one person in front of a trolley to save five?" While there may be better and worse answers to such dilemmas, what they primarily reveal is how strongly we prefer not to "solve" them, because we value all the people in the dilemma equally and we resist having to sacrifice any one. That is what makes the situation difficult. It is a dilemma because we are strongly committed to the worth of each one, of each potential victim of a "solution." Eager students rush to solve the dilemmas, and to construct ever more inventive hypotheticals. But from the point of view of foundations, the interesting question is what makes a dilemma a dilemma in the first place – what is the origin of the competing considerations that give each horn of the dilemma its moral weight? Typically, that weight results from the worth of the different persons affected.

Given that the worth of persons is essential to at least the most important ethical rules and considerations, two questions arise about the relation of worth to rules. First, what exactly is the relation of worth (a feature of entities such as persons) and rules (commands about what actions are right)? Second, does the worth of persons imply or explain all moral rules, or only some? If only some, where do the rest come from?

It is true that some of the later commandments of the Decalogue, such as "Do not bear false witness" and "Do not steal" are not easily explained directly in terms of the worth of persons, at least in the obvious way of "Do not kill." While in normal circumstances, to lie to someone or steal from them in some way treats them as a means and not an end (in Kant's terminology), and hence regards them as of lesser worth, there must be some further explanation of why those particular actions have that implication. Indeed, even the very basic ethical rule that it is wrong to cause pain to people, without good reason, is not obviously reducible to the worth of persons: It needs also some premise about why pain is an evil for people. We will consider how rules of obligation arise from worth in Chapter 8.

In the meantime, we continue to develop the theme that the worth of persons is essential to morality, without asserting that it is the whole of it.

ASSUMPTIONS UNDERLYING COMMON MORALITY

Intuitions can be firmed up by noticing that a sense of the worth of persons is implicit in how almost all of us (at least in modern Western society) think about morality. That is a theme of Alan Donagan's *The Theory of Morality*. The definite article in his title is important. He argues that there is a coherent theory underlying the general moral outlook and behavior of all (normal) people, though it is not necessarily consciously expressed. Rules of ethics are not basic. Instead, the normal rules of behavior are generated by the more fundamental assumption that persons are valuable in themselves. He writes:

> I take the fundamental principle of that part of traditional morality which is independent of any theological presupposition to have been expressed in the scriptural commandment, 'Thou shalt love thy neighbour as thyself', understanding one's neighbour to be any human being, and love to be, not a matter of feeling, but of acting in ways in which human

beings as such can choose to act. The philosophical sense of this commandment was correctly expressed by Kant in his formula that one act so that one treats humanity always as an end and never as a means.[17]

All moral rules, Donagan maintains, even very detailed ones about specific cases, should be deducible from this general principle, with enough effort. Thus it is possible to say why the prohibition against murder might be reconsidered in the case of capital punishment: The destruction of the life of one person is balanced against the destruction of life of the criminal's victims, actual or potential, and that is a consideration of the same nature as the one that led to the prohibition of murder in general. Rights arise in the same way: A right to life is simply the wrongness of destruction of a life, seen from the point of view of the person living the life.

So if we start with the conception of ethical theory, common in analytic philosophy since Sidgwick, that its task is to start with "intuitions" about particular cases, refine and clarify them, and extract principles from which they follow,[18] then, according to Donagan, what we arrive at is an ethic based on the worth of persons. (Whether this promise can be fulfilled will need more discussion.)

A similar thought is found in Bernard Gert. His aim, like Donagan's, is to analyze the common system of morality. He is impressed with Hobbes's view that the system of morality has one main purpose, namely peace. That is, its purpose is much more about the avoidance of serious harms than the promotion of important goods. "Morality," says Gert, "is an informal public system applying to all rational persons, governing behavior that affects others, and includes what are commonly known as the moral rules, ideals, and virtues and has the lessening of evil or harm as its goal."[19] Plainly the common rules of morality do have at least a strong focus on reducing harm, such as prohibitions on interpersonal violence and the deliberate infliction of risks. The notion of harm – Gert lists the basic harms as death, pain, disability, loss of freedom, and loss of pleasure – is meaningful only if there is a being of intrinsic worth to whom harm can happen.[20] Harms are only of serious concern if they happen to something of worth. It does make some minimal sense to speak of the disability or loss of pleasure of a cockroach, but it matters very little. Correspondingly, harm to humans is objectively important because of the worth of humans themselves.

A third author is Sam Harris. In *The Moral Landscape*, he suggests that the technical vocabulary of "metaethics," "noncognitivism," and the like fails to engage with serious issues and urges concentrating on the difference between an obviously very bad and an obviously very good human life. In one scenario, a young widow is about to be killed in the jungle after a life witnessing little but abuse and atrocities. In the other, a happily married, healthy, and privileged Westerner has won a large grant to help children in the Third World. The obvious difference between the two lives he describes as one of "well-being."[21] That may be a weak word, but it rightly calls attention to the state of being of humans, a state which is objectively of concern because humans are inherently worth being concerned about.

KANT AND MOORE

These recent authors, however, lack the clarity of two classical writers on ethics. These older writers serve as a reminder that the focus on action in ethics since their times is not the only possible direction for ethical inquiry.

Donagan's reference to Kant is to the point. Behind his action-oriented remarks about universalizablity and duty that have been the inspiration of much later "Kantian" ethics, Kant himself is insistent on the fundamental dependence of ethics on the moral importance of the human person[22]:

Man regarded as a *person*, that is, as the subject of a morally practical reason, is exalted above any price, for as a person he is not to be valued merely as a means to the ends of others, or even to his own ends, but as an end in himself, that is, he possesses a *dignity* [*Würde*] (an absolute inner worth [*Werth*]) by which he exacts *respect* for himself from all other rational beings in the world. He can measure himself with every other being of this kind and value himself on a footing of equality with them.[23]

That represents an uncompromising commitment to the worth of persons as essential to ethical foundations, a commitment that must be revived.

G. E. Moore does not speak of the worth of persons or any equivalent. What he does is to distinguish clearly between the *good* (whatever it is that has worth absolutely) and the *right* (concerning actions). In the Preface to *Principia Ethica*, he breezily ascribes the ills, past and present, of ethical theory to moral philosophers' failure to keep separate two different questions, namely, "What kind of things ought to exist for their own sakes?" (or "What is good?") and "What kind of actions ought we to perform?" (or "What makes an action a morally right one?"). He writes:

I have tried in this book to distinguish clearly two kinds of question, which moral philosophers have always professed to answer, but which, as I have tried to shew, they have almost always confused both with one another and with other questions. These two questions may be expressed, the first in the form: What kind of things ought to exist for their own sakes? the second in the form: What kind of actions ought we to perform? I have tried to shew exactly what it is that we ask about a thing, when we ask whether it ought to exist for its own sake, is good in itself or has intrinsic value; and exactly what

it is that we ask about an action, when we ask whether we
ought to do it, whether it is a right action or duty.[24]

While self-evident truths alone are capable of grounding answers to
the first question, he contends, solutions to the second question will
need to incorporate, in addition, causal empirical truths pertaining
to the results of actions.

Whether or not we accept Moore's further views that good is
indefinable or that what has intrinsic value is mainly states of consciousness – the choice of category for the bearers of intrinsic worth
will be considered in Chapter 4 – his identification of intrinsic worth
as a basic topic of ethical inquiry, independent of any connections
with action, is essential for starting ethics in the right place.

CHAPTER TWO

Rights, Duties, Virtues, Values, Consequences, Dilemmas

◈

We saw that rules of ethical behavior, or at least many of the most basic ones, led back to and were explained by the worth of persons.

We next examine how many of the other fauna in the ethics zoo keep leading back to the worth of persons and do not make sense without it. That is so despite the best intentions of those who defend them as the central concepts in ethics without reference to worth.

The aim at present is not to deduce anything about virtues, rights, values, and so on, from the first principle of worth of persons. (How exactly obligation relates to worth will be considered in Chapter 7.) It is just to show that the worth of persons is an essential component of discussion of those things – that it is a necessary part, rather than a sufficient foundation for solving all the problems.

It is sometimes said that there are three major approaches to ethics: the deontological (emphasizing rules or duties); the consequentialist (emphasizing outcomes); and virtue ethics (emphasizing character). From the point of view of worth, all three are superficial if they are meant as accounts of foundations. For all of them, on examination (and no very deep examination either), point to worth as a necessary and deeper ingredient of ethics.

RIGHTS

The concept of human rights has become a mainstay of objectivist views of ethics, and rightly so. The late twentieth century saw two long-term trends in popular thinking about ethics. One was an increase in relativist opinions, with the "generation of the Sixties" spearheading a general libertarianism, an insistence on toleration of diverse moral views (for "Who is to say what is right? – it's only your opinion."). The other trend was an increasing insistence on rights. The gross violations of rights in the killing fields of the mid-century prompted immense efforts in defense of the "inalienable" rights of the victims of dictators, of oppressed peoples, of refugees. The obvious incompatibility of those ethical stances, one anti-objectivist, the other objectivist in the extreme, proved no obstacle to their both being held passionately, often by the same people.

The account of the Helsinki rights movement in Tony Judt's magisterial history of late-twentieth-century Europe, *Postwar,* demonstrates the huge power of rights as a moral and political weapon in the major historical event of the late twentieth century, the fall of the Soviet empire:

> In August 1975 the Helsinki Accords were unanimously approved and signed [between the major Eastern and Western countries]. On the face of things, the Soviet Union was the main beneficiary of the Accords.... it was agreed that the 'participating states will respect each other's sovereign equality....'
>
> But also included ... was a list of rights not just of states, but of persons and peoples, grouped under Principle VII ('Respect for human rights and fundamental freedoms, including the freedom of thought, conscience, religion or belief') and VIII ('Equal rights and self-determination of

peoples'.) Most of the political leaders who signed off on these clauses paid them little attention – on both sides of the Iron Curtain it was generally assumed that they were diplomatic window dressing, a sop to domestic opinion, and in any case unenforceable....

It did not work out that way.... From this wordy and, it seemed, toothless list of rights and obligations was born the Helsinki Rights movement. Within a year of getting their long-awaited international conference agreement, Soviet leaders were faced with a growing and ultimately uncontrollable flowering of circles, clubs, networks, charters and individuals, all demanding 'merely' that their governments stick to the letter of that same agreement.... Hoist on the petard of their own cynicism, Leonid Brezhnev and his colleagues had inadvertently opened a breach in their own defenses. Against all expectation, it was to prove mortal.[1]

Reference to rights serves as a reminder of how strongly most people are committed to objective ethics – most people believe that basic rights cannot be overridden by anyone's decision (even, for example, a majority decision of a parliament). Healthy legal systems act to protect rights from violations by powerful interest groups, including states. Less healthy polities disparage human rights as "Western values," despite heroic attempts by some of their own citizens in defense of their rights.[2]

The way appeal to rights works in political and legal discourse is as bedrock, as a moral notion of last resort. The Universal Declaration of Human Rights was so successful partly because it laid down rights without any explanation of where they come from. The Declaration did go so far as to say that "all human beings are born free and equal in dignity and rights,"[3] but offered no philosophical explanation of why. In fact, that was because its drafters agreed on the rights themselves but failed to reach agreement on the source of rights. When the Lebanese Thomist delegate wanted God included and the Brazilian delegation suggested reference to man being made in the image of God, the Chinese delegate absolutely refused to consider any such Western metaphysical and theological extravagances, with the result that the origin of rights was left out entirely.[4] In retrospect, that was fortunate, as it allowed the Declaration to be widely accepted. That makes sense politically, but not philosophically.

For surely rights, too, are not basic. If rights are thought of as free-standing, as if they themselves could serve as a basis for ethics, they would deserve Bentham's jibe that they are "nonsense upon stilts," since they would be anomalous entities not fitting into any wider theory. But reference to the worth of persons can supply an explanation. What is it about humans that means they have rights? We have a right to life *because* our life is valuable, not vice versa. As Wolterstorff writes, "The UN declarations are all dignity-based documents. All of them affirm or assume that human rights accrue to human beings on account of the dignity that human beings possess, the worth, the excellence, the estimability" (and he adds that that must lead to a search for what it is about humans that gives them that worth or dignity).[5] The Helsinki Accords themselves say that human rights "derive from the inherent dignity of the human person."[6] The rights of the Universal Declaration, such as the right to education, refer to the human beings for whom those goods are necessary. Humans have a right to education because they have the rationality to be educated, while animals don't. That is a fact about humans, necessary and sufficient to support the right to be educated. Simply being human is sufficient and necessary to possess a right to life, because the worth of humans is what places a moral barrier in the way of any attempt to destroy human life. If there were no such thing as the worth or dignity of humans, there would be no purchase for the concept of rights; there would be nothing about humans in virtue of which they would deserve rights.

Gregory Vlastos links worth to those rights which are independent of merit. Certain rights may depend on merit, such as rights to reward, but a right to a fair trial is not like that. He writes:

> We acknowledge personal rights which are not proportioned to merit and could not be justified by merit. Their only justification could be the value which persons have simply because they are persons: their "intrinsic value as individual human beings," as Frankena calls it, the "infinite value" or the "sacredness" of their individuality, as others have called it. I shall speak of it as "individual human worth," or "human worth," for short.[7]

The concept of a right is also tightly connected to the concept of being wronged, which itself involves the concept of an insult to or violation of one's worth. As Jean Hampton explains:

> What is it that really bothers us about being wronged?... However much we may sorrow after bad fortune, when the same damage is threatened or produced by natural forces or by accident, we do not experience that special anger that comes from having been *insulted*. When someone wrongs another, she does not regard her victim as the sort of person who is valuable enough to require better treatment. Whereas nature cannot treat us in accord with our moral value, we believe other human beings are able and required to do so. Hence when they do not, we are insulted in the sense that we believe they have ignored the high standing that value gives us.[8]

Dworkin similarly argues that the most basic human right, a right more abstract and lying behind particular rights such as those in the Universal Declaration, is the right to an attitude, "the right to be treated *as* a human being whose dignity fundamentally matters."[9]

It is true that the prevalence of rights talk has led to certain justified complaints about the overuse of the notion. The language of rights has been subject to "strong inflationary pressures on the term that have brought about its debasement,"[10] and thus often co-opted for political purposes so as to support a great range of implausible claimed entitlements.[11] Those hijackings are a tribute to the inherent political power of the idea of rights; they are not good reasons for doubting the whole idea of rights.

It is true also that in a sense the notion of rights is not an appropriate foundation of ethical obligation in general because it is morally thin. Simone Weil explains why the appeal to rights does not bear enough weight in important cases:

> If you say to someone who has ears to hear: 'What you are doing to me is not just', you may touch and awaken at its source the spirit of attention and love. But it is not the same with words like 'I have the right...' or 'you have no right to...' They evoke a latent war and awaken the spirit of contention. To place the notion of rights at the centre of social conflict is to inhibit any possible impulse of charity on both sides.
>
> Relying almost exclusively on this notion it becomes impossible to keep one's eyes on the real problem. If someone tries to browbeat a farmer to sell his eggs at a moderate price, the farmer can say: 'I have the right to keep my eggs if I don't get a good enough price.' But if a young girl is being forced into a brothel she will not talk about her rights. In such a situation the word would sound ludicrously inadequate.[12]

That is true, but it does not imply that there is anything wrong with the notion of rights. It is just that the concept is a kind of shadow on the public world of what is really essential to ethics. When the Helsinki Rights movement demanded the Soviet government "merely" respect the rights that had been agreed to, they meant that rights were a minimal standard, the last barrier to transgression. And Weil's comments belong to the 1930s, before rights talk had the moral significance it later came to have. Only after the Holocaust and similar events did the phrase "violations of human rights" come to be used of the gravest of assaults on persons.

Nor is it relevant that rights talk "tends towards individualistic accounts of society and underwrites a view of human relations as exchanges rather than cooperative endeavours."[13] Oppressed people demanding their rights would welcome cooperative endeavors on their behalf, but minimal respect for their rights is much less than that and will suffice. Cooperation and love are desirable add-ons, but a right is a hard boundary. Talk of rights alone is certainly a one-sided view of ethics, but one that highlights a particular kind of attacks on the worth of persons.

Those misuses of rights talk highlight what is correct about the central notion of rights. What is valuable about rights talk is exactly that it focuses on the "recipient-dimension, the patient-dimension"[14] of action, unlike, for example, obligation talk or guilt talk or virtue talk. "The reason the language of rights has proved so powerful in social protest movements is that it brings the victims and their moral condition into the light of day."[15] It sees actions or potential actions from the point of view of the person being acted on. Does the worth of that person, their inviolable dignity, place any limit on the proposed action? That is the first question to be asked, before any inquiry as to the place of the action in the moral code, or in the life of virtue or flourishing of the actor.

What has been said so far does not imply that humans have *equal* rights, or that, if so, they are based on equal worth. There are difficulties with that notion.[16] The question of equality of worth will be examined in Chapter 4.

DUTIES

In one way, duties are correlative with rights and so any story about rights will flow through to an account of duties. For example, a right to asylum does not mean much unless it imposes on some actual persons the duty to grant asylum. The right and the duty arise from the person's need existing at the same time as the ability of someone else to deal with it. So duties refer to intrinsic worth if and only if rights do.

The origin of duties in the worth of persons is confirmed by the existence of duties for which it is hard to pin down correlative rights. If I have the normal wealth of a first-world adult, I have a duty of charity, a duty to give some of my surplus wealth to help those in need. It may be hard to identify any particular individual who has a right to a portion of my wealth or a right to be admitted to my country as a refugee. Nevertheless, the existence of the poor, whose poverty is in many cases so severe as to prevent their living lives worthy of humans, is a standing reproach to my indulgence. If there were no such people, or if it were impossible to work out how to aid them effectively, I would have no duty of charity – I might as well use my wealth to fund my champagne lifestyle. My duty, imprecise as it is, thus arises from the worth of the persons who lack something important to being human and who could be aided by people in positions like mine. Their needs propagate through the network of possible actions by many actors, generating duties when they reach actual people.

Nevertheless, Kant's theory of the special place of duty in human moral perfection suggests there is something more to the moral quality of duties than just as correlates of rights. Kant asks, What are the ends that are also duties?, and answers, They are *one's own perfection* and *the happiness of others*.[17] Neither of those is closely related to correlative rights (except that part of the "happiness of others" that concerns avoiding the violation of their rights).

It makes no sense to say I have a right against myself. But if I willfully fail to learn anything when provided with normal educational opportunities, I have failed in a duty to myself. That is because the kind of being I am requires knowledge for its excellence (as described further in Chapter 8). The worth of humans, as is commonly believed and will be argued in Chapter 6, is closely tied to their rationality, so any contempt shown toward my rationality as such, by myself just as much by others, diminishes my worth. So my duty to educate myself arises from my worth in a different way from the duty of others not to violate my right to life. But its grounding in worth is still clear.

Therefore, while a commitment to duty is admirable in itself – perhaps, as Kant says, the most admirable thing in itself – it is still true that duty is not morally freestanding or an appropriate starting place for ethics. Something is a duty only if there is a need for the action (or refraining from action) which there is a duty to do. If I see someone fall in the river and get into difficulties, my action to help them is admirable, but the duty is generated directly by their need. (An account of why one person's need does generate moral obligation on another will be given in Chapter 8.) No need on the recipient's part, no duty on another's. And "need" only has moral significance if the being having the need is of moral worth.

VIRTUES AND CHARACTER

According to "virtue-based ethics," the main point of ethics is neither rules nor individual right actions, but living the "good life" of justice, courage, temperance, and so on. It was a dominant approach of ancient ethics, relegated to near obscurity in the nineteenth century in favor of rules, duties, and consequences,[18] revived in recent decades.[19] Ethical endeavor, on this view, should primarily aim at creating a right character, which will then issue in right action. "Ethics may be briefly defined as the doctrine of human character."[20]

The strength of virtue theory is to point out that what is

especially admirable is not just a series of right actions or the consequences of right actions, but the inner disposition from which they issue. A series of right actions, all chosen for the right reasons, are indeed individually admirable, but they do not have the unity that comes from their being expressions of a fixed inner disposition. A hero or saint that we are inspired to imitate, or feel we ought to be inspired to imitate, is not a collection of actions but a person whose qualities are revealed by those actions.

Virtues are important, but they, too, on examination, point to something more basic than themselves, based in the fundamental worth of persons. They do that in two ways: first, by their orientation to action, and second, via the ethical value of the creation of character, which only makes sense if the entity possessing the character is itself of ethical worth.

First, the connection between virtue and right action is logically tight. True, which comes first is debatable. It may seem that virtue is logically prior to the rightness of actions. It may be argued, in Aristotelian fashion, as Gary Watson summarizes it:

(1) Living a characteristically human life (functioning well as a human being) requires possessing and exemplifying certain traits T.

(2) T are therefore human excellences and render their possessors to that extent good human beings.

(3) Acting in way W is in accordance with T (or exemplifies or is contrary to T).

(4) Therefore W is right (good or wrong).[21]

To the contrary, it has been argued that "the concept of a moral virtue is conceptually posterior to the concept of a morally admirable act. A moral virtue is the habit of performing morally excellent acts of a certain sort in a certain way."[22] Either way, plainly the interrelation between character and right action is very close. It need not be decided here whether one is prior to the other. Virtue theory certainly concentrates on that aspect of right action according to which it is an outcome of a fixed disposition of a person. In that case, what has already been said about the reliance of right action on the idea of the worth of persons is inherited by the virtues.

More than that, however, surely virtues are *for* something outside themselves. A virtuous character by itself would be a kind of Heath Robinson machine, narcissistically active for no external purpose. A proposed virtue that does have an inward-looking character, like asceticism, is regarded with suspicion or at best ranked low among virtues. In general, a virtue is a habit of right action, or at least a disposition to try to act rightly. For example, the point of courage is to enable necessary action to protect life or health in dangerous situations. The worth of the life to be protected is what gives ethical point to both the courageous action and courage itself. A similar character trait such as foolhardiness is not a virtue because it does not have that connection to what needs to be done for the sake of persons. Courage, justice, and charity are generally outward-directed, to the protection or benefit of persons other than the actor, while temperance largely benefits the actor himself and prudence benefits both the actor and others. But the point of all of them is benefit to a person, who possesses worth.

That is still true if a virtue is taken to be directed not so much toward individual actions as toward the "good life." "A virtue," it is said, "is a character trait a human being needs for *eudaimonia,* to flourish or live well,"[23] a definition that summarizes the classical tradition from Homer to Aquinas.[24] In that case, virtue has a point because of its relation to what is good for humans, and thus depends on humans themselves and what happens to them being inherently worthwhile.

But the other-directedness of virtue is not the whole story. The concept of a "human excellence" is crucial to the theory of virtues. Virtue theorists are right to say that there is something admirable about a virtuous character over and above the right actions that it enables. We rightly admire a person's reliability that we can lean on when our backs are to the wall. We do so even if no occasion arises for the exercise of that virtue.

The Greek *arete* means "excellence" as much as "virtue." The point of an excellence is that it is not for something but admirable in itself (even if it serves some purpose as well, as in "well-oiled machine"). It is not just a tool for living the good life, though it will help with that. Virtues are qualities admirable, or beautiful, in themselves in Homer, and in the list Saint Paul chooses to associate with the word, "whatever is true, whatever is honorable, whatever is just, whatever is pure, whatever is lovely, whatever is gracious, if there is any excellence (*arete*), if there is anything worthy of praise, think about these things."[25]

As virtues are human excellences, humans have duties to develop them, over and above duties to perform individual right actions. Someone who neglects the development of moral virtue, for example by allowing themselves to become arrogant and self-centered, thereby offends against their own worth. Someone who struggles to do what is right and realize their potential, as their circumstances allow, is admirable irrespective of how many right actions they are able to achieve. In that sense, virtue ethics has the advantage of being applicable to the disabled.

It is true that too much focus on one's virtue may tend toward self-centeredness or narcissism. That in itself is not a problem for virtue theory. Almost any good may be taken to excess, without that implying it is not a genuine good. But it does suggest that virtue theory should at the very least be complemented by some other ethical perspective, such as rights theory, that reminds us that "it's not all about me."

Much the same comments as made about virtues also apply to values. It is important to have good values, but what are the reasons why some values are better than others? Like virtues, the point of values lies in something beyond themselves.

In the era of modern nervousness, the word "values" has come to be used in the mission statements of schools and other institutions in place of more robust moral language. The word can have the dangerous suggestion that we can all choose our own values as we please. It is often used with the implication "I do not criticize your values but I am committed to (rather than assert) mine." If there is no ethical standpoint from which one can criticize values as better or worse, more or less in accord with the worth of persons, then anything goes, including offenses against human worth. Heidegger rightly complains:

> Precisely through the characterization of something as "a value," what is so valued is robbed of its worth; that is to say, by the assessment of something as a value what is valued is admitted only as an object for human estimation.... thinking in values involves the greatest blasphemy imaginable against Being.[26]

Replacing worth by values – with their inevitable suggestion that values are created by acts of valuing – is a frivolously idealist move, like replacing properties of things with our "perspectives" on them. So regarding ethics as fundamentally about human valuings would be like regarding science as about constructions from experience.

Worse, to start with "value" is to prejudge the issue as being about our interests instead of about worth.

Regarding "values" as a result of acts of valuing has also had an unfortunate effect on discussion of the "fact/value" distinction. As will be argued in Chapter 5, there is something correct about the "is-ought gap," a fundamental dichotomy between the factual and the moral aspects of the universe. But debate in the twentieth century was vitiated by seeing it as a dichotomy between objective facts studied by science and "the normative" or "value judgements," conceived of as "empirically unverifiable and objectively unjustifiable,... relegated to what is simply subjective, relative, emotional and contingent ... lying outside the domain of reason."[27] That is not correct. If worth exists, it exists in the things that have worth just as much as mass does, not in the observer, and it is not subjective, relative, emotional, or contingent. There may be in addition to worth acts of valuing it and normative conclusions drawn from it – just as there can be acts of measurement of scientific facts and conclusions on their usefulness – but that does not impact on or replace the worth itself.

"Values," then, contrast with worth by showing the need for a more solid grounding for acts of valuing and for rendering objective the distinction between right and wrong acts of valuing.

ETHICS OF CARE

Some ethicists in recent decades, especially feminist ones, have argued that the virtue or practice of care is given short shrift in traditional ethical theories concerning autonomous agents, obligations and rights, and the more abstract virtues such as justice. "Care is the new buzzword," Annette Baier remarks in "The Need for More than Justice."[28] We need not take a position on that comparative thesis or whether care and justice are rightly contrasted to agree that care is central to ethics, in that so much ethical action involves care – for children, for the vulnerable, for ourselves.

The connection between the ethics of care and the worth of persons is particularly obvious. The point of care is that the person cared for is a being of value who needs it.

It is that connection that makes it obvious why an essential element of the ethics of care is competence. "Making certain that the caring work is done competently must be a moral aspect of care if the adequacy of the care given is to be a measure of the success of care."[29] Caring is a response to the needs of someone, which makes sense if they are valuable in themselves so that their needs have moral standing and give point to caring for them. They require actual care, that is, successful care, not the useless empathy of a bleeding heart. So they deserve a competent response (where that is possible with the resources available).

AUTONOMY AND LIBERTY

Respect for the autonomy or liberty of persons has had a high profile in ethics in recent decades. It refers to one aspect of persons, their capacity as free agents.[30] That is unlike the ethics of care, which refers to the good of persons in general. Nevertheless, the ability to act freely is a particularly important aspect of being a person (as is widely accepted and will be explained in Chapter 6). Respecting the worth of *persons* requires attention to what persons actually are, and being a free agent is essential to that. It is possible to care for cats, as good and harm can come to them, but one can respect only the autonomy of humans because only humans have it.

Much of the moral discussion on autonomy and liberty concerns its claims relative to other requirements. Mill, for example, holds "that the sole end for which mankind are warranted, individually or collectively, in interfering with the liberty of action of any of their number is self-protection. That the only purpose for which power can be rightfully exercised over any member of a civilized community, against his will, is to prevent harm to others."[31] Those of more socialist bent advocate more restrictions on liberty in the name of this or that other good. The purpose here is not to calculate the balance between liberty and other claims, but to understand why liberty weighs in the moral balance at all. The liberty of a person is morally significant because the person is significant. It is strongly morally significant because the ability to act freely is a central property of a person, part of what makes something a person. Thus it can only be curtailed for a reason itself strongly based in the worth of persons, such as self-protection and the harm of others.

CONSEQUENCES AND THE SOURCE OF DILEMMAS

Some ethical theories, such as utilitarianism, found ethics on some notion of the *consequences* of actions, for example by laying down "the greatest happiness of the greatest number" as the sole criterion of right action. While there have been many well-known and justified criticisms of such views, it is undoubtedly true that in many cases the point of an action is its consequences, and the existence of evil consequences is a substantial reason to avoid an action.

Consequences for whom? Consequences are themselves evil because they happen to an entity that is itself significant. They are consequences *for* someone, which is why they matter morally. Downie and Telfer remark, "There is surely no point in organizing action to maximize happiness unless we think that happiness matters, and it is unintelligible to suppose that happiness matters without supposing that the people whose happiness is in question matter. But to say that they matter in this way is to say that they are objects of respect."[32]

Similarly Velleman writes, "What's good for a person is worth caring about only out of concern for the person, and hence only insofar as he is worth caring about.... his interests wouldn't matter unless he mattered – that is, unless he had a value that was prior to, and not commensurable with, the value of his interests."[33] (Substance as the bearer of worth will be defended further in Chapter 4.)

And that is so even if, as argued in Chapter 6, worth supervenes on properties which include the capacity to have interests.

(The only alternative for utilitarianism would be to count pleasures and preferences in abstraction from the beings that have them. That is exactly what is done in Peter Singer's "preference utilitarianism,"[34] which is the source of its offensive corollaries such as the allowability of infanticide.)

Many of the objections to utilitarianism involve certain dilemmas to which it gives rise. In these cases, the recommendations of utilitarianism conflict with common, more deontological, moral intuitions. Yet a purely deontological theory appears to neglect something important, too. We examine some of these dilemmas, with a view to showing that only a "worth of persons" perspective on ethics shows why such dilemmas are genuine.

An extreme form of deontology is summed up in the dictum "Let justice be done though the heavens fall." This is a saying that a few ethical hardy souls are prepared to back very literally, while for others it is a saying to be interpreted ironically, as indicative of an implausible fanaticism in anyone who would assert it without misgivings.

Few ethical theories can give a coherent account of why there is a real dilemma in this dictum. According to "deontological" theories, right action is right action, rights (to justice, for example) are absolute (or at least absolute subject to conflict among them), and there can be no "ends justifying the means," such as avoidance of collapsing skies justifying deviations from justice. Those theories, even if one in the end agreed with them, fail to give adequate weight to the moral force of consequences. Insisting on our morally clean hands despite the horrendous cost to others really is ethically dubious, and more so as the cost of the consequences mounts up.

On the other hand, "consequentialist" theories such as utilitarianism hold that actions are to be morally evaluated *solely* in terms of the goodness or badness of the consequences, such as the falling of the heavens. They thus fail to give any weight at all to the doing or otherwise of justice in itself. That is as implausible and morally repugnant as giving *only* justice weight.

Various cases, imagined and real, give flesh to these abstract considerations. A classic is the case of a sheriff in a town of the old South who is faced with a choice between executing an accused black he knows is innocent, or allowing a white mob to riot and kill many.[35] According to utilitarianism, he must kill the innocent man to prevent the greater evil. But the problem is not merely that this is a difficult case, but that utilitarianism gives no weight at all to the injustice. (The utilitarian J. J. C. Smart writes, "However unhappy about it he may be, the utilitarian must admit that he draws the consequence that he might find himself in circumstances where he ought to be unjust,"[36] but fails to explain why the utilitarian should be unhappy about a violation of justice.) Even someone who thinks the sheriff ought to hang the black if the riot will be bad enough feels there is some problem of injustice that the size of the catastrophe must outweigh. On the other hand, a sheriff committed to justice might justifiably feel his nerve shaken as the number of innocent victims of the riot he could prevent becomes larger and larger.

The dilemma is genuine. It is clear why it is genuine. The two sides of the dilemma are both grounded in the worth of persons but in different ways. The gross violation of justice to the victim is an outrage because he is a valuable human being. But the deaths of innocents in a riot are also a grave evil because that involves their destruction. They are equally human beings of immense value. It is the worth of persons that explains why there is a genuine dilemma.

Real and urgent cases arise in the course of "behind the scenes" political decisions where there is some genuine moral pressure to consider deviations from normal moral principles for "reason of state." Cardinal Richelieu's many crimes in the name of public security were defended in Jean de Silhon's *Minister of State* as necessary for "reason of state" ("a mean between that which conscience permits and affairs require"). It is all very well for the Prince to keep to high-minded moral principles like keeping his word, but ought he do so when the safety of his subjects is at stake? A private individual only risks his own when he voluntarily suffers loss in order to do noble deeds, but for princes or their ministers to do the same is not noble but imprudent. "They are unjust if they sacrifice that which is not theirs and has been placed in their hands as a sacred trust."[37] Cynical or not, de Silhon is right to point to a substantial moral case for a "mean" because there are morally weighty considerations both on the side of strict conscience and on the side of consequences.

The classic case of self-defense is similar: Consequentialism makes no sense of it (as if I have to weigh my welfare against that of the attackers) while a deontological rule of "no killing of the innocent" is beside the point, too – especially if the attacker is a paranoid schizophrenic who is innocent because he cannot help himself. Self-defense – like euthanasia *in extremis* – is an example of a more general class of "emergency ethics," where a sudden and serious crisis creates pressure to stretch normal moral rules to avoid a horrendous outcome.[38]

In recent times, the case of torture has concentrated discussion on the problem. Many ethicists resist the suggestion that it might be necessary in some cases to discuss whether torture might be justified. Torture, they say, should be unthinkable.[39] Yet to rule out of court even considering torture in some extreme cases fails to allow on the table the claims of victims who might be saved if torture were used. The moral stresses in the discussion are shown by the fact that opponents of torture (for moral reasons) are very keen to maintain that ticking bomb scenarios never happen (a factual question). But such cases do occasionally occur, and in a world where weapons of mass destruction have the potential to cause casualties up to six orders of magnitude higher than 9/11, there is a moral need to take seriously the competing claims of how bad torture is and how bad mass casualties are.[40] Again, the moral weight of the competing claims exists irrespective of what conclusion is eventually reached on the issue. That is what standard moral theories like pure utilitarianism or pure deontology or pure virtue theory fail to account for. What accounts for the moral weight of competing claims is their grounding (in different ways) in the worth of persons.

CONCLUSION

That still leaves many questions about worth unanswered, of course. They include whether everyone has equal worth (and who counts as "everyone," such as humans with dementia or ones who are microscopically small), whether animals or rainforests or paintings or gods have some worth (or worth of a quite different kind), and what having worth implies for detailed rules of morality. Those are far from easy questions, but they are secondary questions. Doubts on them are no reason to let slip the firm grasp we have of the truth that good and evil matter because they happen to people of inherent worth.

CHAPTER THREE

Five False Starts and One True One

THE PERSPECTIVE THAT bases ethics on the worth of persons can be better understood by contrasting it with a range of rivals. As we saw, the deontological, consequentialist, and virtue theory approaches to ethics at least incorporate a commitment to worth, even if less explicitly than one might wish. Five other approaches on how to start in ethics do not. They can be called the Darwinian, the Calvinist, the Humean, the Socratic, and the Aristotelian. They are all siren songs, inviting the ethical theorist to explain away rather than explain real worth.

They all suit different aspects of modern currents of thought. They are all theories that lie at the backs of people's minds as bolt-holes, inviting retreat into ways of believing that we can do ethics (or something that superficially looks like ethics) without a robust commitment to objective worth.

These views cannot be examined in detail. But enough can be said to explain why they are not promising directions to pursue, in the search for what ethics is about. The aim in reviewing them is as much to display the virtues of a worth of persons perspective by contrast as to show what is wrong with those false theories in themselves.

EVOLUTIONARY ETHICS

The idea of naturalist, usually evolutionary-based, ethics, is that ethics is just *custom*. The rules that happen to evolve (genetically and socially), as tribes experiment to make social life livable, are the ones that evolve, and that is all there is to ethics. "Morality is constituted by the rules, whatever they are, that society enforces."[1] Sacrifice yourself for your tribe; drive on the right – those are essentially the same kind of social rule. Altruistic habits are said to have evolved because it helps the survival of human tribes (or human genes). Different tribes might evolve different customs.

The theory is expressed in purely scientific terms. It lends itself to the usual pseudo-scientific "Darwinian fairytales" purporting to explain this or that prohibition in some tribe (or in some other tribe, its opposite). Some of the evolutionary stories may even be true, that is, true causal stories about how certain behaviors were reinforced and selected for.

Its difficulty, as a theory of the *foundations* of ethics, is that it is really a form of ethical skepticism. That is explicitly so in the "error theory" of John Mackie, which holds that ethics is about *nothing at all*: We are completely mistaken in thinking there is any such thing as ethics (there are only customs, which don't oblige us in any way to follow them, but we mistakenly attribute obligatoriness to them).

One might wonder if other versions of naturalistic or "evolutionary" ethics differ from Mackie's really or only cosmetically. Only cosmetically, if we accept accounts such as E.O. Wilson's in *Sociobiology*:

> Self-knowledge is constrained and shaped by the emotional and control centers in the hypothalamus and limbic system of the brain. These centers flood our consciousness with all the emotions – hate, love, guilt, fear, and others – that are con-

sulted by ethical philosophers who wish to intuit the standards of good and evil. What, we are then compelled to ask,
made the hypothalamus and limbic system? They evolved by
natural selection. That simple biological statement must be
pursued to explain ethics and ethical philosophers, if not
epistemology and epistemologists, at all depths.[2]

The argument is invalid. It is: "We cannot know ethical truths (if
there are any) except through the urgings of our back-of-brain
plumbing, therefore, we cannot know ethical truths at all." This is of
the same form as "We cannot know mathematical truths except
through the calculations of our frontal cortex, therefore, we cannot
know mathematical truths at all." It is an example of the argument
form identified by David Stove as the "worst argument in the world."
It has the general form "We can know things only: as they are related
to us/under our forms of perception and understanding/insofar as
they fall under our conceptual schemes/etc., therefore, we cannot
know things as they are in themselves."[3] Of course we need our brains
to work correctly to know ethical truths, just as to know perceptual
or mathematical truths, but that in itself is no reason to doubt them.

Evolutionary ethics is full of talk about a sense of obligation (for
example, that we feel obliged to help others in our tribe) in place of
actual obligations. What is especially disturbing about evolutionary
"ethics" is how a hidden and unadmitted reference to the worth of
persons in this discussion permits an indefinite amount of ethical
"vacuum activity" (in the sense of animal behavior studies, where
dogs long deprived of earth "bury" fictitious bones in the corner of
rooms).[4] In particular, if a behavior contributes to survival (of an
individual, a tribe, or a species), that is taken to be a purely factual
matter of Darwinian "fitness," without any allusion being made to
survival's being a good for someone. Yet surely the reason evolutionary ethics appeals is its combination of apparent scientific standing

with the comfort arising from its alignment with what we know to be the good of staying alive.

This is particularly evident in the choice of which human behaviors to expatiate on and "explain" and which to sweep under the carpet. Altruism has been a particular favorite; a rosy glow suffuses the great number of mathematical models generated to explain how altruistic and sometimes self-sacrificial behaviors might be selected for in evolution. There has been much less talk about certain less savory patterns of action that have also contributed to the spread of the genes of those so behaving. Rape and ethnic cleansing offer obvious advantages for "selfish genes" wishing to spread themselves in future generations – advantages well realized by Genghis Khan, who has an estimated 16 million living descendants.[5] The most salient indicator of whom one shares genes with is race, so racism is a behavior to be expected as a result of evolution.[6] But rape, racism, and genocide are evils and their role in evolution is entirely incapable of providing an excuse for them. Whatever evolutionary traits, tribal customs, or individual acts exist, moral criticism of them from an outside standpoint is necessary. That outside perspective can be provided by a theory of personal worth (and possibly by some other objectivist moral theories). It cannot be provided by a purely scientific theory.

If ethics is just whatever has evolved, there is no standpoint from which one can say that one tribe's customs (for example, those of the Nazi tribe) are worse than others, or that there has been moral progress (for example, in abolishing slavery). Any standpoint would itself be the parochial view of a certain tribe, evolved by chance. If racism has evolved (as is to be expected if altruism derives from helping those with whom one shares genes), there will be no way of criticizing that. The impartiality of the "moral point of view" is very unlikely to evolve.[7] Nor will there be any reason why I should do as my tribe says (if I can get away with not doing it). For the theory just says, "What happens, happens."

Evolutionary "ethics" thus encourages a trivialized and ethically unpleasant view of what ethics is about. Since its only (surrogate for) good is survival, it must approve all and only what contributes to that. The resulting "ethics" is, at best, "workable traffic rules for self-assertors, so that they do not needlessly frustrate one another,"[8] at worst, a series of sycophantic congratulations to those who do "whatever it takes" to survive and multiply.

Some philosophers have not so much covered up as rejoiced in the supposed anti-ethical consequences of evolutionary theory. Bernard Williams, for example, wrote that "The first and hardest lesson of Darwinism, that there is no teleology at all, and that there is no orchestral score provided from anywhere according to which human beings have a special part to play, still has to find its way into ethical thought."[9] In recent decades, such thinking certainly has found its way into ethical thought. The leading thesis of that kind is the influential argument of Sharon Street that Darwinian evolution is incompatible with realist moral theories, on the grounds that if there were moral truths, there is no reason to believe that evolution would have shaped our evaluative attitudes so as to make them correspond to those moral truths.[10]

That cannot be right in general. Evolution must track survival, and on realist theories the survival of a being of positive worth is an objective good, indeed the most basic objective good since it is a condition for all others.[11] It is perfectly clear why evaluative attitudes evolved by Darwinian means will see as a strong positive the survival of the organism itself and at least its close kin. It is likewise clear why an organism will take its own learning and cooperation with its group to be good, again creating a synergy between what Darwinian theory predicts and what realist ethical theories assert.

However, there is no guarantee, or even expectation, that evolutionarily evolved attitudes will usually track the moral good. In fact, moral realists hold that they do not. It is predictable, evolutionarily speaking, that tribes will naturally believe that the tribes over the hill are subhuman and deserve extermination. That is, on a realist view of ethics, a mistake. Evolved attitudes fail to track the right. They can only be corrected by rational reflection, which can use a symmetry argument to show that the people over the hill are relevantly similar to us and so deserve survival if we do. Our abilities to reflect rationally may be evolved as well, but they can conflict with evolved emotional attitudes.

Tribal custom resulting from evolutionary history produces systems of evaluatory attitudes and behavioral rules which sometimes coincide with ethics and sometimes not. It is not itself ethics.

DIVINE COMMAND ETHICS

An equally simplistic theory is that what is right is by definition what God commands. The "divine command" theory of ethics is held to some extent by Calvinist Christians and Muslims.[12] It is no surprise that these religious traditions find little place for an inherent worth of persons, and merely hold that for inscrutable reasons God chooses to superadd some worth, or overlook its lack, for a subset of humanity freely chosen by himself.

It has the same problem as the naturalist theory – a lack of an independent moral viewpoint for saying that God has got it right (or wrong). Perhaps we think that God, if he exists, is good and will always act rightly, but that is not the same as saying, as the view being considered here does, that if God commands something, then it is right by definition. Socrates cunningly exposed the difficulties of the divine command theory in the "Euthyphro dilemma," asking "Is something good because the gods command it or do the gods command it because it is good?" The difference is evident if we ask whether, for example, God could command that murder be right.[13] Given that we have understood why the wrongness of murder is an implication of the worth of persons, we can see why that is impossible – as impossible as his ordering that $2 + 2$ should equal 5. (The religious traditions that favor divine command theory are inclined to insist on God's omnipotence, but that does not apply in such cases: The symbols "$2 + 2 = 5$" fail to describe a possibility on which he could confer being.[14])

He cannot make murder a good or trivial matter. (And certainly, if we believed he could make murder right, we would have to believe that he could just as easily make lying right, in which case we would have no reason to believe any revelations he chose to make.) As a thought experiment, we could consider what we ought to do if we came to believe that God did command murder – as, indeed, some youths under the influence of radical imams do come to believe. We ought not to believe in any God who commands murder or genocide – or ought not to follow his commands if he does exist. As Sartre says, if Abraham believes himself commanded by an angel to kill his son, his first reaction should be to question whether the voice is really from an angel.[15] (Or as Kant puts it from the opposite direction, "Even the Holy One of the Gospels must first be compared with our ideal of moral perfection before we can recognize Him as such."[16]) That is, we must have some independent grasp of the good before we can judge whether a particular religious message deserves to be followed.

Of course, not all religious traditions with a personal God hold a divine command theory of ethics. The general Catholic view has been that what is good is inherent in the nature of things and that God, while on the side of good, cannot change it, for example by commanding genocide. Pope Benedict XVI's 2006 Regensburg speech praised the medieval Greek emperor Manuel II for saying, "Not to act reasonably, not to act with *logos*, is contrary to the nature of God." That is, God's moral commands are not freestanding but (necessarily) in accordance with the ways things must be. We will consider natural law theories such as those in the Catholic tradition later.

It is true that some Protestant theories that describe themselves as divine command theories reject the "discretion thesis," the claim that God could make murder or any other wrong action right. They restrict what God could command, given his nature, and are better called divine resemblance theories.[17] Those are substantially different theories, which we do not examine here.

The fundamental problem, though, with divine command theories lies at an earlier stage than their issues with arbitrary commands and commands to act abhorrently. It lies in the absence of an inherent worth of persons. If that is established, the source of ethics is clear and there is no motivation to add God's command to it, especially if God's command might contradict the ethics arising from the worth of persons. (Though there is still the possibility that God's command may help us know or somehow round out ethics.) It is only if "fallen" humanity is thought to have no inherent worth that God's command is needed to fill the gap – and since no ethics exists prior to the divine command (for example, one that would support the rights of persons), "anything goes," and to judge God's commands would simply be impious.

THE HUMEAN ERROR: ETHICS AS ABOUT
ACTION AND MOTIVES

Introducing his views on ethics, Hume says without argument:

> Philosophy is commonly divided into speculative and practical; and as morality is always comprehended under the latter division, it is supposed to influence our passions and actions, and to go beyond the calm and indolent judgments of the understanding.... Since morals, therefore, have an influence on the actions and affections, it follows, that they cannot be derived from reason; and that because reason alone, as we have already proved, can never have any such influence.[18]

That is tradition, but not the truth. Before we get to the issue of whether reason is motivating or not, there is a prior and undefended assumption in Hume: that ethics is essentially about action and its motivation. That would rule out the possibility of ethics being about something not fundamentally about motivation and action, such as the worth of persons.

But as we saw in the previous two chapters, there is every reason to think that the ethics of action – what is the right and wrong thing to do – depends on deeper questions about the worth of persons, which explain what, for example, makes wrong the action of harming someone. Hume's thought does not argue against that, but merely assumes it is false.

Modern Humeans, such as Roger Teichmann, are a little more aware of the need to head off alternatives. Having asserted in Humean fashion that "Its [ethics'] subject-matter is human life and what is humanly important,"[19] meaning what we happen to find important, he is quick to dismiss talk of "value." He denies that we help humans before dolphins because "we impute more value to them than to dolphins. Whatever such phrases mean – and they generally mean very little – they do not help us; for it is not as if there can *never* be a reason for preferring a dolphin to a human being – e.g. if choosing a creature to train to carry coded messages under water."[20] The instrumental value of dolphins is not to the point of whether we value (or ought to value) them in themselves, any more than the instrumental value of slaves is relevant to their rights.

The Humean perspective is restricted to the distinction between instrumental value and what we ultimately want, which is ungrounded in anything ethical. It is ungrounded because Humeans have specifically ruled out any possibility of reasons or grounds for our ultimate wishes.

Certainly, the "worth" perspective makes trouble for itself by denying the close conceptual connection between ethics and obligatoriness, yet having to explain the nevertheless necessary connection (see Chapter 8). The connection is more like the connection between numbers and counting. The necessary truths about numbers determine that there is only one right way to count, but the truths about numbers are just the way they are, preexisting human activities in conformity with them (or not), like counting. As Plato says, it would be ludicrous to interpret mathematicians' talk of actions like adding numbers, constructing circles, and extracting square roots as implying that mathematics is really about action. It is pure knowledge, "the knowledge of that which always is, and not of a something which at some time comes into being and passes away."[21] Arithmetic is normative for the actions of adding up by accountants, but it is not itself essentially normative nor about actions. It is the same with ethics: Eternal truths are normative for action but are not themselves norms.

THE SOCRATIC ERROR: REPLACING VIRTUE WITH REASON

The "Socratic" approach to the foundations of ethics is inspired by Socrates's saying that virtue is knowledge – that is, that rationality is all that is needed to found ethics and that errors in ethics are fundamentally mistakes of reason. Evil, on that view, always rests on some kind of mistake. (The approach is also inspired by Kant's universalizability criterion, but it would be wrong to call it simply "Kantian" in view of the other strands in Kant's ethics.)

That idea appeals to the class interest of philosophers, who are inclined to think that "all is reason." A number of analytic philosophers of the late twentieth century, disillusioned with all "big" metaphysical ideas like inherent worth or rights, pursued the idea that the "moral point of view" just involves symmetry between humans –

I put my interests on a par with others' because there is no *reason* why mine should be preferred to theirs. Thus ethics is to be founded in pure symmetry arguments, and the symmetry is a symmetry only of reasons for a social animal.

Thus Kurt Baier's *The Moral Point of View* poses the fundamental question "Why should we be moral?" His answer is that we should be moral because (and solely because) being moral is following rules designed to overrule self-interest whenever it is in the interest of everyone alike that everyone should set aside his interest.[22] Michael Smith, too, hopes to reduce ethics to (ideal) rationality, "an account of moral judgments in terms of what one would desire if one were fully rational." He puts forward, as a requirement of rationality: "If there is a normative reason for some agent to φ in certain circumstances C then there is a like normative reason for all those who find themselves in circumstances C to φ."[23]

Symmetry or equality is a certainly a good idea in itself, as is consistency in reasoning, in the sense of reaching like conclusions in like cases. And it is useful to inquire how much of ethics is derivable from equality – justice, for example, is heavily dependent on the "equity" of treating people alike. But appeals to symmetry are meaningless without establishing what, at the bottom level, symmetry is a symmetry *of*. Symmetry merely of "reasons" is a will-o'-the-wisp. Whenever the going gets tough, there is a hidden assumption of equality of moral worth, without which it all falls in a heap. When I ask who gets to be "symmetrized with" – whose interests are to be regarded as on a par with mine – it becomes clear that some criterion is needed of who counts as morally equivalent to me, that is, who has equal moral standing. If, for example, I take animal interests to be not symmetrical with mine, that is because I recognize something fundamentally different about them, that is, their worth. They and their interests are not normatively on a par with me because of something morally that they lack.

Thus Smith finds himself obliged to add something to mere symmetry of reasons. What is *moral* is further constrained by some "platitudes": "'Right acts are often concerned to promote or sustain or contribute in some way to human flourishing', 'Right acts are in some way expressive of equal concern and respect', and the like."[24] True, but as Aristotle shows, digging into what appears to be platitudinous can be revealing. Perhaps "equal concern and respect" is expressed because the objects of concern and respect have some properties that imply they are owed it.

The problem is made plainer by another definition of the moral point of view: that it "consists in seeing in another's good, considered just as such, a reason for action on our part."[25] That should encourage inquiry into what the good of a person is, and what it is about a person that makes their good a reason for action. Without that, the "moral point of view" cannot pretend to be an account of the foundations of ethics.

ARISTOTELIAN ETHICS

Aristotle is a valuable writer on some ethical topics and has important things to say about the virtues. But when it comes to what ethics is about, something goes wrong at the very beginning. The *Nicomachean Ethics* opens with the remark that "the good is what all things aim at." It is not entirely clear if this is meant as a definition of the good, an analysis, or a statement of a property of the good. But it orients everything that comes later and gives Aristotelian ethics its characteristically teleological direction. It is all about the aim of activity. Aristotle asks what a human life is for, and considers answers such as pleasure, or honorable action in the service of the state, or contemplation. Virtues are human excellences that contribute to whatever it is that human life is for, in something the same way as organs serve various purposes in the life of the human body. As reason is the unique feature of humanity, its exercise is the most excellent human function. As often with Aristotle, his views agree with common opinion and the way the word "good" is used.[26]

The natural law ethics of Thomas Aquinas adopts the same perspective,[27] though adding a more religious cast to the answer to what human life is for. It attempts to answer questions of right and wrong by reference to what is in accordance with human nature, and the conception of human nature is teleological – lying is wrong, he argues, because it is a misuse of human cognitive and communicative capacities, whose purpose is oriented toward truth.

There is something correct, as will be argued later, about seeing virtues as serving a purpose in human life and in giving an account of the virtues as perfections of humans that animals do not have. There is also something correct about Aquinas's picture of the relation of right and wrong to what is natural. It will be argued in Chapter 8 that much of natural law ethics is implied by the ethics of worth.

But as a *foundation* of ethics, these ideas are inadequate. The problem is the lack of account of why the smooth running of something of a kind is good, without a prior account of why a thing of that kind is valuable (if indeed it is valuable, absolutely). A well-oiled tank or a fast-running cockroach are good of their kind, but is their kind a good one – and if it is a good one, is it as good as the human or divine kind? Aristotelian ethics does not ask or answer those questions. Although it is taken as obvious that humans and God have "perfections" that animals do not, gradings of worth are not the subject of explicit discussion. Aristotle and Aquinas start from "things in the universe of which it makes sense to say that things go well or badly for them,"[28] without explaining first what kind of things those are, or why what happens to them should be of moral concern.

A symptom of the problem is the strong divorce in Aquinas between "practical reason" and speculative reason. Aquinas dichotomizes "theoretical reason" and "practical reason" and assigns everything to do with the Good to the latter. "Good has the nature of an end," he says, repeating Aristotle, and "the precepts of the natural law are to the practical reason what the first principles of demonstrations are to the speculative reason."²⁹ On a worth-based conception of the foundations of ethics, that is quite wrong. The discovery of worth in individuals is as much a function of the "speculative reason" as the discovery of length or mass in physical things. While worth has moral consequences that length does not (for reasons to be explored in Chapter 8), in itself it has no orientation to practice, or what is to be aimed at. Like an aesthetic good, it is just there and can be known and admired. It is not "for us" or for anything.

This mistake of Aquinas (and Aristotle) is explained by Dietrich von Hildebrand as a failure to distinguish two kinds of (genuine, objective, non-instrumental) good, the good in itself and the good for us. Gratitude to my benefactor, he points out, is different from the admiration of generosity in a third party. Gratitude refers to the giving of a gift that is an objective good for me; admiration is of a virtue that is an objective good in itself.

> When someone is saved from a danger threatening his life, or is released from imprisonment, his joy and his gratitude toward God clearly refer to the kind of importance which we have termed the objective good for the person. . . . it also differs clearly from the important-in-itself. Life and freedom are here considered not only in their intrinsic value, but also insofar as they are great gifts for *me*. If I adore God's infinite bounty and mercy which bestowed these goods upon me, I clearly respond to something important-in-itself, to an infinite value. Similarly, I am motivated by a value when the moral goodness of a human benefactor moves me. In these cases I am not directed to the importance which implies a relation to a subject, but to a pure importance in itself. In the importance which my life, freedom, health etc have for me

there is, on the contrary, an essential relation to my own person: they are objectively important *to* me.[30]

Similarly Roy Holland explains that Aristotle makes the mistake of conceiving of absolute goodness on the model of (a limit) of relative goodness (as in a good knife), so the absolutely good is what is for the absolute end (for example, for human flourishing, or contemplation). But our sense of a notably magnanimous or heroic action has nothing to do with what it is for. "The recognition of an absolute value … where one is struck by the egregious fineness of an action like the rescue of an innocent person who is harmed or wronged – acknowledgement of such an action involves the awareness of a demand that can as readily obstruct as further any purpose howsoever elevated and irrespective of whether the purpose be conceived as private or communal."[31]

Von Hildebrand's and Holland's examples of what has absolute value are actions or virtues rather than entities like humans, but they suffice to make the point against the Aristotelian purely teleological view of ethics. The point applies even more strongly to the worth of entities. While actions and virtues can be admirable absolutely, that is so only because of the absolute worth of the entities possessing them and benefited by them.

The problem with Aristotelian approaches in ethics lies in trying to rely on an objective good-for (which is relative to the nature of the thing for which it is a good), with minimal reference to the good-in-itself, the worth of the thing for which an action is good-for.

Two recent authors, Philippa Foot and John Post, have developed a minimalist Aristotelian approach to ethical foundations which is designed to avoid the main problems with Aristotle and also to avoid, or paper over, Hume's is-ought gap. It is a valuable attempt as showing the possibilities and limits of the Aristotelian idea of grounding ethics in nature.

Foot's *Natural Goodness* invokes the idea of "Aristotelian necessities" for a species. For humans, an example is the need for promise-making to ensure human life, for example, having one's children cared for after one's death. She writes:

> We invoke the same idea when we say that it is necessary for plants to have water, for birds to build nests, for wolves to hunt in packs, and for lionesses to teach their cubs how to kill. These 'Aristotelian necessities', depend on what the particular species of plants and animals needs, on their natural habitat, and the ways of making out that are in their repertoire. These things together determine what it is for members of a particular species to be as they should be, and to do that which they should do. And for all the enormous differences between the life of humans and that of plants and animals, we can see that human defects and excellences are similarly related to what humans beings are and what they do.[32]

Foot is thus explicitly "likening the basis of moral evaluation to that of the evaluation of behaviour of animals." A free-riding wolf that feeds but does not help with the hunt is a defective wolf, as is a human who breaks promises (without a good excuse). A human form of life is different from a wolf form, notably in that humans understand the rules, but the basis of moral evaluation lies in what is natural for the life of the species. Moral behavior like keeping promises is a necessity for human life as cooperative hunting is necessary for wolf life, and that necessity is what makes it moral. That only applies to living things: "On barren Mars there is no natural goodness."

John Post similarly defends "an important kind of normativity some think is objectively in the world – the primitive normativity involved in a biological adaptation's being for, or designed to do this or that."[33] While not the same as moral normativity, and while created by a natural process of evolution, it is not purely factual but properly normative. The "reduction" of such primitive normativity to biological facts about what adaptations are for is to be seen on the model of the reduction of water to H_2O or of lightning to an electrical discharge in the clouds – it simply gives a scientific account of what the experienced phenomenon really is. The "folk" role of a heart's being for pumping is identified with the scientific property of the pumping of hearts having been selected for in evolutionary history.

The difficulty for Foot's and Post's identification of some form of normativity with what is natural for members of a species lies in a dilemma. We understand scientifically what it means for the heart to be for something: It makes survival more probable. So does promise keeping among humans – the human form of life being social in the way it is, human survival depends on it. So what is good about human survival? Human survival is a good if and only if it is worthwhile that humans survive. That is, they have an inherent worth that gives point to their survival. If it were otherwise – Foot mentions mosquitos – there would be no such story. The beating of the mosquito heart can be called a good for mosquitos, and certainly contributes to there being more mosquitos, but whether there is any point to it absolutely cannot be established by scientific facts about the survival of mosquitos.

The whole Aristotelian edifice of "natural goodness" rests on the assumption that the organisms for whom things are a good are things worth having on the planet. That assumption is often true, in which case the inherent worth of them does explain the derivative worth of their health, survivals, and forms of life. Without that assumption, the Aristotelian superstructure is a house of cards.

Another problem for Aristotelian ethics also stems from its foundation concepts being "practical rationality" and what is apt for flourishing. It is fundamentally unserious and egocentric. As Anscombe observes, Aristotle's own ethics is hardly ethical at all. "Most noticeably, the term 'moral' itself, which we have by direct inheritance from Aristotle, just doesn't seem to fit, in its modern sense, into an account of Aristotelian ethics."[34] What is practically rational for me is what contributes to my flourishing. That explains why it would be nice, perhaps even morally worthwhile, for me to take certain actions that would make me flourish better. It does not explain the terribleness of murder or the urgency of justice, or the overriding character of moral obligation in general. It does not explain why altruistic actions are reasonable for me (except when the beneficiaries of those actions will in turn do my flourishing a favor). Its defender Mark Murphy admits that he wishes he "could defend a more stringent principle of impartiality as a requirement of practical reasonableness," but confesses that he cannot do so.[35] If then we attempt to fill the gap by appealing to some symmetry between myself and others, which would make their flourishing a motive for me, we have gone beyond Aristotelian ethics, as we have implicitly imported a principle of equal (or at least comparable) worth of persons.

In short, Aristotelian ethics is too much "what about me" and my life. As Wolterstorff writes, "The focus of the eudaemonist is entirely on action; how to live one's life well is the question that shapes all eudaemonist thought. From among candidates for ends in themselves in our structure of action we are each to make that selection that holds the greatest promise of making one's own life well lived. Insofar as the 'passivity' of *being treated* a certain way is seen as having significance, that significance lies entirely in whether being so treated contributes instrumentally to living one's life well. That one might be wronged in being so treated does not enter the thought of the eudaemonist."[36] Too much of the serious business of ethics is left out.

The five false starts on the foundations of ethics – Darwinian, Calvinist, Humean, Socratic and Aristotelian – have each their own problems, but they share two features that prevent them from seeing the basics of ethics clearly. The first is their emphasis on action and motivation, as if that is the whole of ethics and what needs principally to be explained. That aspect is worst in Hume, who starts with the unargued claim that ethics is as a conceptual matter only about "passions and motives," but it infects the others as well. All regard their task as done if some explanation (evolutionary, divine, rational, or whatever it may be) is given of patterns of behavior. For reasons explained in the first chapter, that misses the main sources of ethical seriousness, in the worth of persons and hence the importance of what happens to them.

The second feature which these false starts share is a focus on the feel-good aspects of ethical behavior. Evolutionary ethics is proud of its explanation of altruism but hides its equally plausible explanation of genocide, the Socratic approach likewise labors to reduce unselfishness to reason, the Humean invokes natural motives of sympathy for others, and the Aristotelian asks what acts and virtues will contribute to human flourishing. Even Calvinism, which certainly has its darker aspects, takes the main content of divinely commanded ethics to be Jesus's rules of love. Tragedy is missing. Remorse is missing. They are missing because they are not relevant to the story these approaches are telling about ethics. Since tragedy and remorse are at the center of what is important about ethics, an account of ethics that willfully or negligently leaves them out reveals itself as merely frivolous.

. . . AND ONE TRUE START: KANT

The present approach to ethics obviously has much in common with Kant. So we explain where it agrees with and where it differs from the Kantian perspective.

It distinguished sharply between worth or value in the abstract, and morals in the sense of what ought to be done. It agrees wholly with Kant as to the former, less so with regard to the latter.

Kant makes several claims that he seems to intend as foundational (perhaps some more so than others):

(1) Humans have a dignity, an absolute inner worth.

(2) Humans deserve respect.

(3) Humans should be treated as ends and not means.

(4) One should act on maxims that could rationally be willed as universal laws.

(5) One should obey absolute deontological rules such as the wrongness of lying.

The first of these has a logic quite different from the others. It states a property of humans, their dignity or worth. The others state something about how other humans should relate to them, which is something quite different from a property of them in themselves. Such "oughts" might follow from worth, but they are relations concerning humans, not properties inherent in them.

[Note also that even the formulation "end in itself" does not exactly have the same meaning as "of (high or supreme) worth." "Worth" is a property of a thing; "end" expresses its relation to the action of something else.]

Kant's first claim, that humans have a dignity, an absolute inner worth, is the same as the foundational claim of the present project. We simply expand on it and try to explain the metaphysical commitments involved, the source of that worth, and the compatibility of it with theories of the nature of the universe.

Kant's other claims, about the rightness of action, he claims follow from or (he sometimes says) are equivalent to the fundamental dignity of persons. These principles are about something other than the worth of persons – namely, the rightness of actions. One may or may not agree that the worth of persons implies them (and if so, with or without further premises).

The point of view taken here is that these Kantian principles are acceptable as general orientations or heuristics, and as such are suggested by the inherent worth of persons. The second, "Humans deserve respect," is true just because respect means recognition of the facts, namely the worth of persons. But the others are not correct if taken as strict universal generalizations that determine exceptionless rules of right action. Indeed, the worth of persons explains why there should be exceptions to them.

The point is easily illustrated with the claim that persons should always be treated as ends and not means. The fundamental idea of that is correct: The worth of persons means they ought to be regarded as good in themselves and so there is a limit on what can be done to them for one's own purposes; their own needs require to be taken into account when dealing with them. But there is still the possibility that, from some urgent necessity itself arising from the worth of persons and perhaps involving their survival, one might need to treat a person as a means, and solely as a means, to an end, disregarding their own interests. An artificial case, designed specifically to test the principle, is given by Derek Parfit:

> *Third Earthquake:* You and your child are trapped in slowly collapsing wreckage, which threatens both of your lives. You cannot save your child's life except by using *Black*'s body as a shield, without her consent, in a way that would crush one of her toes. If you also caused Black to lose another toe, you would save your own life.[37]

Less artificial cases involve (just) wars and self-defense. There is no use pretending that one's firing at an enemy soldier is treating him as an end in himself. One is treating him not only as a mere means but as a mere obstacle to the achievement of one's objective. But one greatly regrets being forced to do that. Such cases do not call into question the worth of persons – survivors of earthquakes, enemy soldiers, or anyone else. Nor do they call into question that there is extremely strong reason to treat people as ends in themselves rather than means to one's own projects. It is just that the necessity to survive is also of extreme moral urgency, and that, too, follows from the worth of persons. What such cases call into question is the possibility of using the Kantian dicta as exceptionless rules of action.

Work on the foundations of ethics will not resolve those dilemmas. That is not its purpose. The business of foundations is not to resolve difficult cases, but to explain why they are difficult in the first place.

The present project is closer to natural law theory than Kant in its derivation of rules of action from principles of worth, as explained in Chapter 8, "The Source of Obligation." That is unlike attempts to tweak Kant's principles to try to make them exceptionless, such as Parfit's "It is wrong to impose harm on someone as a means of achieving some aim, unless (1) our act is the least harmful way to achieve this aim, and (2) given the goodness of this aim, the harm we impose is not disproportionate, or too great."[38] Projects of that sort may be justifiable for some purposes (such as a liking for deductive structures, or because one's grant application has promised software for computational casuistics), but foundations of ethics they are not. A suggestion such as the one given is also incomplete as a guide to action without going into the measurement of the goodness of aims and what is proportionate to them (unlike Kant's own principles, which guided action without that). Such measurement will require reference to the worth of persons and of what is good for them and to what degree, which is better done, it will be argued, in a natural law perspective.

Rai Gaita points out how conceptions of ethics such as the ones in the previous chapter, if taken to be accounts of what is basic, fall foul of our experience of remorse, when we ask, in full realization of what we have done, "My God what have I done? How could I have done it?"

Nowhere, he says, is the moral sense more sober than in lucid remorse. But trying to understand remorse in terms of the more superficial views on ethics just produces parody:

> 'My God what have I done? I have violated the social compact, agreed behind a veil of ignorance.' 'My God what have I done? I have violated rational nature in another.' 'My God what have I done? I have diminished the stock of happiness.' 'My God what have I done? I have violated my freely chosen principles.' An answer must surely be given as to why, at one of the most critical moments of moral sobriety, so many of the official accounts of what it is for something to be of moral concern, the accounts of the connection between obligation and what it means to wrong someone, appear like parodies.[39]

True. However, it would be wrong to conclude that every attempt at a foundation of ethics must fail the remorse test: "My God what have I done? I have destroyed or irreparably damaged a living, breathing soul." That justifies remorse.

CHAPTER FOUR

The Search for a Foundation of the Worth of Persons

❖

If the worth of persons is to be founded in reality, it should be possible to state what it is about persons that gives them that worth. Their rationality, for example, seems relevant to worth but their size does not. But before we come to the range of possible answers to the question "What gives humans worth?" it is necessary to consider some more abstract and metaphysical aspects of the issue. The most basic one is whether the project should be undertaken at all, or whether there is some fundamental mistake in trying to found moral worth on properties that people have. Then, since any suggested property to found worth might be partly or wholly lacking in some humans, problems arise over the presumed equality of persons and the sufficiency or otherwise of capacities or potentialities (for example, capacity for rationality). Finally, could worth be constituted by a relation to something else, such as being loved by God?

These issues are largely independent of and more abstract than the question of what exactly is the property of humans that founds worth, so it is better to treat them separately.

One initial positive reason for looking for a basis for ethics is the "supervenience thesis": One of the very few widely agreed principles about ethical foundations is that there is no difference between two things in worth (or ethical properties generally) without a difference in their natural properties.[1] If true, that suggests both some degree of objectivity of worth[2] and also the supervenience of it on some base. If there must be a difference in natural properties to found a difference in worth, then worth must be at least in part founded on natural properties.

SHOULD ONE LOOK FOR PROPERTIES
WHICH ACCOUNT FOR WORTH?

Anti-foundationalist views of ethics are common outside philosophy, as in Clement Attlee's saying "Believe in the ethics of Christianity. Can't believe in the mumbo-jumbo."[3] They are rampant within philosophy, too.

It has been maintained that "What properties give humans worth?" is the wrong question, and that one should not look for properties on which to "found" ethics. Two serious reasons have been advanced. One is that ethics does not admit of or benefit from foundations at all. The second is that any occurrent property, such as rationality, might be lacking in some of the beings to which one feels it right to attribute worth, such as permanently comatose humans.

Rai Gaita argues, from a Wittgensteinian perspective, that the search for foundations of ethics is a mistake. While strongly objectivist about ethics, he maintains that any putative foundations could not possibly cast light on ethics. Speaking of the case of a nun who showed love for severe psychiatric patients at a hospital in which Gaita worked when young, he writes:

> As someone who was witness to the nun's love and is claimed in fidelity to it, I have no understanding of what it revealed independently of the quality of her love. . . . I can only say that the quality of her love proved that [the patients] are *rightly* the

objects of our non-condescending treatment.... But if someone were to ask me what informs my sense that they were
rightly the objects of such treatment, I can appeal only to the
purity of her love. For me, the purity of her love proved the
reality of what it revealed.... To speak of those patients as
'fully our equals' is not, even implicitly, to pick out something
about them that could be known or even specified independently of this kind of love.[4]

Surely it makes no sense to say of the patients that they are rightly the
objects of some attitude or action, while at the same time denying
that there is something about the patients themselves that makes
that right. If love "reveals" something about its objects, there must
be something, however minimal, about the objects themselves that it
reveals. The word "reveal" has a success grammar and is meaningless
without some reality revealed. Conversely, if a "love" is freestanding
and has no relation to the true worth of its object, it is delusional,
a simulacrum of the real love of a lovable object.

So while Gaita speaks of our recognition of "a common humanity" as crucial to ethics and even speaks of "experiences that all
human beings share in virtue of their common humanity,"[5] his
unwillingness to inquire into what it actually is that humans have in
common undermines the apparent content of his position.

That is confirmed by Gaita's own comments elsewhere on the
inappropriateness of elaborate obsequies for pets.[6] Certainly it is
excessively sentimental to build a large monument to one's dead cat
and lay flowers annually. Surely there is a fact of the matter about the
inherent moral difference between cats and humans that underlies
and explains why obsequies for one are appropriate and for the other
are not. It cannot be simply a contingent matter of culture, as no
amount of cultural change will allow cats to become members of
our culture. To deliberately avoid inquiry into what that difference

consists in would be to adopt a know-nothingist approach, unworthy of the inquiring mind.

Surely, as Wolterstorff puts it, "Worth or excellence or dignity is not something that just settles down here and there willy-nilly. An entity has worth on account of some property it has, or some capacity it can exercise, or some activity it has performed or is performing, or some relationship in which it stands. Its worth supervenes on its properties (capacities, activities etc.) or standing in certain relationships."[7] As he argues, "If the piano sonata that you composed is a fine sonata, then there's something about your composition that makes it fine. We may find it difficult if not impossible to put into words what that is; but it makes no sense to say that it's a fine sonata but that there's nothing about it that makes it fine. The project of accounting for the worth of something is the project of identifying that about the thing on which its worth supervenes, the project of identifying that feature of the thing by virtue of which it has its particular worth."[8] There must be some story to tell. If there isn't, there's no account of what we recognize, or how we recognize it, or why we should react to what has worth differently from how we react to what doesn't.

METAPHYSICS PHOBIA: RAWLS AND OTHERS

Indeed, a phobia of metaphysics is widespread in ethical theory. We examine it because it is such a barrier to progress on the foundations of ethics. We look at one of the most influential theorists of the last half-century, John Rawls. He speaks for many ethical theorists in his attempt to steer clear of metaphysics, and the defects in his attempt are shared generally. In this debate, "metaphysics" is understood widely as encompassing any substantial realist claims about the nature of persons.

Rawls's distinctive thesis is that adequate principles of justice are those which would be chosen by rational agents concerned to maximize their share of such things as "rights and liberties, opportunities and powers, income and wealth" and "a sense of one's own worth."[9] Such rational agents are to design the just system without knowing what position they will hold in it, thus behind a "veil of ignorance" which is fair to everyone by putting them in the same initial position. The inherent reasonableness of his proposals and the ability of his simple axioms to generate them have been the source of their popularity. Everyone loves a model, especially one with deductions from symmetry principles.

But "sense of one's own worth" is ambiguous. Does it have success grammar, meaning "a recognition of the truth that one has worth," or is it a purely psychological entity, a possibly deluded and transient "feeling good about oneself"? If the former, then inherent moral worth would be a foundational concept for Rawls. He appears to prefer the latter reading, offering a very upbeat and action-oriented picture of what a sense of self-worth implies:

> Perhaps the most important primary good is that of self-respect.... it includes a person's sense of his own value, his secure conviction that his conception of the good, his plan of life, is worth carrying out. And second, self-respect implies a confidence in one's ability, so far as it is within one's power, to fulfill one's intentions.[10]

But a purely psychological notion simply raises the question, Is one's secure conviction, or one's plan of life, or confidence in one's ability, justified or deluded? If it is not justified, it is a shaky "primary good" indeed. But if it is justified, it must be justified by something about oneself, which threatens to be "metaphysical," in the wide sense used in this debate. Critics of Rawls have said rightly, "Whether Rawls can have liberal politics without metaphysical embarrassment is one of the central issues posed by Rawls' conception."[11]

Critics have queried especially the equality of persons in Rawls's initial position. Equality of what, and why? Dworkin argues: "Justice as fairness rests on the assumption of a natural right of all men and women to equality of concern and respect, a right they possess not by virtue of birth or characteristic or merit or excellence but simply as human beings with the capacity to make plans and give justice."[12] On what basis are they attributed that right?

Rawls replies to such accusations with arguments that his conception of justice is "political not metaphysical." His attempts in these arguments to avoid "metaphysics" completely are less than convincing and provide a lesson for all such attempts. He writes:

> A conception of the person in a political view, for example, the conception of citizens as free and equal persons, need not involve, so I believe, questions of philosophical psychology or a metaphysical doctrine of the nature of the self.[13]

Surely that is impossible. If, as a matter of fact, humans are not equal persons, there is no justice in conducting politics as if they are (except perhaps for Hobbesian reasons that such a delusion may contribute to public safety, but that is not Rawls's position); and if they are not, in fact, free, there is no point in giving them choices such as votes. But whether persons are free and of equal worth are basic metaphysical questions. Rawls admits that "The representation of their freedom seems to be one source of the idea that some metaphysical doctrine is presupposed," but replies, "Citizens are free in that they can conceive of themselves and of one another as having the moral power to have a conception of the good."[14] Indeed, they can so conceive of themselves, but is that conception correct? If so, it is a substantial metaphysics of the person. If not, it does not support a claim of justice for political institutions based on it.

As in the case of Gaita, thinking about the comparison with animals is useful. Rawls hopes to begin with the concept of "just distribution" without inquiring into the metaphysical difference between the "us" included in the distribution and the "them" not included. Merely having a life plan is taken to be sufficient legitimacy to be included in the distribution that one can rationally consent to. Yet the metaphysical difference between humans, who can have a life plan and rationally consent to distributions, and animals, who cannot, is immense. Founding ethics and politics on that difference while avoiding discussion of it is not honest.

And, in fact, avoiding foundational questions in philosophy is not so easy and Rawls does have a brief discussion on the "basis of equality," which raises the question of why animals are not included. It might be expected that he includes as participants in the initial position exactly those who can understand it, but instead he writes that "equal justice is owed to those who have the capacity to take part in and to act in accordance with the public understanding of the initial situation."[15] His use of "capacity" to extend rights beyond those who can actually understand to infants and the severely disabled indicates a degree of metaphysical stance on human nature.

Dworkin, in many ways the opposite of Rawls when it comes to the objectivity of ethics, shares with him a phobia of metaphysics – or in his own euphemism, his theory is "not a metaphysically ambitious one."[16] In defense of the "independence" of ethics from anything scientific or factual, he caricatures the search for metaphysical foundations of moral realism as "some nonmoral metaphysical argument showing that there is some kind of entity or property in the world – perhaps morally charged particles or morons – whose existence and configuration can make a moral judgment true."[17] That is not how it works. There *are* morally charged particles – the entities who used to be called morons (and other humans, too). They are not, however, "nonmoral," but inherently of worth, the nature and source of that worth being what has to be inquired about.

Rorty, too, argues against "rights foundationalism," but his reason is merely that the whole approach to human nature is "outmoded":

> We are much less inclined than our ancestors were to take 'theories of human nature' seriously, much less inclined to take ontology or history as a guide to life. We have come to see that the only lesson of either history or anthropology is our extraordinary malleability. We are coming to think of ourselves as the flexible, protean, self-shaping animal rather than as the rational animal or the cruel animal.[18]

The "we" whom he hopes to sweep into agreement with these thoughts will not include everyone. What makes "we" we, and us flexible and protean? We are not so protean as to turn into ferns or sponges, presumably. Indeed, the limited range of behavior of ferns and sponges is part of the nature of ferns and sponges, whereas the self-shaping abilities of humankind, such as they are, are supplied by human nature and are part of what makes humans something special. It is the possibility of human choice to shape oneself one way rather than another that leads to there being human ethics. There is no sponge ethics, and taking a theory of sponge nature seriously explains why.

Rorty's belief that history has anti-metaphysical lessons is shared, and to a higher degree, by the deeply historicist mainstream of continental philosophy. A foundational presumption of that tradition is that since some past philosopher, such as Kant or Hegel, "the basic condition of philosophizing changed; since then there has been no alternative to postmetaphysical thinking."[19] That is a large debate, but for present purposes we just need to note that only humans are subject to historical social and cultural pressures via language, and that is so in virtue of the nature of humans (and its difference from animal and rock nature). That very crude metaphysical difference is all that is needed to show why we cannot be "postmetaphysical" in general.

Yet another objection to metaphysics is based on the idea that metaphysics is theoretical and ethics is practical, so the former cannot imply the latter. That objection is advanced by the Grisez-Finnis school of Thomists: "From a set of theoretical premises, one cannot logically derive any practical truth, since any sound reasoning does not introduce what is not in the premises. . . . Therefore the ultimate principles of morality cannot be theoretical truths of metaphysics and / or philosophical anthropology."[20] But as argued in Chapter 1, the central thing in ethics is not practice but an inherent property, worth. It is true that some explanation needs to be given of how metaphysical properties do imply anything about practice, such as obligation; that will be done in Chapter 8. But obviously there is no problem in general about metaphysical properties having a bearing on practice, in, for example, the way that causality bears on the advisability of stepping off a cliff.

In the end, we are committed to inquiry into "metaphysics," in the basic sense of distinguishing the morally relevant from the morally irrelevant properties of things, as soon as we agree that a person's color is morally irrelevant to their rights but whether they are alive or dead is not.

Once we have explained what is wrong with anti-foundationalism about ethics, we may still wish to understand why it is so prevalent. Metaphysicians themselves may be tempted to speculate unkindly that the sort of philosophers who move into ethical and political theory are those with limited ability in more abstract areas. Perhaps some avoid looking into metaphysics for fear of what they might find. Others may have a genuine concern for public order, worrying that digging too vigorously in the foundations of ethics may cause them to collapse. But there is a simple explanation which requires no such alleged insights into the minds of theorists. It is the ubiquity of the view that ethics is really about human interests and their coordination. If that were so, there would be no need or scope for going deeper. As argued in previous chapters, that is not so, because what is most central in ethics is not human interests but why humans and their interests should matter in the first place.

EQUALITY OF WORTH

The second and more serious problem with looking for a property or properties that would be the explanation for their moral worth, is that any credible candidate is one that some humans might lack, wholly or partially. That would threaten the principle of equality of worth. So first we should consider whether the widespread commitment to equality is justified or whether we should consider relaxing it in favor of some conception of human moral worth as coming in degrees.

For example, if one chose rationality as the source of worth, and even if it is a threshold concept so that one is rational or not, it certainly seems that the range of rationality is considerable between the severely disabled and the genius. That could lead to unequal worth of persons, *prima facie* to grossly unequal worth.[21] The "great-souled" one or moral paragon may seem truly the one of worth and lesser mortals vermin or at best tools of the great. "The basic concern is that if status is grounded in certain valued traits that persons have, and these valued traits are present to different degrees in different persons, then it is hard to see how persons generally can have the same status."[22] Or again, "Whichever higher cognitive or practical capacity we choose, there will always be some humans who have *not yet* acquired it, others who *no longer* possess it, and those unlucky few who can *never* have it.... Once the religious dogma that all human beings were created in God's image has been excluded from scientific and philosophical discourse, there is no good reason left for assuming that all humans *qua humans* do possess an inherent moral worth."[23]

A positive aspect of the debate is that asking about equality has directed attention to worth, much more explicitly than has happened in other ethical topics. To ask about the basis of equality is most naturally taken to be a question about the equality of worth – although it is certainly possible to change the question to one about equal treatment in the absence of any inherent equality, or about equality only in the eyes of God or society, it is most natural to search for something inherent to humans, the having of which equally will support equality of rights. That is especially so since there is not much point in having equality in the case of zero worth. As Waldron writes, "Without this second dimension of worth [that is, positive ethical worth], basic equality might be taken to recommend treating all human lives as equally inconsequential and all human interests as equally matters of little or no concern."[24] Or in Larmore's words, "After all, when we realize that our own good does not, absolutely speaking, matter more than the good of others, we might perhaps conclude that therefore neither theirs nor ours matter at all. Being impartial has been known more than once to produce indifference."[25]

So the debate on equality is generally situated within the assumption of, or at least the search for, positive ethical worth of persons.

Equally crucial to the debate is the widespread and firm moral commitment to equality, in some important sense.

"Our equality of birth by nature impels us to seek equality under the law" is a thought as old as Plato, and Western law since ancient times has made serious efforts to implement that principle, including the removal of legal institutions incompatible with it, such as slavery.[26]

Although pure deductions from the abstract principle of equality cannot solve all questions in ethics, due to the diversity of qualities and circumstances of people, the principle of basic equality always has strong purchase in deciding real cases. As one typical example, an equal right of children to a fair share of educational resources will require different actions in the cases of a musical or mathematical prodigy, a well-adjusted child of average intelligence, and an intellectually disabled child. All have rights to education, but the plans must be tailored to each child's abilities to profit from teaching, and one plan may cost more than another. The equality of right is the driving force behind the complex planning.

It might seem, in such cases, that the principle of equality is so qualified in practice as to be close to vacuous. That is not true. To adapt a principle to circumstances is not to qualify it, but to work out its implications, in combination with other premises. The inability of the abstract principle of human equality to resolve complex disputes does not mean it plays little role. As Amartya Sen remarks in discussing the "equality of what?" question, if someone disputes an egalitarianism of economic outcomes with a theory of the equality of libertarian freedoms, the plausibility of both sides of the debate depends on their connections to a more basic equality of concern. If there were not some credibility to the contentions that equality of basic concern implied equality of economic outcomes and also equality of freedoms, then the dispute would not be able to get under way.[27] It is a natural temptation to wish to decide for either equality of outcomes, or resources, or opportunities, or initial positions in order to get down as soon as possible to the business of issuing policy prescriptions, but that avoids the hard work of discovering what the implications of basic equality are, as well as giving up any place from which to argue against those who make a different choice.

Similarly with the lifeboat cases that are staples of undergraduate teaching on the topic of equality. The stress of having to consider who should leave a lifeboat in which not all can survive is itself testament to the strength of our commitment to equality, and there is always a strong vote for the proposal that all should stay in the lifeboat and hope for the best. It is also possible to keep to a strict equality by deciding who is to go by lot. Even if we were to decide that (other things being equal) the old should go first on the grounds that they have less future to lose, a certain equality of consideration is preserved, in that the decision is proportional to the loss to be sustained, not proportional to any alleged superiority of personal worth or quality.

Although the complexity of real life makes for many hard cases in these fields, appeals to equality of consideration are always very powerful. And that does not mean merely that equality is weighted heavily in comparison with other considerations. It means that any other consideration, such as skin color or age or wealth, is by default of absolutely no weight, and the moral relevance of any consideration must be established in the face of the strong presumption against its relevance. Further, such a consideration, if relevant to one person, must be equally relevant to another; for example, if intellectual disability tells against one person's chance of gaining an academic position, it must tell equally against another's. In cases like these, different treatments of relevantly different people are not backslidings from the principle of basic equality, but workings-out of it in different circumstances.

That explains how the equality of worth of persons plays such a crucial role in normal moral deliberations, but not yet who counts as equal or why.

PROPERTIES TO FOUND WORTH:
OCCURRENT OR CAPACITIES?

While it is agreed that dead people do not have worth (though we treat human remains respectfully out of respect for what they were when living), simply being alive with human DNA seems doubtful as a sufficient basis for worth. Even those who attribute a full right to life to human zygotes are inclined to emphasize the potentiality of those beings to become full humans with normal properties like rationality. The agreement of the Catholic Church to the disposal of surplus frozen embryos, rather than calling for their adoption, suggests that even the most intransigent of supporters of the right of all biologically human entities to life will make exceptions. At the other end of life, too, it is accepted that sufficient evidence of brain inactivity is enough for the turning off of life support from a mostly living human body.

The problem is that if one chooses an occurrent property such as rationality or consciousness as the foundation of moral worth, one risks denying the moral equality of persons, since humans can differ widely in how currently rational they are. Even those in a temporary deep sleep could risk having their right to life challenged, if one takes occurrent rationality seriously enough.

Yet it is especially those lacking in occurrent rationality, freedom, and general ability to look after themselves whose interests need to be protected by moral theory.

It is not a sound move either to cobble together some attempt to include all humans via species membership, such as "belonging to a species such that maturation of its properly formed members includes possessing the capacity for rational agency."[28] First, that is a very thin description of individuals, making it unclear why such a complex description should be a sufficient ground of something as morally important as human dignity.[29] In any case, a species is, as the scholastics said, a being of reason. It is a class to which one belongs on the basis of properties one has, not vice versa, and what is owed to members must be in virtue of those properties. If an individual lacks those properties, it is unclear why it should be considered to belong fully to the species or to inherit the rights of full members of the species.[30]

It is natural to then turn to an account involving capacities, such as founding worth on the capacity for rationality or rational agency.

It is easy to think that any capacity theory can be dismissed as easily as any occurrent-property theory, on the grounds that "some human beings do not have the capacity for rational agency, newborn infants, for example, and those sunk deep into dementia. The capacity is not ineradicable."[31] Some disabled have not, never had, and never will have any real ability to exercise rationality. So one is tempted to conclude that no capacity account is possible.

It is not so easy to dismiss all capacity theories. "Capacity" is relevant, but difficult to define; there's capacity and capacity.[32]

The problem is to explain why it is a tragedy for an Alzheimer's victim to be unable to exercise rationality, whereas it is not a tragedy for a cat to be unable to exercise rationality (or a teratoma consisting of human cells either). It is something about them and the difference between them. It is not that Alzheimer's sufferers will have or did have the property of rationality either, nor being in the same species as beings that have the property. It is something they now have, something about being human, inherent to them, something which is now defective in expression.[33] Something has gone wrong with them, implying a capacity, in some sense, for it to have gone right and hence an evil in the defect. And it is not a Platonist abstract human nature or "design plan"[34] that they fail to participate in, but something in them that is in a defective state.

If some expensive medical technology could be found to restore them to normal human rational functioning, we would pay the money. So would we to prevent their condition worsening. They are humans – not "members of the human species," but actual humans – and so they deserve it. We don't pay money to do that for animals.

It is necessary to bite the bullet and draw a distinction. One can choose a property like rationality or consciousness or living a full human life as the moral ideal and the true story about what makes humans morally worthwhile. Then humans strong in those ways are in one sense genuinely morally superior; that is the point of their striving to improve themselves in those ways. "Appraisal respect," as it is sometimes called, must be of occurrent properties, which some humans lack.[35] The aim of moral life is to transform potency into act, because act is better. Those who fall short in those respects but are still human lack something important, but what gives them moral equality in a more basic sense is their (sadly unrealized) potentiality to realize those properties.

The point can be made with two examples.

The first example is the human embryo. Even if it is maintained that an early embryo is not a full human being with the rights of a human, there is still something tragic about the loss of early miscarriage. The grief it causes may not be identical to that from the loss of a newborn baby, but it is not like the pain of involuntary childlessness either. The entity would have grown into a definite human being, in the normal course of nature. The potentialities of an existent being, even if unrealized, are morally significant. In general, what someone could have been is what makes a tragedy of not being that (as when anyone dies young or goes seriously wrong in life).

The second example is what Gaita calls Judge Moshe Landau's "inspired intervention" at the trial of Adolf Eichmann in 1961.[36] There was no dispute that Eichmann had led a life among the morally worst possible, but Landau insisted that there should be no show trial and the only purpose of the trial was to see justice done. As Gaita interprets it, the meaning of his remark was that Eichmann, despite his overwhelming and obvious guilt, was owed a fair trial just because he was a human being. He was entitled, in Kantian terms, to respect but not reverence.

The same point is made by the Christian theory that humans, made in the image of God and equal in his sight, are subject to a Last Judgment, which separates the sheep from the goats. Are the damned morally equal to the blessed? Well, yes and no. It is their inherent equality, as persons, with the blessed that gave them the potentiality or opportunity to live lives like the blessed, and it is that same equal potentiality that gives point to their damnation for choosing to do the direct opposite.

It may help to ask, "What lacks for a human are most tragic?" Loss of cognition (for example, in dementia); of basic health; of consciousness (for example, when heavily drugged with morphine); of a minimal sense of pleasure and well-being (in depression or chronic pain); of basic social interaction (in solitary confinement). Those losses are terrible things to happen. It is wrong if people of Nazi temperament accuse such humans of having "lives not worth living." What is tragic is that they do have lives worth living, but are unable to live them. On the other hand, if they themselves find their lives unbearable and commit suicide, then, even if we think that is strictly speaking wrong, we have sympathy and wonder whether we might do the same if so afflicted. The fact that those outcomes are terrible is what makes the loss for those who sustain them catastrophic – not by deleting the basic humanity of the victim, but by resulting in the tragic combination of a continuing life and its being lived under terrible afflictions.

That has not answered the question of where to draw the line between humans and non-humans. At some point we may say that a mass of tissue with human DNA is not really a human being and does not have worth or rights. It is not the business of the foundations of ethics to decide exactly where to draw the line, or even whether there is a definite line to be drawn. It seems obvious that teratomas are on one side and babies soon before birth are on the other, but beyond that, it is for ethical reflection on medical facts to determine.

IN WHAT CATEGORY ARE THE BEARERS OF INTRINSIC VALUE?

If we do allow inquiry into the morally relevant properties of things, or "metaphysics," then before discussing which properties exactly are to the point, it would be advisable to have straight what *kinds* or categories of things could be the bearers of intrinsic value. Full-blooded entities (substances, in traditional terminology) such as people? Properties of people such as beauty or height? Mental experiences? Properties of the mental such as "the good will"? Whether a whole life is well lived? States of affairs such as justice in the distribution of goods? Relational properties such as being approved by society or loved by God? Events?

It could turn out that this question can only be answered by identifying the origin of moral worth itself. But *prima facie*, it ought to be more obvious what category/ies the ultimate bearer/s of worth is/are in. Failure to consider that question first can only result in confusion. At the very least, the debate will clarify what sort of answer we should be looking for when we ask, "What makes something have moral worth?"

Debate on this question has proceeded, but without clear issue. The problem may be false dichotomies in the alleged alternatives.

Elizabeth Anderson puts the case that the primary bearers of intrinsic value must be concrete particulars such as persons. Persons, she says, are what we actually care about – and while our caring does not create worth, it is an often reliable sign of what we take and ought to take to have worth:

> It makes sense for a person to value most states of affairs only because it makes sense for him to value persons, animals and other things.... All states of affairs that consist in someone's welfare are only extrinsically valuable. If it doesn't make sense to value the person (in a particular way), then it doesn't make sense to care about promoting her welfare.... states of affairs which consist in the existence of something are valuable only if it makes sense to care about the thing that exists....
>
> It makes sense for a person to value most [states of affairs] only because it makes sense for a person to care about the people, animals, communities, and things concerned with

them. This follows from the fact that our basic evaluative attitudes – love, respect, consideration, affection, honor, and so forth – are non-propositional. They are attitudes we take up immediately toward persons, animals, and things, not toward facts. Because to be intrinsically valuable is to be the immediate object of such a rational attitude, states of affairs are not intrinsically valuable if they are not immediate objects of such attitudes.[37]

A further reason for considering things as the primary bearers of worth is the observation of an important difference between the concepts of intrinsic worth of states of affairs ("Moorean" value in Ben Bradley's phrase) and that of intrinsic worth of persons ("Kantian" value). "Moorean intrinsic value can be either positive or negative – a state of affairs can be intrinsically good or intrinsically bad – but Kantian intrinsic value does not have that feature."[38] Surely the reason why states of affairs like a person's being disappointed can have negative value is that the value in question is not basic – it matters that someone is disappointed only because of the role of that state of affairs in the life course of that person. Or if it is maintained that, for example, pleasure is intrinsically good only when experienced by someone who deserves it,[39] that is a case of the positive or negative value of the experience being explained in terms of the more basic life of the possessor. On the other hand, the "Kantian" worth of a person is not subject to a negative because worth has "bottomed out." The worth of persons is where the buck stops, just because persons are substances. There are no negative substances.

Yet it is a false dichotomy to see a contrast between "Kantian" and "Moorean" intrinsic value. It is possible (and it will be argued below) that the ("Kantian") worth of things holds in virtue of the properties they have (hence of the "Moorean" value of their having those properties). The dichotomy must be a false one at least to some extent, because of the general metaphysical truth that a fact has a thing as a constituent. A fact or state of affairs, "*a*'s being F" has the object *a* as a constituent. So a thing and a fact about it are not separate or separable beings (to which one might, for example, take opposing attitudes). It makes no sense to admire someone for their courage while not admiring their courage.

Similar remarks apply to the theory of the Thomist William E. May that what gives humans worth is their soul, as the "principle" in them that makes rationality possible. He writes:

> The ultimate reason why *some* human beings are capable of becoming minded entities (i.e. moral beings) is something rooted in their being human beings to begin with, something that they share with those members of the human species who are *not* actually minded or moral beings, and something that is the root reason why they and *all* members of the human species (including neonates, infants, raving maniacs and fetuses) are beings of moral worth. This "something" has been variously named. It is the *ruach* of the Old Testament and the *pneuma* of the New Testament; it is the *nous poietikos* of Aristotle, the *mens* of Augustine, the *anima subsistens* of Aquinas, the *memoire* of Bergson, the *Geist* of Rahner. However named it is the principle immanent in human beings, a constitutive and defining element of their entitative makeup, that makes them to be what and who they are: beings of moral worth capable of becoming minded entities or moral beings; it is a principle of immateriality or of transcendence from the limitations of materially individuated existence.[40]

The theory that rationality needs an immaterial "principle" may or may not be correct. It may be that rationality is indeed not possible for purely material objects. But for present purposes it would not matter if the "principle" of rationality proved to be something material in brain activity. What is significant is that what has moral worth is a whole human being, but in virtue of whatever "principle" is in the human being that gives it powers of rationality (or whatever the worth-conferring property or activity is).

There are indeed alternative theories as to what has worth that are genuinely different from a substance-in-virtue-of-its-properties theory. The main one is that it is experiences themselves that have value. That is, experiences themselves are the items of value, and the beings that have them are merely their carriers. Aristotle's eudaimonism tends to value life-goods, like being magnanimous and how life goes, rather than the humans that have it; at least, that is the impression it gives, even if it does not explicitly deny worth to humans.[41] G. E. Moore says that "personal affection and the appreciation of what is beautiful in Art and Nature," are not only "the most valuable things which we know or can imagine," but they are also "good in themselves"[42] – and his theory has no worth of persons separate from that.

In favor of the experience theory and against the theory that humans themselves have value, several authors have put the "dreamless sleep argument." Noah Lemos argues: "Imagine a world with only people in a dreamless sleep. There is no value in the existence of that world: only people's being wise or happy is of intrinsic value."[43] Put that way, there may appear to be a conflict between the theory that people are the bearers of intrinsic value and the theory that states of consciousness are. But the apparent starkness of that conflict depends on some metaphysical assumptions. If, for example, people just *were* (a succession of) states of consciousness, as one version of a Cartesian philosophy of mind might hold, the conflict would disappear. In fact, people are not a succession of states of consciousness, as being embodied is essential to them. But neither is it true that there exist, on the one hand, people as bare particulars and, on the other hand, separate entities, states of consciousness. The relation between persons and states of consciousness is more intimate than that. Their states of consciousness are part of what they are.

If one took rationality or happiness or something similar as what gave people worth, then the conflict would be largely resolved. People in dreamless sleeps are in a position similar to the severely disabled discussed above: Though potentially rational and hence having worth (and having rights not to be murdered), they lack occurrent rationality. The reason for their worth nevertheless makes essential reference to occurrent rationality, and true benefits to them can only supervene on their rationality being exercised. That does not detract from worth being a property of them – but it is a property they have in virtue of their capacity for rationality.

The debate may be compared to that on the bearer of causality. What kinds of entities are causes – things, properties of things, events, processes, states of affairs ...? [44] The answers are not necessarily incompatible alternatives. If the earth causes the moon to revolve around it, it is rightly said that the cause is a thing. But the earth has that effect in virtue of its mass, which is the causally relevant property of it. And if one separates the history of the earth into time-slices, and observes that the earth's position and mass at one time moves the moon at a slightly later time, one can equally regard events as the causes involved. The relations between these ways of speaking are not especially metaphysically opaque. It just means that objects behave causally in virtue of the properties they have, and that properties in order to act must be properties *of* existing objects. It is similar if it is maintained that persons have value in virtue of, say, rationality or in virtue of their actual or potential conscious states (or in virtue of some properties of the latter such as awareness or pleasure). Those are not incompatible positions but specifications of a single position.

There is, however, still an important difference between maintaining that people have worth in virtue of their experiences and the capacity for them, and true "experientialism," the view that it is just loose experiences that have value. It is Peter Singer's unswerving commitment to experientialism that has resulted in his many deviations from normal moral views. His "preference utilitarianism" consists in holding that what is right is what maximises the satisfaction of preferences or interests, which are conceived of as conscious occurrents. All interests are equal; "an interest is an interest, whoever's interest it may be"[45] (as opposed to equality of the entities having the interests). So what is right is determined solely by counting and balancing interests, in abstraction from the entities having them. That explains Singer's derivation of the daring ethical theses for which he is well known, such as that a human infant has no conscious interests and hence no inherent right to life, especially if there are no adults who wish it to survive. The difference between his extreme version of experientialism and philosophy of the worth of persons in virtue of their experiences is evident in his endorsement of replaceability: He argues that if painlessly killed animals are replaced by similar ones, there is no net moral loss, and the same for humans; indeed, killing a disabled child and replacing it with a newly conceived healthy child is a net gain in experiences and so ought to be done.[46] That corollary, or reductio, of pure experientalism exposes why it can give no weight, even *prima facie*, to the life of the disabled child who is to be done away with.

The same problem arises for more classic versions of utilitarianism. If taken literally, the ideal of "the greatest happiness of the greatest number" implies loading the ills of the many onto a single scapegoat if possible, or favoring those with special talents for enjoying a champagne lifestyle. That is because happiness is valued as a kind of stuff to be calculated with and maximized, in abstraction from the people possessing the happiness. That is, it values experience in abstraction from the experiencer. Those are the conclusions where utilitarianism most directly clashes with ordinary moral intuition.

In fact, if experience is a stuff valued in abstraction from the experiencer, utilitarianism ought to advocate maximizing total happiness rather than average happiness – that is, increasing the population at the expense of average happiness.[47] For obvious reasons, this position has been downplayed in utilitarian circles. As Rawls and others put it, classical utilitarianism does not respect the "separateness of persons."[48] Doing so would, of course, imply some commitment to the worth of persons as such.

By valuing the person in the first instance, the theory of moral worth stands against any version of replaceability. In that way it agrees with love. The "lover" on the lookout to "trade up" to a better partner is not doing love the right way. An entity having worth in virtue of some properties is not replaceable by one with the same properties, because the replacement involves disposing of *its* worth.[49]

A foundation of ethics in the worth of entities such as persons will not be tempted to those novelties, even when it agrees that the worth of persons depends on the properties and potentialities they have.

The upshot is that we can investigate what gives humans worth without having to obsessively watch our metaphysical back concerning the category of the entities involved. We can agree that substances have worth primarily, but if we are careful, we can still agree with G. E. Moore, who variously attributed intrinsic value to individual things, states of consciousness or their qualities, the existence of things, types of things, and states of things.[50]

COULD WORTH BE A RELATION TO SOMETHING ELSE?

A few authors have argued that the worth of humans, though real, is not intrinsic to them but is conferred by something external. Richard Rorty, after asserting that there is no "human nature" for rights to be grounded in, holds they are socially conferred.[51] Nicholas

Wolterstorff, whose account of human rights and their connection to worth in many ways agrees with the present one, argues that there is no intrinsic feature common to all humans (for example Alzheimer's patients would lack any version of capacity for rationality) and concludes that the only possible foundation for human worth is being loved by God.[52] The "conferred by society" theory has the defect, not shared by the divine conferral theory, that "society" is just other people, so if they themselves have no inherent standing as beings of worth, it is hard to see how they could confer any worth on anything else. But the theories share the view that worth is conferred by a relation to something external.

One problem for the theory is to explain why those outside forces, society or God, should choose to confer worth on some things but not on others. Surely it is not a purely free decision of society or God to choose certain entities on which to confer worth and to ignore others? If God were to choose to confer worth on female humans and male cockroaches and to deny it to male humans and female cockroaches, his will would be not only arbitrary but a violation of what we know about the nature of humans and cockroaches. Cockroaches do not have sufficient properties to bear the weight of conferred worth. It just does not fit. God, if he is to confer worth, ought to attend to the antecedent differences in, for example, the capacity for rationality or ability to be grateful to God.

Wolterstorff concedes, in fact, that crocodiles could not be chosen by God as his friends, since "being friends with God is incompatible with crocodilian nature. To be a friend with God one has to have the nature of a person."[53] But then, having the potential for friendship with God is high up in the scale of things, seriously of worth. Surely a being which God would think worthy of friendship (or even, on a Christian view, worthy of being incarnated as) already has inherently quite sufficient worth to ground the usual human rights such as the right not to be tortured.[54]

As Wolterstorff says, conferred worth is something like the "sentimental value" of a relic. If I value a ring because my mother wore it at her wedding, that value does not arise from any inherent properties of the ring. That sort of value can be conferred on almost anything. But that is called "value" (in distinction from inherent worth) just because of its arising from an act of valuing by an outside valuer. It does not arise from properties of the item valued. Surely that is quite unlike human or divine love. That attaches to its object because the object is worth loving. Loved persons may be flawed, but a flaw is a defect in something which is inherently of worth. Love, as opposed to sentimental valuing, only has point when what is valued is worthwhile in itself. Sentimental value is inherited by something via its historical connection with what does have inherent value: My mother's ring has value to me because my mother wore it, and I loved my mother. *Her* worth is of a different kind. It is inherent to her.

How will one know what has the relational property, if not by looking at inherent properties? In principle, revelation might determine it, but the Bible and the Quran do not discuss matters of marginal humanity like dementia.[55] God is portrayed as addressing commands to humans in general, but infants and the demented cannot understand or obey the Ten Commandments. How could we know where the boundary is of what entities God loves, if not by looking at the qualities they have that make them sufficiently human?

My love cannot bestow worth on an Alzheimer's patient, and neither can God's. It must respond to, or as Gaita says reveal, something which, though perhaps hidden, is already there. That can only be the inherent worth of the whole person.

CHAPTER FIVE

The Supervenience of Worth on Natural Properties

◈

THE NATURE OF the relation between worth and its grounding properties, such as rationality, is a difficult one. *Prima facie,* potential grounding properties like rationality (agency, individuality …) are specifiable without explicit reference to anything ethical (evaluative, normative …) while the worth that arises from them is paradigmatically ethical. Yet it will be argued that rationality (agency, individuality …) are wholly sufficient to ground worth. That appears to conflict with Humean intuitions about the is-ought or fact-value distinction, according to which an unbridgeable gap lies between the two.

Supposing we are able to identify some (metaphysical) properties of humans that ground or account for their worth, what exactly is the relation of worth to the grounding properties? What does the supervenience of worth on those properties mean? The supervenience or grounding relation that holds between rationality (etc.) and worth will have to be a metaphysically powerful one. Though to an extent *sui generis,* we can hope to partly understand it through a comparison with a number of other, non-moral, relations of supervenience, especially that between logical relations and the normativity of reasons for belief.

WHAT DOES "GOODNESS" ADD?
WHAT ACTUALLY IS "GOOD"?

In fact, there are two separate questions about the relation of grounding properties to worth. The first question is, What does an assertion of being "good" add to just being rational, emotive, or whatever natural properties are the grounds of worth? What is actually being claimed by the goodness-as-well claim? (The second question, to be considered in the next section, is how to explain what the relation is between supervenient goodness and "base" or "grounding" properties such as rationality.)

As usual, thinking that ethics is fundamentally about action or attitudes muddies the waters. As discussed in Chapter 3, Aristotle's disastrous "definition" of the good as "what all things aim at" got things off on the wrong foot by linking the good essentially to action. Similarly, thinking that the good is what is admirable would be to put epistemology before ontology. We wish to know what the good is, that makes admiration an appropriate attitude to it, and that makes aiming at it the right thing to do.

Similarly, thinking that ethics is fundamentally about reasons for action encourages a "buck-passing" theory of the good, whose conclusion is that there is no distinct property of goodness needing explanation. Such a theory holds that once we understand the reasons for action, such as that murder is murderous, we do not need any further quality of "badness" to be possessed by murder. That would add nothing to the reasons for action that we already have. "In short, value adds no reasons to those generated by the ground for that value."[1] Hence there is no need to posit a property of goodness or badness as such, over and above non-ethical properties. Frank Jackson writes:

> It is hard to see how the further properties could be of any ethical significance. Are we supposed to take seriously someone

who says, 'I see that this action will kill many and save no one, but that is not enough to justify my not doing it; what really matters is that the action has an extra property such that only ethical terms are suited to pick out'? In short, the extra properties would be ethical idlers.[2]

The problem is that, as has been argued in earlier chapters, the buck can be passed along for a while, but stops at worth. What is wrong with murder is a moral wrongness, and the reasons for that are not simply that it has the descriptive features collected under "is murderous." The fact that an action will kill many renders it bad solely because the death of many is an evil, as they have intrinsic worth which will be destroyed by their death. If that were not true, murder would matter no more than stone breaking and hence would not be wrong. That worth is an ethical property, and still needs explaining.

G. E. Moore directly addressed the question of what goodness is, but gave an answer widely regarded as unhelpful if true. He said that "good" is a property that is indefinable, unanalyzable, like "yellow" or "pleasure."[3]

The comparison with "yellow" has proved misleading, as it carries the suggestion that good is a property, so to speak, painted on the surface of objects. Plainly that is not right, and it is not what Moore said. The similarity that Moore intends us to seize on is just the aspect of being unanalyzable in terms of any simpler concepts. It is not surprising if language does have unanalyzable concepts, admitting of no further analysis just because they are absolutely simple. A concept's being unanalyzable is not a sign of something being wrong with it.

In fact, according to one line of linguistic investigation, all languages share some sixty-five "semantic primes," which are atomic and which can be combined to make all concepts in all languages – concepts such as "I," "big," "part," "before," "can," "if," and so on. "Good" and "bad" are among them.[4] The details remain controversial, but it is reasonable that concepts like those listed are simple, and that there is nothing problematic about them on that account. No one complains they cannot understand "part," or claims it is a mysterious notion, just because it is primitive. If "good" is, as Moore thinks, simple and its meaning is just intuited, it is in good company.

However, just as yellow, even if simple, may be compared with neighbors in its "spectrum" like "green," good may be usefully compared with other "transcendentals" such as "being," "truth/logical relations," and "beauty." Reductive analyses are unlikely to be had, but considerable understanding of them is near-universal, in a sense appropriate to each.

THE GOOD AS PERFECTION OF FORM?

There has, however, been one important attempt to analyze the good, which if not totally successful, has yielded valuable insights.

If we are in search of theories of what good is, theories which will apply to a basic and non-relational property like the worth of persons, we will find there are very few products on the market. But there is one – a very old and powerful theory, though not often taken seriously in recent times. It is the doctrine of Augustine and Aquinas, based on Plato and Aristotle, that the good is perfection.[5] The meaning of this is that everything has a nature, the working out of which without defect is a self-realization of its nature. The full actualization of any nature has a kind of radiance, appreciable by a rightly formed ethical perception. For example, learning and justice are perfections of the rational nature of humans and are good, while admiration of learning and justice comes naturally to any mind not clouded by a defect such as prejudice.

The theory is not intended as a definition of the meaning of "good." It is an analysis of what good is actually found to consist in, and a criterion of identifying the good (for each kind of thing). It is not intended to reduce the good to something non-evaluative, as "perfection" retains the evaluative connotations it has in ordinary language. But it is claimed that the good as perfection removes any mystery from the good, as it is recognizable, of any thing (that is, substance), what its form is, and hence whether it is realizing it or has failed to do so. The form provides a measure of whether the good has been attained. The theory thus fits best with an Aristotelian world picture in which the world is uniquely divided into things which are, in turn, uniquely divided into species; but since that is true of the entities to which we are most concerned to attribute worth, such as humans and related species, that is not a serious limitation.

That theory requires accepting that every nature is good. The convertibility of being and goodness is indeed accepted by Augustine and Aquinas, along with its corollary that all evils are defects, that is, failures of a nature to realize itself fully. Certain lower natures, such as that of rocks, are not as impressive as some higher ones, but the realization of even rock nature is claimed to be a minimal sort of good. The perfection of some natures, such as that of mosquitos, may tend to cause a defect in the development of others, such as humans, but that is no objection to recognizing their perfection in itself.

The Aristotelian aspects of the theory connect perfection with teleology – the perfection of a thing's nature is its *telos* – what it actually aims at in its developmental unfolding (or, in the case of free natures, what it ought to aim at but can decide to frustrate). A thing will realize its nature unless some impediment prevents it. The Platonist and Neoplatonist aspects of the theory connect it to the perfection of the highest form – the Good, or the One, or God. The Good is the highest perfection and necessarily expresses itself in creation, while the good of creatures participates in that of the highest reality.

The theory has certain problems, some of which are surmountable. It is certainly defensible that every existing thing is good, to some minimal degree.[6] Popular contemporary theories like deep ecology strike a similar note and express the theory in a style more congenial to the contemporary mind than deeply alien ancient philosophies like Neoplatonism, where the theory was originally most at home. It is natural to see evils as mattering because they happen to things that themselves matter, or have intrinsic worth, and to that degree at least the Augustinian theory that evils are defects of what is inherently good is reasonable.

The problem is more the failure of the theory to address the grading of good, as in the kinds of good there are. On a theory of the intrinsic worth of humans, it was the difference between the worth of humans and of rocks that chiefly needed explaining. If rocks have worth, it is hardly to an ethically significant degree. A vanishing asteroid is not a tragedy, even a small one. But the theory that all things have a form whose perfection is their good addresses what rocks and humans have in common, not what distinguishes them. A rock and a human may each realize their nature, but an imperfect human is worth more than a perfect rock. What makes that so? It must be that some forms are more perfect than others – where "perfect" here cannot mean simply "realizing themselves fully" but must have an irreducibly moral element. As John Crosby explains it:

> Let us think of the goodness, or value, or dignity that is proper to human beings in distinction to plants and subhuman animals. We readily see that this is not good in the formal sense [that is, perfect relative to its form] at all. For the formal sense presupposes the distinction between an individual and its kind: in calling something "good" we want to say that it is a good one of its kind, or that it eminently fulfils the idea of form of its kind. But when we speak of the dignity of man we speak of good that belongs to a kind. Every human being equally possesses this dignity as a result of being human in

kind, and there is no such thing as an eminent or a deficient possession of this dignity. And there is another highly significant kind of good which also does not have this "good one of its kind" structure. It has been said (by Joseph Pieper, among others) that in loving another I say in effect to him or her: "How good it is that you exist." There is no such thing as an eminent or deficient possession of this good; what we have here is good that goes with this person being the unrepeatable, incommunicable person that he or she is. So here too good is not formal but "contentful."[7]

Also, gratitude, justice, and the like may be, in fact, perfections of humans, but they are not good *because* they are perfections of humans. They perfect human nature because they are themselves good (in a way that is possible for humans).[8]

So we will need an additional theory of the grading of forms, to explain why some forms such as rationality confer a great deal of worth and others such as rockness a nugatory amount. That must explain what it is about the form that issues in its worth, so will be some form of supervenience theory, as described below.

The second problem faced by the perfection theory is its implications for the worth of defective members of species. If the good is perfection of form, species members who fail to reach that perfection appear to have no source of worth, so the scrap heap looms for them as it does for broken pots. That consequence was certainly evident in Aristotle's assumption that the great-souled one was a higher being that the ordinary human, who was in turn much more deserving than those naturally slaves. Equality of worth of humans (or of any other species) is hard to reconcile with a theory that bases goodness on perfection of form.

It is possible to address that concern with the Aristotelian theory of "first and second act."[9] "First act" is just being a kind of thing, such as being a human. "Second act" is the exercise of operations proper to that kind, such as thinking. Humans could then be equal in first act but not in second act. But that simply transfers attention to first act itself. What is good about being a human that is different from the goodness of a rock? It is not perfection relative to form. So again we need a theory of the goodness of kinds.

It should be concluded that the perfection theory of goodness has a use in exhibiting the importance of perfection and defect as ethical notions, but not as a reductive analysis of "good." Some supervenience theory is still needed to explain how being a certain way, naturalistically, necessarily results in its being of ethical worth.

SUPERVENIENCE/GROUNDING

The second question to be answered about grounding properties and worth is what the relation is between supervenient goodness or worth and its "base" or "grounding" properties such as rationality. (In current philosophical argot, the relation is usually called "grounding" and the word "supervenience" is used of a wider class of relations of necessitation,[10] but we do not keep to this distinction here.)

There is one basic reason for the thesis that the ethical supervenes on some non-ethical base. Almost the only thesis agreed nearly universally in metaethics is that entities the same in all natural properties are morally equivalent.[11] As G. E. Moore puts it, "If a given thing possesses any kind of intrinsic value in a certain degree, then not only must that same thing possess it, under all circumstances, in the same degree, but also anything *exactly like* it, must, under all circumstances, possess it in exactly the same degree."[12] Intrinsic value thus differs from aesthetic value, or at least art-market value, which varies according to relational properties such as "having been painted by Leonardo."

Before examining the nature of supervenience in the abstract, we should address an initial suspicion that the whole project is fraudulent.

It can at first appear special pleading, or even a paradox, to assert that the good is so strongly connected to its grounding properties as to be necessitated by them, yet is somehow fundamentally different from and additional to them. *Prima facie,* rationality, capacities for free action, individuality, and so on, are non-ethical properties while worth is ethical, so there is an is-ought gap and the threat of an open question argument (asking whether anything with those properties is really good). So is that not an attempt to have one's cake and eat it, by asserting a significant (moral) addition to (natural) being, yet at the same time reducing it to "nothing more than" the base on which it supervenes? And the bigger the gap asserted, the more suspicious the relation of supervenience would seem to be.

That concern is best addressed initially by comparing ethical supervenience with some examples of supervenience which are better understood – if not perfectly, then at least without the apparently special problems of ethical supervenience. Some possible comparators are:

- The supervenience of (spatial) symmetry on the position of parts

- The supervenience of the meaning of words on spoken and written marks

- The supervenience of chess strategy on the rules of chess

- The supervenience of algorithms on their software implementations

- The supervenience of the betweenness relations among colors on the colors themselves

- The supervenience of the singleton set {Socrates} on Socrates

- The supervenience of the truth of p^q on the truth of p and the truth of q

- The supervenience of a statue on its shaped material (the relation of material constitution)

- The supervenience of truths on their truthmakers: that "truth supervenes on being, and that successful predication supervenes on nature."[13]

- The supervenience of God's approval on the goodness of an act (and of God)

- The supervenience of the rationality of belief on logical relations

- The supervenience of the social world on the mental worlds of individuals

One might also be tempted to consider:

- The supervenience of the mental on the physical[14]

but for present purposes it would be better to leave that aside as it is too poorly understood, and it may be that the relation of emergence in that case is unlike supervenience. If Cartesian dualism were true, which *prima facie* it could be, the mental would not supervene on the physical. But there is no analogue of Cartesian dualism that would render the singleton set of x not supervenient on x, or goodness not supervenient on natural properties. The supervenience relation we are considering has a tighter and more transparent necessity than (on present knowledge) the relation between the physical and the mental.

In each of these cases, the supervenient entities are substantially different in kind from the supervenience base. Yet we can under-stand – in principle fully and purely by thinking – how the base nec-essarily gives rise to the supervenient entities or properties, and how these entities/properties are therefore not "queer" in Mackie's sense, nor supernatural. It is argued that the supervenience of moral worth on the natural properties of persons is fundamentally the same as these kinds of supervenience. At the very least, these cases provide models for the supervenience of moral worth, and show there is nothing misconceived in the notion of supervenience itself.

Certainly it is a substantial philosophical project, in each case, to give an account of how the supervenient entity is grounded in the base. Some have progressed further than others. Any lack of progress does not motivate dismissing the supervening entity as "merely" the base. Instead it motivates work to explain why simple reductive strategies have poor prospects and what it is that the supervenient entity adds ontologically.

With those examples in mind, we can examine attempts to explain the relation of supervenience in general. Work has proceeded apace, and with some success, in recent decades on the nature of the relation of metaphysical grounding or supervenience.

First, supervenience relates properties "out there," not concepts or words. It is a feature of how the world is, not how we think or talk about it. Of course, supervenience is possible for mental entities, too, such as the supervenience of rational belief on logical relations, but it is a relation of entities, not a relation between concepts.

Second, supervenience is not just necessary connection, and it is asymmetrical between ground and superstructure. Necessarily, Socrates exists if and only if the singleton set {Socrates} exists, but the set supervenes on Socrates, not vice versa. But it is a strictly *necessary* connection, not merely a nomic connection subject to miraculous exception. [15]

Third, it is not reduction: It is not true that the supervening entity is "nothing but" the base. Supervenience involves an "addition to being." As Paul Audi describes it:

> One of my assumptions is that there are certain non funda-
> mental properties, properties that are never instantiated
> brutely, but always because some other properties are. It is in
> making sense of the force of this 'because' that grounding
> earns its keep. I will assume that there are normative proper-
> ties, semantic properties, aesthetic properties, determinables,
> and dispositions, and that none of these is instantiated
> brutely ... my ethical example presupposes a nonreductive
> view of wrongness because if wrongness should reduce to
> some natural property, then the relation between the natural
> fact and the normative fact would be identity.[16]

Fourth, supervenience is not contingent identity either, as in the identification of lightning with an electrical discharge in the clouds, or water with H_2O. In those cases, there is really only one entity (respectively electrical discharge and H_2O) and what "lightning" and "water" add is merely how they initially present to humans. The dif-ference is conceptual rather than ontological – ontologically, there is no difference whatsoever between water and H_2O. Good is not like that, relative to its natural base, nor are the other cases listed above. Good is not identified with a natural property, but is said to arise of necessity from natural properties. It is the same with singleton sets and the other cases.

Whether supervenience is the same as emergence, as in the emer-gence of chaotic behavior from simple equations or the emergence of life from biochemistry, is not easy to say. Emergence is less well understood than supervenience (and will be considered briefly in the Epilogue). For present purposes, there is no need to determine that.

We conclude that supervenience is a sufficiently well-understood notion to perform the task of grounding the ethical in the non-ethical or natural. It is true that attempts to do so directly with right actions have proved implausible. If we attempt to ground, say, the wrongness of stealing in natural facts about acts of stealing, we will not succeed. Acts of stealing surely do not possess metaphysical properties that distinguish them from acts of non-stealing, and in any case, we are well aware that the wrongness arises from something external to the action itself, in its relation to the moral standing of the victim. Hence, it is rightly said that "the claim that some set of non-normative facts F makes a particular action wrong hangs in the air as an explanation of why the action is wrong without some further account of where F gets the wrong-making force it bears."[17] But the situation is very different when a further account has already been given through the process of passing the wrong-making buck back to the worth of persons. Persons have certain natural properties, such as rationality and the capacity for free action. We have a strong intuitive sense both of how those properties confer moral worth (in that something identical to a person in those properties could not fail to have the same moral worth), and also how that worth underpins or generates the rightness and wrongness of actions. The theory of supervenience in general provides an explication of that intuition, and an explication that is not an ad hoc posit just for the case of moral worth.

Whether a supervenience theory such as this results in an ethical theory that should be called "naturalist" is not easy to say. If colors are natural, then presumably so are the betweenness relations that supervene on the colors. But if Socrates is natural, it is unclear whether the singleton set {Socrates} that supervenes on him is also natural. Philosophies of set theory could differ about that. Given that the word "naturalism" has normally been used in ethics to describe theories that are reductionist, a supervenience theory, which denies the strict reduction of ethical to non-ethical properties, should probably count as non-naturalist. But nothing important hangs on the name.

THE MORAL/WORTH AND EPISTEMIC/LOGIC PARALLEL

Developing just one of the above parallels will make clearer the nature of the supervenience of the ethical on the natural, especially by showing how supervenience is not an ad hoc posit for the moral case but is unavoidable anyway. The supervenience of right belief on good reasons is (up to a point) well understood. And if it is not fully understood, that is our fault, not any defect on its part.

The parallel with belief and reasons is a good pick because the space of reasons and the moral space both contrast with the space of natural causes in the same way. The base in each case consists of observable scientific properties, of brains and societies going about their causal business and issuing moral (respectively rational) conclusions, while the superstructure of absolute demands of morality (respectively rationality) appear *prima facie* to float free in a Platonic realm which imposes objective standards on the outputs of the causal processes. Whatever is, is caused, but "Whatever is, is right" is equally false in the moral and logical worlds.

This parallel has been defended in recent times, but in the more usual ethical context where ethics is taken to be about (moral) reasons for action. The parallel is then between moral reasons for action and logical or evidential reasons for belief, both said to be "normative." Terence Cuneo argues:

(1) If moral facts do not exist, then epistemic facts do not exist.

(2) Epistemic facts exist.

(3) So, moral facts exist.

(4) If moral facts exist, then moral realism is true.

(5) So, moral realism is true.[18]

Commitment to epistemic facts (premise 2) means, for example, that "'Sam's belief about UFOs is irrational' and 'Beliefs based on good evidence are justified' are examples of epistemic sentences."[19] They are true sentences, expressing how things stand objectively in the space of reasons.

Cuneo's reasons for accepting premise 1 are simply the close parallels between the moral and the logical cases. The usual reasons for holding that moral facts do not exist is that they possess features taken to be objectionable, such as being categorically demanding, being (causally) explanatorily idle, and supervening on naturalistic facts in an apparently mysterious way, without seeming to fit into the naturalist picture of the world. But epistemic facts have those features as well, so any objections to moral facts would carry over to epistemic facts. But epistemic facts are widely accepted and are unavoidable (and, as Cuneo argues at length, not reducible to anything naturalistic).[20]

Similar ideas are found in T. M. Scanlon's "reasons fundamentalism," in which reasons (especially for action, but also for belief) "are not reducible to or identifiable with non-normative truths, such as truths about the natural world of physical objects, causes and effects, nor can they be explained in terms of notions of rationality or rational agency that are not themselves claims about reasons."[21]

The ideas behind this parallel need to be transposed from an action-based into a worth-based ethics. Indeed, the parallel becomes clearer there. To parallel worth we would want something "not about us," but reasons in the absolute and external sense of pure logic. There are such reasons, existing in logical space (whatever that is), independent of our desires and interests – logical facts such as "the evidence in court did not reach proof beyond reasonable doubt of the defendant's guilt," "modus ponens is valid," "the ontological argument is worthless," "Fermat's Last Theorem is proved." They are authoritative or prescriptive in that for thinking to be right it must conform to them, but that is secondary their obtaining as facts in the logical realm.

It is unfortunate that it is not possible to back up these claims with an agreed philosophy of logic, in the sense of a theory of the nature of logic, nor is there even a leading contender. So we have a poor grasp of the metaphysics of "facts in the logical realm." Philosophers not in the area tend to adopt by default a Fregean Platonism, in which logical relations are abstract entities holding between "propositions," which are themselves abstract entities in the Platonist sense. Other views are defended, but remain controversial.[22] But for present purposes, that does not matter. Even if we have not found it yet, there must be a correct philosophy of the nature of logic which explains its independence from our desires, interests, institutions, and mistakes in thinking. Philosophers would be the last people in a position to deny that logical reasons exist and give us good reason to think something, since dealing in such reasons is what their work consists in. If moral realism can establish its similarity to logical realism, it is looking very solid.

SUPERVENIENCE, HUME'S IS-OUGHT GAP, MOORE'S NATURALISTIC "FALLACY," AND MACKIE'S "QUEERNESS"

Since worth is an ethical property that is claimed to supervene on properties such as rationality that are not explicitly ethical, some discussion is needed on Hume's is-ought gap and whether supervenience bridges it.

But first, we should recall that "Humean intuitions" on the gap between the natural and the ethical are just that – intuited only from the time of Hume. Since then it has seemed natural to write such things as "It is obvious that a normative feature of persons (such as intrinsic worth) or a normative rule that is said to apply to all persons (such as an injunction to respect persons as such) cannot be derived solely from a descriptive metaphysical characteristic."[23] That is not obvious, and was denied at least implicitly by almost everyone before Hume gave it a thought. The orthodox view before then was of a Great Chain of Being, with the world's entities arranged in a scale of increasing perfection, from minerals to plants to animals to humans to angels to God.[24] It was taken to be obvious that the higher entities in the Chain were more perfect, so that increasing metaphysical sophistication implied increasing absolute importance, or worth. (We will consider the Chain further when discussing the worth of the non-human in Chapter 7.) Even today, those deep ecologists who argue that all species are equally valuable, or that rocks are as worthwhile as animals or people, usually recognize an air of paradox in their position of "ontological egalitarianism."[25] But if it really were obvious that metaphysical differences did not support moral ones, that would not be so.

Hume's passage is quoted here, despite its familiarity, in order to examine how its claims relate to supervenience, which is, of course, not a concept found in Hume.

> In every system of morality, which I have hitherto met with, I have always remark'd, that the author proceeds for some time in the ordinary ways of reasoning, and establishes the being of a God, or makes observations concerning human affairs; when of a sudden I am surpriz'd to find, that instead of the usual copulations of propositions, is, and is not, I meet with no proposition that is not connected with an ought, or an ought not. This change is imperceptible; but is however, of the last consequence. For as this ought, or ought not, expresses some new relation or affirmation, 'tis necessary that it shou'd be observ'd and explain'd; and at the same time that a reason should be given; for what seems altogether inconceivable, how this new

relation can be a deduction from others, which are entirely different from it.... [So] the distinction of vice and virtue is not founded merely on the relations of objects, nor is perceiv'd by reason.[26]

As stated, Hume's is-ought gap is expressed in terms of logical deducibility. But it is implausible that the relation of natural properties to moral ones is either logical like "All bachelors are bachelors" or via "analytic bridge principles" involving meaning, like "All bachelors are unmarried." "By the same token, you can't derive non-vacuous 'hedgehog' conclusions from 'hedgehog'-free premises."[27] Claims about deducibility do not bear on claims of supervenience, since logic relates concepts and supervenience relates properties. Also Hume's gap as stated is about the gap between the factual and the normative, "is" and "ought," and as explained in Chapter 1, worth is not fundamentally about the normative or oughts. So it is unclear whether Hume's gap, if it exists, refers to that between the scientifically factual and worth or that between worth and obligation. (The latter gap will be discussed in Chapter 8.)

Nevertheless there is something correct, as has been widely felt, about Hume's assertion of some gap between "relations of objects" or the purely scientific properties of the world, and ethical properties. The nature of that gap, since it is not a matter of logic, is not very clear. But it is clear that the property of rationality lies on one side of the gap, the scientific side, and worth on the other. Piling up scientific facts about an object fails to include any facts (if facts they are) about its moral worth. Even if it is maintained that moral facts somehow supervene on nonmoral facts – for example, if it is maintained that anything with all human nonmoral properties, such as rationality and consciousness, is necessarily worth as much as a human – the moral facts are not found in the nonmoral facts. The gap requires some explanatory bridge. Supervenience is intended to bridge that gap. If rationality confers worth, something important has happened, even though necessarily.

The parallel with the case of causes and reasons is again helpful, because that case lacks the special difficulties that are felt to accrue to the moral case. There exists a causes-reasons gap, similar to the is-ought gap. No amount of scientific facts about the causes of belief (such as Darwinian explanations of why we believe one thing or another) constitutes any reason for those beliefs. The evidence, in say a court of law, is a sum of statements of fact, and the reasonableness or otherwise of the verdict supervenes on those (claimed) facts – with the evidence as it is, only one verdict is rationally justified. But the causes of the jury's verdict in their upbringing and neurology are not part of that supervenience. We may feel we do not fully grasp how reasons supervene on facts, but that cannot be because of any "queerness" of the logical. The logical will have to fit into the scientific world picture somehow, since science depends on – in fact, largely consists of – logical inferences. We understand the supervenience of reasons on facts sufficiently to provide an encouraging parallel for the ability of supervenience theory to bridge Hume's gap.

Similar comments apply to the relation of supervenience to Moore's "naturalistic fallacy," which refers to the same "gap" between the factual and the ethical.[28] Moore's open question argument says that of any natural property X that might be advanced as an analysis of "good" (for example, what we desire to desire), we can always intelligibly ask "Is X good?" Therefore, he concludes, "good" cannot mean X.[29] That is correct, but like Hume's remarks on deducibility, it is about concepts, so it does not bear on whether worth or other moral qualities might supervene on natural properties. Moore's argument is about concepts and meanings, as he emphasizes ("My business is solely with that object or idea [of good] . . ."). Reduction and supervenience are about properties "out there."[30] Supervenience is unrelated to meaning and deducibility. Nevertheless, Moore's argument, like

Hume's, has been widely felt to identify some sort of gap between the non-ethical and the ethical, a gap not well expressed in terms of meanings or deducibility. Supervenience is intended both to admit that that gap exists and to bridge it. Moore, unlike Hume, thought that a real property of good existed, though he did not attempt to explain any relation it might have to natural properties.

Mackie's central argument for his "error theory," which maintains that there is really no such thing as ethical obligation, is that moral properties would be metaphysically "queer" in the materialist universe he takes us to be living in. He writes, "If there were objective values, then they would be entities or qualities or relations of a very strange sort, utterly different from anything else in the universe."[31] And "moral facts would be 'queer,' in that unlike other facts, they cannot be explained in terms of arrangements of matter, or logical constructions out of sense-data, or whatever the particular theorist takes to be the general form of real things."[32]

Mackie does not expand much on those remarks, presumably feeling there is no need to. As with Hume's gap, it is necessary to distinguish different aspects of ethics that could be considered "queer" in a naturalistic universe. Obligation is one thing, inherent worth another (whose relation will be considered in Chapter 8). Mackie sometimes says that the problem is the relational aspects of the moral world, its "objective prescriptivity," "built in to-be-pursuedness," "absolute action-guidingness." If that were the problem, intrinsic moral worth would escape his objections, since in itself it is not relational. But Mackie's phrase "objective values" appears to be designed to cover all such possibilities, relational or not, and although Mackie does not explicitly speak of worth, it is clear he would take it to be as metaphysically queer as objective moral obligation. It is clear, too, that there is a case for its being so, if we take naturalism strictly enough.

Mackie pointed out, as Hume did about "ought," that the relation between a natural fact (for example, being cruel) and a moral fact (being wrong) cannot be an entailment, a logical or a semantic necessity. That is true. Yet, as he says, the "wrongness must somehow be 'consequential' or 'supervenient'; it is wrong because it is a piece of deliberate cruelty. But just what *in the world* is signified by this 'because'?"[33] Mackie's followers such as Richard Joyce profess themselves unable to make any sense of the "pre-wired superstition" that morality really binds independently of any institutional facts, saying, "Perhaps Mackie and I fumble to dissect something that by its very nature cannot be brought into the light to be picked over by philosophical scrutiny."[34] The theory of supervenience has offered an answer to that question. The wrongness of cruelty results from the worth of the victim, which is a constituent of the world, itself supervening on the victim's human or animal properties.

As in the parallel cases above, opponents of Mackie have followed a "companions in guilt" strategy, to show that supervenience is no more problematic in the moral cases than in other cases where it is hard to avoid accepting it. And, rightly, they have tended to choose as a parallel the case of the epistemic force of reasons.[35]

In summary, Hume's is-ought argument, Moore's open question argument, and Mackie's allegation of queerness do point to a genuine gap in meaning between naturalistic predicates and ethical ones, and to a metaphysical gap between naturalistic properties and ethical ones (a gap that does not exist between H_2O and water). The notion of supervenience, if it is doing its job – as we have argued it is – bridges those gaps.

CHAPTER SIX

The Properties of Humans Which Ground Their Worth

❖

If it is accepted that the search for what it is about humans that gives them worth is in principle a sound one, it remains to establish which properties of humans are relevant. Size and color are obviously not relevant. So what properties are?

The traditional answer is rationality. It remains a strong contender as it appears to distinguish what is uniquely human. Apart, however, from the fact that some animals have a degree of some kind of rationality, it is unclear quite what counts as human rationality, or rather how widely rationality is to be understood. Significant properties enabled by rationality, such as the possibility of free action, the ability to fit actions into a life narrative, the whole emotional as well as rational structure of the human person, and individuality, are crucial to what makes humans human. They all contribute to giving humans worth. The complex package made possible by embodied rationality, rather than rationality itself narrowly understood, is what being human means and is what gives humans worth. There is no reason why a single feature of humanity should be sought as the sole ground of worth. As Robert Audi puts it, "The dignity of persons is multidimensional, involving at least rationality, the capacity for normative judgment and moral agency, a kind of sentience, and other values warranting respect for persons."[1]

It might, indeed, be possible to maintain that *all* features of humans contribute to worth – that although being some specific color or shape is not significant, being colored and shaped somehow (or in general embodied) is significant. Of course, sinning is a common feature of humans that does not contribute to worth, but the capacity to do so might. But even if it were true that all features were morally relevant, it would be necessary to distinguish foreground from background – which features are central to worth and which peripheral? Whether there is a sharp division between worth-conferring properties and others is a secondary question. What we want to know are which human properties are most fundamental in making humans what they are.

How will we recognize which features are relevant (or most relevant) to worth and which not? We have some sense of which are a tragedy to lose: Changing color or becoming invisible is weird but harmless while declining into dementia removes the core operations of a human being, leaving only the basic respect owed to what might have been. With each of the following suggestions for properties that found human worth, we can easily appreciate how devastating the loss of that property is. Typically, there is also psychiatric literature on the effects of partial loss. Complete loss of that property leaves one unable to operate as a human being, even though one is still human.

Thus the appropriate attitude toward human excellences is not the minimalist one of the last chapter, which anxiously sought something common to all humans, even disabled ones. Here we aim to understand how humans might be maximally abled, as in Shakespeare's eulogy:

What a piece of work is man, How noble in reason, how infinite in faculty, In form and moving how express and admirable, In action how like an Angel, In apprehension how like a god, The beauty of the world, The paragon of animals.[2]

"Be ye therefore perfect," Jesus says. At least let us try to grasp what human perfection consists in. The point of action by humans is to change things, including the actors themselves, so we need to look at the "developable" as well as "inherent" aspects of humanity. [3]

While the question "What is human perfection?" is not exactly the same as "What gives humans worth?" one would expect a close connection. Surely those features which enable perfection to be reached are central to conferring worth. Some preconditions or enabling causes for perfection may turn out to be more important than others, but all have some claim.

(THEORETICAL) RATIONALITY

A classic answer to the question "What gives humans worth?" is "rationality." "Man's excellence," says Saint Augustine, "consists in the fact that God made him to His own image by giving him an intellectual soul (*mentem intellectualem*) which raises him above the beasts of the field."[4] A person is an "individual substance of a rational nature," according to Boethius.[5] Kant (though his view of rationality is more inclusive than the purely intellectual) says, "*Rational nature exists as an end in itself*. In this way the human being necessarily conceives its own existence.... In this way, however, also every other rational being conceives its existence owing to just the same rational ground which also holds for me."[6]

One reason why this answer is *prima facie* attractive is that it is the most obvious difference between ourselves and animals. The worth of animals, on the face of it, is less than ours, and that appears due to their lack of a full version of rationality since they resemble us closely in so many other respects. Conversely, too, we value especially those animals like cats which are highly cognitive and inquisitive, and so have a trace of some kind of rationality. That is a large part of what makes them attractive as companion animals. If animals really did have the rationality attributed to them in anthropomorphic animal tales, we would not eat them, and we would treat them as real colleagues.

Another initial consideration in favor of rationality is its crucial role in enabling other human perfections, such as free action. Finnis writes:

> The radical capacity and act(uality) which each human being has by virtue of his or her individual rational soul makes each of us superior in the straightforward sense that we thereby have and instantiate every level of being – the physical solidity and dynamisms of a star or a galaxy, the chemical and biological complexity and self-directedness of a tree or lion, and more: the capacity to understand all these other realities, to reason about them and about reasoning itself, to replicate and transform other beings on all those levels of reality, and with self-mastery's freedom choose how to live.[7]

These initial considerations are not entirely convincing. Animals differ from humans in other ways, too, for example in their emotional repertoire, and those differences are *prima facie* morally relevant. Or again, it may be that for some reason it is the combination of animality and rationality in humans that is valuable rather than the moral weight falling solely on rationality. Nevertheless there is sufficient reason to examine rationality in the first instance, as a putative foundation for worth.

To decide fairly whether rationality is the right answer to the question of the basis of worth, it is necessary to take great care with what counts as rationality. Too narrow a definition makes it an implausible foundation, too wide evacuates it of meaning by trying to include all distinctive features of humanity (for example, by trying to include emotions as well).

Alan Donagan, who, as described in Chapter 1, saw common morality as based on an assumption of the (equal) worth of persons, in agreement with the present book, says that worth is grounded solely in humans' rationality. He defines rationality rather narrowly, as "a power, possessed by normal human adults, by which they do such things as propound propositions, assent to them or dissent from them, recognize that if a certain one is true then a certain other must also be true, and the like. . . . a power correctly to perform acts having contents belonging to the domain of logic."[8] That is an excessively narrow view of what is distinctive and valuable about humans, leaving out everything to do with action, emotion, memory, and individuality.

Writers on ethics in the Thomist and Kantian traditions have been eager to insist by contrast that rationality should be understood to include a "practical rationality" or "rational will." It is not pure intellectuality (theoretical reason), they say, that gives humans their distinctive worth, but more their ability to *act* rationally in the sense of choosing actions on the basis of reasons.

That thought is largely correct and will be discussed in due course. But before doing so, we should pause to appreciate that a purely intellectual rationality is distinctive of humans and crucial to their worth. One cannot act for reasons without understanding reasons in the first place, and the ability to understand them, in the full sense, is a crucial part of what makes humans what they are.

Intellectual rationality, as understood here, is distinguished from the kind of "intelligence" that can be handed over to artificial intelligence or found in animals. The major advances in artificial intelligence and the study of animal cognition in the last sixty years have shown the extraordinary powers of both but at the same time the large gap between the complex "adaptive behavior," calculation and search through spaces of possibilities that artificial and animal intelligence is capable of, and the uniquely human ability to genuinely understand.

Experience has shown also that one particular aspect of intelligence, a very central one, is especially resistant to imitation by the formal methods of AI and is apparently lacking in animals. It is understanding. Let us take a very simple example from mathematics, because that is the home ground of pure understanding.

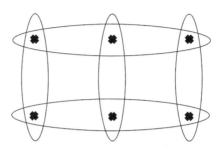

Why $2 \times 3 = 3 \times 2$

Why is it true that $2 \times 3 = 3 \times 2$? It is because two rows of three things are exactly the same things as three columns of two. They are just the same things, considered differently. So we not only *know that* $2 \times 3 = 3 \times 2$ but we *understand why* it *must* be so.[9]

Understanding is not just found in the rarefied realm of pure mathematical truths. It applies equally in, for example, understanding the meaning of texts. Google Translate is very impressive at applying powerful statistical algorithms to huge corpora of language to imitate human translation between different languages.[10] But when it goes haywire, it reminds us that there is no genuine understanding in there, only the cloned results of previous human understanding.

The prospects for putting genuine understanding of that kind into software or hardware are as close to zero as they were in the 1950s. There is just nowhere to start. After sixty years of experience, it is time to face the fact that understanding is essentially entirely unlike rule following, the manipulation of uninterpreted symbols, and the application of statistical algorithms. We now have a great wealth of experience on what can be done with artificial intelligence, in all its various forms, and the more experience we have, the more unique human understanding looks.[11] The mental act of really grasping meaning, and the necessary connections between one idea and another, is something that keeps escaping the kind of things that artificial intelligence does.

What the correct model of this core of rationality is remains unclear. Older theories include that of Aristotle and the scholastics that the intellect has an immaterial power of knowing universals[12] and Augustine's theory of divine illumination,[13] but theories suitable for a post-Enlightenment mentality are hard to find. We need not decide the question here. It is sufficient to insist on the phenomenon of understanding itself, apparently unique to humans (and any possible super-human entities) and understood as being what it is by the understanding itself.

The classic expression of the value of understanding in the purely intellectual sense is Aristotle's placing of the good of contemplation as the peak of human happiness.[14] "Philosophy or the pursuit of wisdom contains pleasures of marvelous purity and permanence," and is the kind of thing gods would be expected to occupy their time with as they have no need to, for example, act justly while making contracts. The same applies to us, too, in the Christian vision of heaven in which we are freed from the wheel of fate and no longer have any need to busy ourselves with rational decision-making.[15]

It is also the business of our intellects to contemplate aesthetic and ethical realities. As Velleman puts it, "Rational nature is not the intellect, not even the practical intellect; it's a capacity of appreciation or valuation – a capacity to care about things in that reflective way which is distinctive of selfconscious creatures like us."[16] Aesthetic realities require a kind of intellectual interpenetration of sensory splendor.[17] That is true at the high end of aesthetics, where a long development of sensibility is needed to properly appreciate Mozart and Vermeer, but is also true in the more quotidian appreciation of table decorations or birdsong. Those abilities appear to be lacking or vestigial in animals. If a movie shows King Kong as moved by a sunset, that represents him as humanlike rather than truly a gorilla.[18]

Hard thinking is needed to appreciate ethical realities, too. Understanding the worth of persons and what moral needs they have does not in itself have anything to do with the will or action (though it could motivate those). It needs moral understanding, of the kind that can be developed by attention to others and vicariously by the serious study of literature.[19] We will consider the epistemology of ethics further in Chapter 9.

So logical, ethical, and aesthetic matters are all realities to be recognized, and the unified cognitive ability to do so is essential to being human. That is all central to and distinctive of humanity (but possibly shared by gods). We may conclude that a purely intellectual rationality is an essential part what gives humans worth, even if not the whole story.

THE NEED FOR MORE THAN RATIONALITY

Even understanding rationality as widely as reasonable (but not so as to render it vacuous), the human person restricted to its rationality is autistic and not sufficient in itself to be the whole basis of the worth of persons. The first prominent thing it leaves out is the core of truth in Kant's dictum that the only thing good unqualifiedly is the good will. A good will is not "rationality." It is a commitment. And as literary and psychiatric people have said at length, an exclusive focus on rationality omits the crucial emotional aspects of humanity.

There is also the fact that rationality in the human style has preconditions – not just causal preconditions, such as brain activity, but necessary, constitutive, ones. One could argue that the bases of rationality form part of the bases of worth, if the latter supervenes, partly or wholly, on rationality.

For example, understanding, whether intellectual, ethical, or aesthetic, is necessarily an act of a conscious subject, suggesting that we inquire into consciousness as a precondition, at least, of what is essential to humanity. A precondition of both theoretical and practical rationality is a unified conscious self to do the thinking, willing, and acting. Peter Forrest writes:

> Next, we need a theory of what it is to be a full person, with the dignity assigned to personhood by humanism. There are four stages on the way to full personhood. First, there is sentience or consciousness, which I take to be widespread. Second, there is the requisite unity for many bits of sentience to form a mind. Third, there is the requirement that the mind have a sense of self. Finally, there is the way the self at different times forms a person.[20]

Certainly, if those are not in place first, there will not be a sufficiently unified person to conduct rational thought and agency in any more than a fragmentary sense.

Again, actually thinking rationally, as opposed to merely being able to, requires some motivation to translate potentiality into actuality; even extremely rational activities like pure mathematics require passion and commitment to drive them forward. Some degree of emotional and motivational underpinning is necessary to rational activity.

So some more complete account of what makes humans what they are – or what they are over and above animals – is needed. Let us examine those necessary building blocks first, as they must be essential parts of the human person.

CONSCIOUSNESS

Let us perform a thought experiment. Beside a human we place a zombie and a conscious computer. A zombie is an entity biologically the same as a human and outwardly performing like one, but without any inner experience. A conscious computer is a being made of silicon but with an inner experience similar to humans. (There are doubts whether such beings could exist, and other doubts over how to tell from the outside whether a being is a zombie or a conscious computer, but the present thought experiment supposes that such beings are possible and their inner experience is somehow known.) What is their status as moral beings? To focus the question, what would our moral obligations to them be? Since those beings resemble humans, but in different respects, an answer to that question would give us some understanding of what properties of human beings are responsible for, or most closely linked with, their moral worth.

Zombies look like us, but they are not us. They are empty shells. Conscious computers do not look like us, but share what is crucial (if their consciousness is sufficiently like ours). If channels of communication are provided, we can chat to them as person to person, perhaps come to love them (as we can come to love someone met only over the Internet).

We can agree, then, with G. E. Moore's forceful expression of the view that moral relevance requires conscious experience, and that nothing could be more obvious:

> The answer to it, in its main outlines, appears to be so obvious, that it runs the risk of seeming to be a platitude. By far the most valuable things, which we know or can imagine, are certain states of consciousness, which may be roughly described as the pleasures of human intercourse and the enjoyment of beautiful objects. No one, probably, who has asked himself

the question, has ever doubted that personal affection and the appreciation of what is beautiful in Art or Nature, are good in themselves; nor, if we consider strictly what things are worth having *purely for their own sakes*, does it appear probable that any one will think that anything else has *nearly* so great a value as the things which are included under these two heads.... mere existence of what is beautiful has value, so small as to be negligible, in comparison with that which attaches to the *consciousness* of beauty. This simple truth may, indeed, be said to be universally recognised. What has *not* been recognised is that it is the ultimate and fundamental truth of Moral Philosophy.[21]

Similarly W. D. Ross says crisply, "Good is a characteristic belonging primarily only to states of mind, and belonging to them in virtue of three characteristics – the moral virtue included in them, the intelligence included in them, and the pleasure included in them."[22] (Where by "states of mind," he obviously means "conscious states of mind.")

While Moore and Ross both speak of the worth of conscious experiences themselves rather than of the entity having them, Moore's phrase "worth having purely for their own sakes" implies a possessor of the experience to give point to the having of the experiences. They do not mean that states of mind are free-floating and disconnected, but take it for granted they are affections of a unified self.

A person confined to a dreamless sleep or coma would be regarded as a tragedy, because given a person's nature, it could have been otherwise. But an entity like a zombie whose nature was to be in a permanent dreamless sleep could not have worth of anything like the human kind. It could at most have the worth of rainforests, whatever that might be.

THE UNIFIED SELF

Theorists of identity have distinguished two senses of the word "identity," as applied to persons. The prior one concerns the "unity of consciousness" or "unity of agency," which answers the question "Who did that?" The second is "personal identity" across time.

The mental contents of a person (at a time) have a unity that the mental contents of ten people in a room do not have. As Korsgaard explains:

> Just now you are reading this article. You may also be sitting in a chair, tapping your foot, and feeling hot or tired or thirsty. But what makes it one person who is doing and experiencing all this? We can add to this a set of characteristics which you attribute to yourself, but which have only an indirect bearing on your conscious experiences at any given time. You have loves, interests, ambitions, virtues, vices, and plans. You are a conglomerate of parts, dispositions, activities, and experiences. As Hume says, you are a bundle. What makes you one person even at one time?[23]

That unity is necessary for agency; for example, a person's conflicting motives or reasons for a course of action are not separate thoughts that are balanced like weights, but are brought together and compared in some unified faculty.

The significance of that sort of unity for being human is made clear by the deep-seated nature of disorders of it, such as being driven by voices in the head that appear to be external, or more seriously, the disturbances of self characteristic of the worst forms of schizophrenia.[24] More minor defects of unity lead to common moral failings like self-deception and weakness of will.

How such a unity is possible is a difficult question. The classical philosophers agonized over the "unity of consciousness" at length.[25]

The meagerness of the results is no doubt one reason why the problem has had a lower profile in the last century. We do not need to address that question here, since what is important for the worth of persons is the fact of the unity of persons rather than anything about how it can occur.

Agency needs also memory and imagination of the future – of my past and my future. It only makes sense for me to consider an action if its effect in the future bears somehow on my larger plans. There must be some point to the action and its effects in the light of my wish for survival, or eating, or tenure, or love for some others, or some other project; those projects themselves only making sense in a life narrative that is to some degree coherent.[26] I must indeed perceive myself as having some degree of worth; otherwise action in pursuit of my plans is pointless (unless I have to an extreme degree a defect of self-perception such as self-loathing or servility). A solid sense of "personal identity" is needed for moral concerns, such as a feeling for the boundary of the "I" to whom I hope to prevent harm, concern for how I will get through tomorrow, or shame for or pride in what I did earlier. It is because that person will be or was me, and I know that, that I can have such moral concern.[27] Again, disorders such as dissociative identity disorders (involving uncontrolled switching between multiple personalities) deeply disturb agency and highlight how significant personal identity across time is.[28] Knowledge of the unity of the self is reasonably regarded as part of human rationality (and is as far as we know vestigial in animals). If human rationality is taken to confer worth, it must include that central aspect of rationality that knows who we are.

The focus of narrative identity theorists has been on what gives the self unity rather than, as here, what gives it worth. But these are closely related questions. Understanding the unity of a person's life (including one's own) makes possible and determines its right evaluation. "The unity of a virtue in someone's life is intelligible only as a characteristic of a unitary life, a life that can be conceived and evaluated as a whole."[29] Nevertheless one must take care to distinguish between evaluating whether a life has gone well and recognizing the worth of the subject, whether their life has gone well or not. That is, one should distinguish between the worth or excellence of a human being and the relative worth or excellence of a human life and history.[30] As in other cases already considered, the worth of a human makes possible, but does not necessarily issue in, human perfections. Aristotle's eudaimonism was defective in concentrating just on the excellence of a life.

The fact of the unity of the self goes some way to explaining what is wrong and bizarre with the view of Peter Singer and to some extent even Moore and Ross, that what are primarily good are individual mental items like interests or experiences. Experiences do not exist separately except possibly in very disturbed psyches, and the value they have is that of the self of which they are a part (or state).

It is certainly possible to deny the unity of the self. Some theorists have attempted to defend the Buddhist view that there is no unified self in this sense. It is not easy to maintain that coherently; as MacIntyre points out, there is some paradox in Sartre's writing a standard narrative novel about a man alleged to have no unified life narrative.[31] Here we will take it for granted that there is a sufficiently unified self that is the same through different actions. That self is the bearer of worth, and it has that worth partly in virtue of that unity.

THE DIVERSIFIED SELF

The self is unified, but it is also important to humans that there is a great deal of diversity to unify. Humans are not simple, not even their mental parts. Or especially not their mental parts.

Most of what has been said so far would be applicable if humans were simple Cartesian egos, disconnected from physical and social reality. Such an ego could think intellectually, be conscious, and have a conception of itself as unified (at least, if some basic "ideas" to think about could be inserted somehow). In the normal course of nature, an ego and its contents are brought into being by biological and social causes. But it is imaginable that one should be miraculously created by some other cause, such as emerging naturally from a 3D-printed exact copy of an existing human, or by more traditional possibilities such as a brain in a vat or a Matrix-like simulation. Causal history should not be relevant to worth – a copy of the *Mona Lisa* may be cheap but a body-and-soul copy of the real Lisa Gherardini would be a whole person of equal worth. Those created entities, whether really embodied like twin-Lisa or fake-embodied like a real mind in a Matrix simulation, would have normal human worth, and hence the bases of worth should be findable in such strangely created entities. Actual embodiment or engagement with the social world should, therefore, not be included in the bases for worth.

Nevertheless even such a miraculously created human is not a bare Cartesian ego but possesses a diversified self that includes, in a certain (mental) sense, embodiment and social engagement. Even if the "bodies" and "societies" which the mind purports to engage with should turn out to be virtual, the internal representations of them are complex and an essential ingredient in being human. Action occurs not directly on the body but via the body schema, which is essentially mental (a representation of the body and its interactions) as described in the extensive work on "embodied cognition" that is central to recent cognitive science.[32] Mental orientations to the physical and the social are necessary preconditions for action, since action must be on something and normally for some interpersonal purpose.

These are old issues. For all that Descartes is the *bête noir* of embodied cognition theorists, because he took intellection to be disembodied, he thought the imagination (our internal faculty of visualization) was material.[33] Husserl describes how we carry about in our mind a representation of the adjoining world, more complex and complete than what immediate perception delivers:

> I can let my attention wander from the writing-table I have just seen and observed, through the unseen portions of the room behind my back to the veranda, into the garden, to the children in the summer-house, and so forth, to all the objects concerning which I precisely "know" that they are there and yonder in my immediate co-perceived surroundings.[34]

The significance is that a real human being – even just its mental part – is not simple but contains a vastly complex, multifaceted, and changing panorama including a representation of itself (mind and body) and a good portion of the surrounding world, and of the past and anticipated future of both self and world. The human way of being rational is essentially representationally complex.

"Surrounding world" means the social as well as the physical world. If embodiment is a precondition of any action at all, *moral* action that involves, as moral action usually does, other people requires also a basic sociality. The self represents to itself its social as much as physical relations – its appraisal by others, its group obligations, its status, its "identity" in various groups, and so on.[35] Much has been made of language as a uniquely human ability, but it is more a sign of, tool for, and way of enhancing social interaction than a worth-giving feature in its own right. Linguistic signs cannot be read like natural signs, merely correlated like smoke and fire. Understanding language requires a theory of other minds, minds which intend to mean something by their language and intend it to be taken by another mind in a certain way. That social cognition, of which language is an external effect, is the feature of humans that adds to their worth.

If we add that the mind represents to itself also worlds of values, emotions, mathematical, logical, and linguistic entities, and so on, we find an extraordinarily crowded, varied, and complex, yet unified, world "in there." The way human mentality is "infinite in faculty" is data-rich and highly structured. That diversified self is an essential part of what makes humans admirable.

THE RATIONAL WILL AND FREEDOM

According to the Aristotelian/Thomist tradition of "practical reason" and the Kantian understanding of the "rational will,"[36] the point of reason is not just to contemplate truths but to direct freely chosen action. Humans act for reasons and deliberate about the balance of reasons. That is quite unlike acting under the pressure of the strongest instinct or on the instructions of software. I wake up automatically, but my decision on when to get up is something that I consider in the light of whether it is worthwhile right now, how I expect to feel later if I don't get up, how much urgent work I have to do, and so on. Instinct and software cannot literally weigh considerations for and against actions, because they cannot understand reasons and their logical bearing on actions.

Understanding reasons and choosing to act on them are central to "the distinctive endowment of a human being" that Mill sought. He writes, "The human faculties of perception, judgment, discriminative feeling, mental activity, and even moral preference, are exercised only in making a choice."[37] It is so much the core of what it means to be human that we should give considerable weight to "the Kantian thesis that what gives a person absolute worth is his possession of a rational will."[38] If humans have worth at all that is distinctive to them (that is, over and above the different kind of worth that animals may have), it must depend essentially on the possession of a rational will (though not necessarily only on that).

Three things are required about myself, as a matter of metaphysical necessity, for my understanding of reasons to be relevant to my choice of action. First, as mentioned, is that I should *understand* the reasons. Second, as also mentioned, it must be *my* choice of action: I must be, and have a sense of myself as being, a unified self, at the present moment and continuing over time. Third, it must be my *choice* of action: I must have, and know I have, freedom in some sufficiently strong sense.

So the next thing that agency requires is freedom. In order to plan action, I must see myself as able to make a decision one way or another, able to choose to act on the reasons I have so as to make a difference to the outcome. Freedom, in some sufficiently strong sense, is a precondition for rational action – for bodily movements to actually be *actions* of a person. There can be no practical rationality or rational will without the ability, or at least imagined ability, to implement a plan decided on. How strong a notion of freedom is needed – whether a truly libertarian one or a "compatibilist" ability to act on the basis of decisions even if those decisions are determined by hidden neurological causes – is debatable (and will be considered shortly). But some notion of freedom is essential to the structure of the practical rationality that makes humans what they are.

As with other bases of worth, we can appreciate the significance of freedom by calling to mind what it is like when it is missing. A common theme in many of the rights of the Universal Declaration of Human Rights is that they protect "normative agency": the ability of persons to act – the rights to liberty and security of person, the forbidding of slavery and arbitrary arrest, among others.[39] Fights for (external) liberty are a major part of history and heroic actions in the face of tyranny are rightly remembered. But in those cases at least, short of death, those "chained in prisons dark were still in heart and conscience free." We recognize threats to inner freedom as deeper.

They include extremely addictive drugs such as crystal methamphet-amine and voices of command in the head in cases of paranoid schizo-phrenia: The victim retains much of rationality with its awareness of actions, and an ability to plan, but experiences a tragically con-strained freedom.

That applies, too, to the threat to freedom arising from philo-sophical arguments for determinism. F.H.Bradley says that if the "plain man" were to be told that all of his actions were determined and could have been written down in a book before he was born, he "would be most seriously perplexed and in a manner outraged."[40] His objection is that the determinist theory attacks him by making his actions not really his: "He himself might just as well have been anyone else from the first, since nothing remains which is specifically his. The sanctum of his individuality is outraged and profaned."[41] Strong intuitions favor the idea that for moral responsibility and human dignity, we need "sole authorship or underived origination" of our actions,[42] an end to the causal chain, possibly different in an exact copy of ourselves in exactly the same circumstances.

Determinist philosophers, both "hard" (or incompatibilist) and "soft" (compatibilist) have argued that we cannot have freedom in that strong sense, either because it is incompatible with physics or conceptually incoherent (or, oddly, both). This is not the place to resolve that debate, but it is clear why resolving it for determinism would be a loss for human dignity, in the sense of showing we are not the kind of beings we hoped we were.

Kant went further and located the main contribution of freedom to human worth not in the freedom of individual acts, but in our freedom to set the overall moral direction for our acts. If individual acts normally gain their meaning and point from the larger life nar-rative of which they are a part, the ability to decide the overall aim of that narrative is especially important. As Kant puts it, rational beings should be treated as "ends in themselves" because they are "the ultimate creators of their own ends."[43]

That is not to be understood as saying the choice of ultimate ends is a free-for-all, or in any sense arbitrary. We need freedom not just to do what we want, or what we want to want. It is easy to understand the religious view that it is especially the wants we are most attached to that enslave us. We need freedom to align ourselves with those ends that are in accordance with human (and any other) worth. Freedom being what it is, we can misuse it and decide otherwise.

EMOTIONS: LOVE AND OTHERS

What has been said so far concentrates on the reason side of the "reason and the passions" divide. But it is impossible to be human without an adequate development of the emotions. Even to devote oneself to an activity that is wholly reason, like pure mathematics, one needs a passion for doing the hard work.

One emotion (if that is the right word) is crucial: love. An obvious single serious lack in humanity is an inability to (or lack of wish to) love. If extreme, that is something that truly goes to the heart of what it means to be human. Some defect in that area is no doubt near-universal, but a serious defect means something missing from the core of humanity.

One indication of its importance is the credibility of Jesus's "Euclidean" claim, that all the requirements of the law follow from just two axioms: Love God, and Love thy neighbor. Loving one's neighbor implies both wanting their good and taking action to achieve it, which rules out causing harm and commands benevolence. The axioms may not resolve ethical dilemmas, but they do imply the reasons on both sides of the dilemmas. The balance between strict and indulgent parenting is hard because both sides are motivated by love.

It is true that love is based on some kind of understanding. It has a strong cognitive element and so is not rightly regarded as just an emotion. We love not randomly, and if we are lucky not delusionally, but based on understanding of lovability. In Gaita's example of the nun who loved severely psychiatrically disabled patients (Chapter 4, above), love reveals something about the lovability of the object. Iris Murdoch, too, insists that love is a clear-eyed perception of the other, "love is the extremely difficult realization that something other than oneself is real."[44] But love is more than that understanding. As Saint Paul says in his account of love, "If I understand all mysteries and all knowledge ... but have not love, I am nothing."[45] Understanding of lovability, plus laziness or indifference, is not love. Love is something outgoing; it does something. Love necessarily involves a willingness to take action to address what the one loved needs. ("Love is kind, love does not envy..." in Saint Paul's words.) It has also essential emotional components, notably empathy – for example, distress at the loved one's misfortune, especially if one cannot do anything about it (such as with mothers present at the anesthetic-free child dentistry of the 1950s). The Old Testament attributes to God emotions such as anger and yearning for reconciliation when faced with the doings of his chosen people, emotions which are appropriate to love despite some theologians' disinclination to attribute them to a changeless being.

Conversely, we see that psychiatric conditions that constitute major disruptions to love while retaining a high level of some kind of reason, like autism and psychopathy, involve cognitive disorders but are more than that. Empathy is difficult for such people, as is taking other people's needs to be a reason for action on their part.[46]

As psychiatrists know, it is nearly impossible to love without having been loved. The experience of being loved and the attachment that normally arises from it are essential for babies to grow into normal humans. The shocking 1952 film *A Two-Year-Old Goes to Hospital*, with its grim portrayal of a child not allowed parental visits, and John Bowlby's subsequent massive work, *Attachment and Loss*,[47] revolutionized how emotional development is understood. Successful attachment permits the development of a positive model of the self and of others. The ability to recognize oneself as loved is necessary for accepting oneself as a being of worth. To be a being of worth but not to recognize it is a fundamental and tragic flaw in being human.

Many other emotions add to human value. The full story is complex – indeed, part of the point of emotions is the complexity and subtlety of their responses to different situations. Just to take one example of a different kind of emotion, anger is a just response to injustice. A parent of a child whose favorite toy has been forcibly taken from him by bullies is rightly angry and demands justice. So does a slave class who have been trained to see their slavery as natural. Perhaps less unqualifiedly admirable is the anger (Aristotle's *orgē*) of the man whose honor is slighted, such as the academic whose work has not been cited; but it is, as we say, "all too human."[48] Michael Stocker writes, in *Valuing Emotions*:

> Affectivity and emotions have inestimable human value and evaluative importance: put briefly, without emotions it is impossible to live a good human life and it may well be impossible to live a human life, to be a person, at all. An absence or deficiency of affect is a characterizing feature of many neuroses, borderline conditions, and psychoses, as well as such maladies of the spirit as meaninglessness, emptiness, ennui, *accidie,* spiritual weakness, and spiritual tiredness.[49]

"The unfelt life," he adds, "is not worth living."[50]

ALL THE ABOVE: THE COMPLEX WHOLE

As we have seen, many human properties have some show of playing a major role in giving humans their worth. It is natural to conclude that it is the complex of all of them rather than any particular one that is the basis of worth.

In that case, we seek an account of the "structure of the human person," in the sense of Edith Stein.[51] We need some overview of how the ingredients, such as rationality, the will, and love, fit together to make the whole human being. Such theories come in many versions, not necessarily incompatible with one another. Well-known ones include Thomist "anthropology," based on Aristotle's division of the faculties of the soul (itself based on Plato's contrast of the intellect and nobler emotions with the *thumos* or passions)[52]; Freud's id, ego, and superego; and the "biopsychosocial-spiritual" model of health.[53] Here the emphasis is on the recognition and classification of major parts (faculties, aspects, or powers), which give an overall insight as to "what's in there," clarifying what we know already, rather than on technical issues like how separate faculties are, the immateriality of some, the relation of mind to body, and so on. Those are good questions as philosophy, but not directly relevant to worth.

Here it is not to the point to go into details or commit to any one of those theories. But the general direction is clear. If we ask again the contrapositive question "What lacks constitute a serious defect of humanity?" we can deploy the most general insights of psychiatry and psychology. Psychiatry lays out a normal course of emotional, moral, as well as (in general terms) intellectual development. Serious failures to negotiate a stage, whether deliberately or due to a cognitive defect, make someone less perfectly human. (As before, that does not mean they are subhumans who deserve culling, for the same reason that Eichmann as a human being deserved only just punishment.)

A definite complex theory of the person, specially adapted to ethical worth, is advanced by Wolterstorff as a foundation for human rights. The rights perspective is helpful in that, if the violation of any particular aspect of humanity is a serious breach of human rights, it suggests that that aspect is a core one for human worth. Wolterstorff lists twelve essentials for being a "full-fledged human person" (a phrase intended to cover properly developed humans, not infants and the disabled):

- The capacity for rational agency – for enacting intentions based on reasons

- The ability to use language to perform actions such as asserting, commanding, and promising

- The ability to interpret oneself and reality, including "the capacity for some knowledge of necessary truths, for some grasp of the good, the right, and the obligatory, and some apprehension of God"

- The capacity for normative agency, that is, to act for the reason that one judges the action to be good or obligatory

- The capacity for stewardship of the earth and its non-human creatures

- The capacity to go beyond what one knows "to imagine other courses of action, sound structures, visual patterns, mathematical structures, configurations of space and mass, and so forth"

- Having desires about desires, leading to reshaping oneself, and being to that extent self-constituting

- Having an inner life (of thoughts and awareness of thoughts, hopes, regrets, plans, etc.) and some ability to communicate them

- The ability to ascribe certain actions and states and a certain body to oneself

- The capacity to form a "valorized identity," that is, to rank commitments by importance

- The capacity for self-esteem, that is, a sense of one's own worth

- Being inducted into the form of life of some human community

(He suggests that to be also a fully *functioning* human being, one must have also attachment to some fellow humans, capacity for empathy and compassion, and the ability to see things from another's point of view.[54])

These qualities or capacities are distinct, in the sense that one can imagine how one of them could be impaired or attacked without the others (except that damage to rationality would gravely impair all the others). On the other hand, they form a certain unity. The human way of being rational expresses itself in those other particular capacities. In the normal course of development, those capacities are ways in which human rationality realizes itself. These capacities are thus "essential accidents" of rationality in the scholastic sense, like risibility in Aquinas's example: The ability to find something funny has an intellectual aspect and is a necessary consequence of being rational.[55]

INDIVIDUALITY

We have been considering so far various proposals for properties that (developed) humans have in common which may found the worth of persons. It has been argued that that approach leaves out something important, the individuality of persons. Kant's version has been criticized thus (and any other version could be criticized similarly):

> Another source of dissatisfaction with Kant's account has been with his characterization of persons and the quality in virtue of which they must be respected. In particular, Kant's view that the rational will which is common to all persons is the ground of respect is thought to ignore the moral importance of the concrete particularity of each individual.... Rather than ignoring what distinguishes one person from another, it is argued, respect should involve attending to each person as a distinctive individual.[56]

It is the nature of properties to be repeatable. So it is arguable that the search for *properties* as a ground of ethics necessarily misses the individuality or uniqueness of persons. Perhaps properly human worth does not supervene on properties shareable by humans at all (or not wholly so), but on individuality – on *who* a person is rather than *what* a person is.[57]

What "individuality" means is not easily explained in words, since words deal in generalities.

First, individuality may refer either to an individual as he or she exists at a point in time, or an individual with the history of their unique personal narrative (corresponding to the synchronic and the diachronic unity of the self discussed above). But in this case, the connection between the two is close, because the individual at a time is the result of the individual's life history up to that point. Eric Auerbach writes, in his massive work on the representation of humanity in world literature, *Mimesis*:

> The old man, of whom we know how he has become what he is, is more of an individual than the young man; for it is only in the course of an eventful life that men are differentiated into full individuality; and it is this history of a personality which the Old Testament presents to us as the formation undergone by those whom God has chosen to be examples [unlike in Homer]. . . . There is hardly one of [the Old Testament heroes] who does not, like Adam, undergo the deepest humiliation – and hardly one who is not deemed worthy of God's personal intervention and personal inspiration.[58]

Who one is and what one has done is, on that view, essential to (developed) personhood.

Philosophers deal, typically, in the abstract and repeatable. Novelists, on the other hand, even when representing figures who are in some sense types, do so through the individuality of the characters and their histories. Historians and especially biographers attempt something similar with real, particular persons. So we need to look more to literature and historiography than to philosophy to understand the relation of individuality to worth.

Near the end of *Doctor Zhivago*, the character Lara, whose story has been at the center of the novel, is suddenly taken off to the Gulag and never heard of again. With millions of others, she suffers an anonymous death, unregarded by those who cause it, "vanished without a trace and probably died somewhere, forgotten as a nameless number on a list that afterwards got mislaid."[59] The shocking contrast between the richness of her personal story and its end as a non-person is emblematic of the worst of the twentieth century's history. Hannah Arendt, too, points to the crushing of individuality as the worst of the horrors of the camps:

> Once the moral person has been killed, the one thing that still prevents men from being made into living corpses is the differentiation of the individual, his unique identity.... The methods of dealing with this uniqueness of the human person are numerous and we shall not attempt to list them. They begin with the monstrous conditions in the transports to the camps, when hundreds of human beings are packed into a cattle-car stark naked, glued to each other, and shunted back and forth over the countryside for days on end; they continue upon arrival at the camp, the well-organized shock of the first hours, the shaving of the head, the grotesque camp clothing.... The killing of man's individuality, of the uniqueness shaped in equal parts by nature, will, and destiny, which has become so self-evident a premise for all human relations that even identical twins inspire a certain uneasiness, creates a horror that vastly overshadows the outrage of the juridical-political person and the despair of the moral person.[60]

The meaning of "individuality" or "uniqueness" is difficult. Does it literally mean, as suggested by the phrase "We shall not see his like again" often used at funerals, that the point of it is the difference in properties between that individual and others? While diversity of that kind has a minor value in the same way as does species diversity, in realizing different valuable possibilities, it is far from the whole point of "individuality." If identical twins were really wholly identical, or if by some coincidence different persons developed so as to be mentally exactly similar, it would not follow that one of them is "surplus to requirements" and lacks individuality in the sense in which individuality confers worth. The individual character, history, and way of being human that someone develops is inherent in that person and could not possibly be undermined by the existence of a clone, whether on Twin Earth or nearby.[61]

This individuality of persons contrasts with that of things whose repetition is trivial. Borges's story "Pierre Menard, author of the *Quixote*" imagines an early twentieth-century French Symbolist poet who succeeds in writing several chapters of *Don Quixote* word for word – not by copying them from Cervantes's original, but by actually developing the exact understanding of the world that Cervantes had and writing them.[62] That is a ludicrous endeavor because a literary work, however detailed and unique, does not have individuality in the sense in which Cervantes himself had and any clone of him would also have, in the unlikely event that there were one. A copy of a novel is interchangeable with any other and its loss can be replaced in full.

Physical things, too, may differ among themselves, but they do not have individuality in the same sense. "If, however, upon entering the room I see 700 such chairs, then suddenly the particular one diminishes greatly from the point of view of 'worth'. Beings whose 'worth' comes primarily from their common traits are relativized in that worth when placed next to many more exemplars of the same type."[63] (Unless, that is, they have an extrinsic "sentimental value" from a history of association with some individual person.)

The same point about the individuality of persons in relation to worth arises in the old puzzle over whether one is loved or would want to be loved for one's properties or "for oneself" ("Love you for yourself alone / And not your yellow hair," in Yeats's words).[64] While admiration for a person's qualities is appropriate to love for them, any dependence of love on those qualities will motivate "trading up" to anyone who exemplifies those qualities better,[65] and will create justified anxiety in the loved one over what is in store when those qualities fade. Similarly a child will be disturbed if their parents' "love" is conditional on their performance.[66] Love is directed to an individual, not to a set of qualities or even to an individual just in virtue of a set of qualities. Repeatable qualities lead to price, individuality to dignity, in Kantian terms.[67]

While individuality is not encompassed in rational nature in the abstract, there is nevertheless a close connection between individuality and rational nature. Rationality *enables* individuality (and in the natural course of things, will inevitably give rise to individuality: thus individuality is a perfection in relation to which rationality is a disposition). To be an individual of the human kind, appropriate to being loved by a human with a properly human love, one must be a rational human. One must have, as described above, an actual or potential rational understanding and life plan. Being a cat, for example, is not sufficient. Although people do love their cats, and cats have a degree of individuality, to love one's cat as if it were a human is delusional and requires attributing to it human properties which it does not, in fact, have. Being an infant is sufficient for making a start on genuinely human individuality.

Individuality so understood also differs from a simple repeatable property like rationality in that it is a particular in part constructed by the person "owning" it. Theorists of narrative identity such as MacIntyre, Ricoeur, and Schechtman have explained how action only has meaning in the context of a life narrative – in an example of MacIntyre, the action of wielding a spade is part of gardening, which is part of preparing for the winter and also for getting exercise, both of which projects have a point because of their contribution to a more overarching plan of life.[68] The sequence of such deliberate actions, taken in the light of one's life narrative, themselves grow that narrative and create the uniqueness of an individual's life story (or in an older idiom, their character[69]). They may do so better or worse and the individual life story that results is a subject of praise or blame – for example, we admire the person who acts well and creates a virtuous character while carrying the burden of a difficult childhood.

In a previous section we considered the unified self as a necessary precondition of rational action. It is the self in that sense that has agency and is able to determine the direction of actions going forward, thus creating the individuality of the self. The decisions of the self create not only individual actions but the story of what the self in the future will have done. "A person creates his identity by forming an autobiographical narrative – a story of his life."[70] Since persons are free, the specific form of their individual lives is not laid down from the start but is fluid and gradually created by them.[71] What is created is both the life story and the individual at any moment who has had that life story so far and is thus an individual with a unique point of view on the world, an individual whose loss would be a loss to the world absolutely speaking. As the Talmud said in objecting to capital punishment, "Whosoever preserves one life in Israel is as if he has preserved the whole world."[72]

The discussion so far may have given the impression that the "individual" concerned is the autonomous hero of post-Enlightenment Western individualism or the great-souled leader of Aristotle's city-state. It is true that it is primarily Western literature and historiography that has celebrated individual distinctiveness, just as Western art has valued originality over repetitive traditional craftwork. The discovery of the individual as such and the celebration of stories of individuals in novels and biographies is largely a Western obsession.[73]

Nevertheless, like Western mathematics, it has stood the test of time and is a gift of Western civilization to the world.

However, that is not the only way to be an individual successfully, in the sense in which individuality is an element in human worth. Even the modernist intellectual or artist who craves to be special suffers from being deracinated and free of the culture and tradition that could support his strivings. If some other cultures promote an understanding of the course of life that puts a higher premium on identity inherited from family, clan, or religion and less on individual idiosyncrasy, that can work. To have an identity oriented to a wider group or tradition does not prevent one, so to speak, from starring in one's own story. "Even the Agneses and Dorotheas who lead a pale, shadowy existence of support and self-sacrifice on the fringes of solid Victorian Lives of Great Men ... had, one hopes, a firm sense of their own centrality."[74] But some traditions can also be oppressive for those desiring to develop their individuality in their own direction, and that is what is wrong with such traditions.

Other enemies of individuality include extreme poverty, which forces a concentration on immediate ends, and narrow educations, which prevent knowledge of the possibilities of personal development. Again, their constraining individuality in large part explains what is wrong with them. It likewise explains what is tragic about forms of dementia which degrade long-term memory and so take away a person's grasp of their life story.

THE PHYSICAL?

If "man is a rational animal," and rationality is crucial to human worth, why not animality as well? Since free rational action requires a body to act with, is the body, too, part of what gives humans worth? The reasoning would be the same as that above which concluded that consciousness, a unified self, and the like were crucial foundations for rationality and rational action and hence part of what gives humans worth.

A natural reply might be: If humans are rational animals and being an animal does not have (our degree of) worth in itself, then it must be rationality that makes the difference – that causes our worth, and hence animality is not relevant. That does not follow, especially once we have accepted that a complex of properties is the source of worth. If consciousness and emotions are included as part of essential humanity, why not physicality as well?

Popular sentiment, it must be said, is on the side of the body. The vast sums paid to supermodels and star athletes and paid for cosmetic surgery suggest at least a widespread urge to think of human perfection along physical lines. A perfect human should, if we follow the money, be healthy, strong, young, bursting with vitality, and sexually attractive. (It may be that philosophers, typically less well endowed in those respects, have a class interest in denying that, but that in itself is not sufficient reason to entertain their strictures.)

Less easily dismissed as irredeemably vulgar is the artistic tradition. Should we follow the lead of Greek art, where human perfection is heavily physical and the beautiful youthful body is part of the human ideal? The tradition of Western artists painting their attractive girlfriends as Madonnas also represents a view that physical beauty does not just symbolize human perfection but is part of it.

Perhaps even more serious is the bioethical tradition. It has been complained that some libertarian views on public bioethics are premised on "expressive individualism" as a conception of human nature. That would see humans "merely as atomized individual wills whose highest flourishing consists in interrogating the interior depths of the self in order to express and freely follow the original truths discovered therein toward one's self-invented destiny." But a touch of illness or disability will quickly remind us of our embodied nature.

"Because we are bodies, vulnerability, mutual dependence, and natural limits are inextricable features of our lived human reality."[75]

What reason could there be to prefer the Manichean and Cartesian view, that the body is a "muddy vesture of decay" that impedes the real human, the soul – or at least is separate from and really a tool of the true mental human?

There is some reason.

Let us try a thought experiment again. We enter a hospital and meet two patients. One has locked-in syndrome but is mentally alert. The second has advanced dementia. Perhaps both are equally tragic, but in different ways. The first, who has effectively lost their body and ability to act physically, is a whole person and can, in a genuine sense, meet one, even if communication is nearly impossible. If telepathy became possible, true human communication would be enabled. That is not the case with the dementia patient. That person, as a person, has left. That is what their tragedy consists in.

It has been asked, if we found worth on capacities, "can we avoid the equally counter-intuitive consequence that a flying fish is superior to a herring, or that a human-like creature with the ability to fly would be superior to other humans?"[76] The answer simply is that physical differences are not morally important enough.

We may conclude that the core of humanity that forms the basis of moral worth is very complex, but is essentially mental. If, as some Christian theory has it, we exist as separated souls between death and the bodily resurrection, those souls will be us.

CHAPTER SEVEN

Worth of the Non-human

❖

IT MIGHT HAVE been that the only morally significant things in the world of humans were other humans. Much of the world's population lives close to that now, in high-rise concrete boxes without contact with animals or the natural environment and with no thought for gods. If the conclusions of this chapter are wrong and animals and the environment have only instrumental value, it would make very little difference to the conclusions reached in other chapters. But those things are still out there. Their worth needs inquiring into.

We will argue that higher animals resemble us sufficiently to have a degree of the same kind of worth as we do, based on their kind of conscious experience, emotional structure, and individuality, and so they can be said to have certain rights. Other parts of creation, like rainforests and artifacts, have an entirely different but still genuine and objective kind of value. It would be better called aesthetic value rather than ethical, were it not for the almost irredeemably subjectivist connotations of "aesthetic." We will need to recover older, objectivist views of the aesthetic and adapt them to some contemporary environmentalist thought to explain what is meant.

Perhaps surprisingly, the neglect of explicit concepts of intrinsic worth complained of earlier in human-centered ethics has been less evident in discussions of ethics related to the non-human. "Intrinsic value" has been part of the currency of debate in environmental ethics from the first.[1] No doubt that is because worth cannot be left hidden under unexamined assumptions about human equality, as it is in human ethics. Animals, ecosystems, and galaxies are so obviously metaphysically diffcrent from humans and from one another that discussion of their worth has had to be more explicit.

Similarly, many of the common non-worth-based metaethical schemes are immediately rendered out of the question when it comes to the non-human. Ethics related to animals and the environment cannot be simply about following rules or harmonizing interests or instantiating virtues, as cats cannot understand rules, endangered species lack virtues, and rocks have no interests. They are not moral actors, but some may still have interests or rights in virtue of properties they have, while some that do not may still be a moral loss if they disappear. It is harder to be against allowing metaphysics into ethics in principle, when the differences in nature between humans, animals, and rainforests are so obvious and so obviously relevant to their moral status.

SENTIENT ANIMALS

Do animals share enough of the properties that give humans worth to make them rightly said to have a degree of moral worth? It is not for the foundations of ethics to answer that question definitively, as it depends on knowledge of what it is to be an animal that we humans do not totally have. But there is no objection in principle to their having a degree of worth. The properties that have been argued to confer worth, such as consciousness, emotions, and individuality, and possibly rationality, can come in degrees. If animals possess them to some degree, then they have a degree of worth. Some more and some less.

Discussions of the moral status of animals tend to strive either to show that animals are more like us than they seem, or less. Opinions can oscillate between seeing animals as near-automata and an implicit anthropomorphism where we imagine ourselves in their position. That is unhelpful as neither of those positions is right. Animals are like us in some ways and not in others, and both their resemblance and their otherness show us something about worth. They need to be approached and understood on their own terms – both in theory and when it comes to dealing with an individual animal.

Part of the problem is epistemological. We do not know everything about what it is like to be a cat, in the way we know what it is like to be another human. I have a reasonably clear idea of what it would be like to be shot in an act of ethnic cleansing (or more accurately, what it would be like to be about to be shot), because I am a human. But I don't have much idea of what it is like to be a cat stalking a bird, so my ideas on feline rights may be poorly informed. Even so, we do know a good deal, and we know it in the same way as we know about the "other minds" of humans. We know enough to understand that animal physical pain and fear closely resemble ours.

In the area of rationality, argued earlier to be central to human worth, it is especially important to avoid either minimizing or exaggerating the resemblances between humans and the higher animals.

Everyone knows from meeting higher animals that they are highly cognitive, for example very smart in navigating. That has always been generally recognized though occasionally denied. Aquinas, for example, agrees that animals have a certain "semblance" of reason in making judgments of things around them as useful or harmful.[2] Certainly modern research has shown that ape, dolphin, and octopus cognition is considerably more sophisticated than once assumed.

But "cognition" is not exactly rationality. It remains an uphill job to bridge more than a little of the gap. It is surprising that humans share 98 percent of their DNA with chimpanzees. But the chimps themselves are not surprised by that, and they cannot be surprised by it.[3] Xenophanes said that if oxen and horses had hands, they would portray their gods like oxen and horses,[4] but in fact, oxen and horses cannot think of gods. Their mental world just does not have that whole realm of theoretical understanding, abstraction, and reflection on concepts.[5] We can discuss what it is like to be them, up to a point, but they cannot wonder what it is like to be us. As Aquinas puts it, "They have this judgment from a natural estimate, not from any deliberation, since they are ignorant of the basis of their judgment."[6] Modern writers speak similarly, saying for example that animals have hardly any "ability to detach a concept from its role in perception and consider it reflectively, apply it intentionally, and compare it with and relate it to other thoughts."[7] That is, they are cognitive but not properly rational in the sense of understanding.

Similar remarks apply to the "rational will" that Kant thought crucial to human dignity. Again, one should neither underplay nor exaggerate human-animal parallels. Aquinas says that animals have "a certain semblance of free choice inasmuch as they can, according to their judgment, do or do not do one and the same thing."[8] Cats can in a way plan and decide. A cat can plan a route over fences to arrive on the back doorstep at dinnertime, and if we see a cat stalk a bird and then suddenly relax and look around, it is natural to conclude that it decided not to pounce. That makes cats suitable as companions and objects of concern. But that is not the same as making decisions in the sense of acting on understood reasons, nor integrating them into a life narrative, nor being capable of explaining why they did it.

As Korsgaard explains it:

> A lower animal's attention is fixed on the world. Its perceptions are its beliefs and its desires are its will. It is engaged in conscious activities, but it is not conscious *of* them. That is, they are not the objects of its attention. But we human animals turn our attention on to our perceptions and desires themselves, on to our own mental activities, and we are conscious of them. That is why we can think *about* them. . . . And

this sets us a problem that no other animal has. It is the problem of the normative. . . . The reflective mind cannot settle for perception and desire, not just as such. It needs a reason.[9]

In the same way, some of the other bases for worth suggested for humans, like unity of consciousness, emotions, and individuality, are shared to a certain degree by animals, but not completely. They "want and prefer things, believe and feel things, recall and expect things. . . . they too must be viewed as the experiencing subjects of a life, with inherent value of their own."[10] They do lack a life plan into which their choices fit, but then human choices often fail to as well. Animal emotions, especially, are continuous with human ones: "Human life really does have an animal basis – an emotional structure on which we build what is distinctively human. In spite of the differences, quite complex aspects of things like loneliness and play and maternal affection, ambition and rivalry and fear, turn out to be shared with other social creatures."[11] And even more so, animal suffering, as recalled in Bentham's "the question is not, Can they *reason?* nor, Can they *talk?* but, Can they *suffer?*"[12]

It follows that animals can correctly be said to have at least some rights, for the same reason as humans do – their worth puts a moral limit on what can be done to them. Of course, they do not have exercisable rights, like a right to vote, any more than they have duties and responsibilities. That sort of right is possible only for a moral agent.[13] But not all human rights are of that kind, such as the right to life. That sort of right is not exercised by its possessor, but is the way in which inherent worth places a limit on other agents. So it is possible for animals, such as those threatened with human cruelty, to have that right. Their position is more like that of humans with severe dementia, who cannot exercise rights but still have rights to be treated and not treated in certain ways.

As they do have a touch of rationality, we should honor it for the same reason that we honor, though more, human rationality.[14] If (our) rationality is so overwhelmingly precious as we say, surely even a small degree of it is worth something morally. It ill behooves us to stand on our dignity. "When a man boasts of the dignity of his nature, and the advantages of his station, and from thence infers his right of oppression of his inferiors, he exhibits his folly as well as his malice."[15] It is our knowledge that animals have some degree of worth that renders ridiculous as well as offensive a view such as that of Chrysippus that the life in a pig is a kind of salt to keep it fresh,[16] or that animals may be killed purely for sport.

Nevertheless the inequality of worth of animals and humans, whatever degree of inequality it may be, raises questions for morality different from those raised by the equality of humans. If trivial reasons for killing animals are morally unacceptable, what about more serious reasons? Is it permissible to eat animals (if they were raised and slaughtered humanely), and is the answer different in a herding society without alternatives and in a modern society with vegetarian options? Is there a good reason why cruelty to animals is considered much worse than killing them humanely, which is not the case with humans?[17] Those are proper topics for debate (which will not be pursued here), and that is so because of the existence of animal worth but its inequality with human worth.

WEIGHING ANIMAL AGAINST HUMAN WORTH?

If animals have a degree of worth but a lower one than humans, does it make sense to ask how much, exactly, an animal is worth compared to a human? In principle, it is an intelligible question.

When considering the equality of human worth, we noticed that trolley and lifeboat cases concerning the survival of humans create forced dilemmas which are hard or embarrassing to resolve but which at least bring to the surface our deep commitment to human equality. One might pose similar dilemmas which weigh human and animal survival in the balance. Peter Singer was asked whether he would save 200 pigs or one child from a burning house and answered:

> At a certain point, the animals' suffering becomes so great that one should choose to save the animals over the child. Whether this point occurs at 200 or two million animals, I don't know. But one cannot let an infinite number of animals burn to save the life of one child.[18]

Some researchers in pediatric surgery argued that Singer's views had been problematic for the real dilemma they faced, since their research posed the choice of using animal experiments or experimenting directly on children.[19] Some people do risk their lives to save animals in fires, though few would be prepared to order firefighters to do the same.

Any one answer to such dilemmas may or may not be defensible, but the dilemmas themselves are genuine, because animals do have a degree of worth. That inevitably raises the question of how it compares with that of humans. Even if the correct answer is that a single human should be saved in preference to infinitely many animals, the question is still a real one. It is real because animals and humans have a sufficiently similar basis of their moral standing.

THE REST OF CREATION: "AESTHETIC" WORTH WITHOUT CONSCIOUSNESS OR INDIVIDUALITY

The non-experiencing parts of the universe, from gas clouds up to plants and sponges, cannot have the sort of worth that humans and higher animals have. They do not have any degree of rationality, consciousness, individuality, or any of the other features argued earlier to be the bases of worth. They do not suffer. They have no literal welfare or interests. Some of "them," such as corals or ecosystems, are hardly individual entities at all. If they have any worth – inherent worth over and above their usefulness to experiencing beings – it will have to be an alien sort of worth.

One view is that they have no such worth. W. D. Ross says, "Contemplate any imaginary universe from which you suppose mind entirely absent, and you will fail to find anything in it you can call good in itself."[20] G. E. Moore says it would contain only a trace of the good.[21]

An opposite view has been common in both ancient tradition and modern environmentalism. "In the beginning, God created the heavens and the earth," according to the Book of Genesis. He held off creating humans for some days, and in the meantime produced the waters, "plants bearing seed according to their kinds and trees bearing fruit with seed in it according to their kinds," then animals. After each of these creations the biblical writer adds, "And God saw that it was good." Judeo-Christian ethics, though strongly focused on commands and actions concerning humans, has in the background a view of the whole of creation as a work of God and inherently good.

Contemporary deep ecology lacks the God but retains the sacrality of the work. Enthusiasm for robust conceptions of intrinsic value of the non-human world was prominent in the early decades of environmental philosophy, where it was typically claimed that "*intrinsic natural* value recognizes value inherent in some natural occasions, without contributory human reference."[22] It has been less prominent in more recent times but is still present.[23]

Naturally there have been complaints in the environmental literature from those afraid of metaphysical notions of worth, who think "value" has to be introduced into the world by valuers.[24] These are the same arguments that were run against the worth of humans and are equally unsatisfactory. We will not examine them again.

Present scientific understandings of the history of the universe involving self-organization out of gas clouds neither require such an intrinsic-worth perspective nor rule it out. It is certainly possible, and to a point natural, to draw reductivist conclusions from evolutionary theory, taking it to show that complex non-experiencing organisms are the same kind of thing as the atoms out of which they evolved and hence have no more value. But that conclusion is not required, since the properties of a complex whole differ from those of its parts in many ways; there is in principle metaphysical opportunity for worth to supervene on properties of complex systems in something the way it did on rationality, consciousness, and the other properties of humans. The reductivist conclusion does clash with our intuitions, in particular our aesthetic intuitions. It threatens to be aesthetically autistic.

Let us imagine, as Ross suggests, an earth without mind, say that of the early Cambrian era some 500 million years ago. Though the land was nearly bare, the seas were full of burgeoning life. The "Cambrian explosion"[25] saw many variations on the chordate body plan used so successfully and flexibly by later vertebrates (bilaterally symmetric, with mouth, gut, and anus plus basic central nervous system). A proliferation of invertebrates quite unlike present-day ones is visible in the diverse fossils of the Burgess Shale.[26] As far as known to present biological theory, there was no mental experience in that world.

The period ended with some major extinction events of unknown cause, in which a considerable percentage of the species on earth vanished. It might have been that those events had been complete, and all life on earth had disappeared so that the planet returned to dust forever. Surely something of value would have been lost. While we may feel more equanimity over such an event than we do with tragedies involving people, we can still appreciate the loss, in something the same way we do for the destruction of a work of art.

Hard-headed scientists closely involved in such studies are inclined to agree. Richard Dawkins opens *The God Delusion* by describing an experience of a grassed field which he, as a boy, shared with a science teacher of his who had experienced something similar while himself young:

> He suddenly found himself overwhelmed by a heightened awareness of the tangled stems and roots, a forest in microcosm, a transfigured world of ants and beetles and even – though he wouldn't have known the details at the time – of soil bacteria by the billions, silently and invisibly shoring up the economy of the micro-world. Suddenly the micro-forest of the turf seemed to swell and become one with the universe, and with the rapt mind of the boy contemplating it.[27]

The teacher interprets his experience in religious terms, while Dawkins does not. But he does mean us to interpret the experience as of something valuable. He calls attention to similar language in Darwin. Evoking a scene of an "entangled bank, clothed with many plants of many kinds, with birds singing on the bushes, with various insects flitting about, and with worms crawling through the damp earth," Darwin concludes:

> From the war of nature, from famine and death, the most exalted object which we are capable of conceiving, namely, the production of the higher animals, directly follows. There is grandeur in this view of life, with its several powers, having been originally breathed into a few forms or into one; and that, whilst this planet has gone cycling on according to the fixed law of gravity, from so simple a beginning endless forms most beautiful and most wonderful have been, and are being, evolved.[28]

The moral-aesthetic language of "exalted," "grandeur," "most beautiful and most wonderful," is not easily dispensed with or dismissed as mere poetical epiphenomenon or marketing spin. If these ecosystems were the work of an intelligent designer, we would admire the skill of his handiwork and praise the perfection of his work of art. If we think it the result of chance natural processes instead, that should make no adjustment to our view of the worth of the "product," as worth should supervene on the properties intrinsic to a being, not on relational properties like its causal history.

Richard Sylvan's "last man" thought experiment has a similar conclusion. If the last man on earth wantonly destroys all remaining life on his way out, has he, absolutely speaking, done evil by creating a loss?[29] He has, because he has vandalized something of worth. Destruction of that kind of value has been commonly called not only vandalism but pillage, degradation, despoliation,[30] and rape of the environment. Those actions are wrong, but not offenses against people. The notion of vandalism provides an entrée into the worth of non-sentient things, natural or artifacts, in the same way as tragedy does for the worth of humans and cruelty does for the worth of animals. Those concepts are about human response, but they make sense because they are correct responses to losses independent of us.

Vandalism, the "ruthless destruction or spoiling of anything beautiful or venerable" (OED), has an aesthetic aspect to its meaning. But that means the aesthetic in an objective sense, not as a matter of mere taste nor as descriptive of what is in the "eye of the beholder." If we say that our attitudes to sentient life forms are moral whereas our attitude to the rest of the universe is aesthetic, that does not imply less objectivity in respect of the latter. We will consider in a later section what properties of a thing could confer objective aesthetic worth on it.

So a universe of galaxies, rainforests, and zombies – in which, perhaps, evolution proceeded as in ours but by some glitch failed to develop consciousnesses in the brains – would be a universe with a certain kind of intrinsic value. But not our kind. Rainforests and zombies instantiate interesting kinds, but the particulars (particular systems) of those kinds are not irreplaceable. Wipe out a rainforest or zombie and it can be replaced with a copy without loss. Not with a human.

THE GREAT CHAIN OF BEING

If we agree that the biologically diverse world of the Cambrian was indeed a "step up" from gas clouds and plasmas and colliding suns, and bare earth littered with stones, we have begun to take on, if only to a minimal degree, the ancient perspective of the Great Chain of Being with its accompanying doctrine of the convertibility of goodness and being (that is, that every being is good). These are philosophical theses rarely regarded as live options in modern times. But since some version of them is implicit in the environmental perspective, we may recall some of the more dramatic past versions of those ideas to see where the admission of aesthetic worth may lead us.

That view has been echoed by a range of influential philosophies from the Platonic and Neoplatonic Great Chain of Being to versions of pantheism to recent deep ecology. All such theories agree that some kind of inherent worth, of an impersonal kind, is spread much more widely than to the few entities that instantiate conscious or semiconscious experience. Most versions (other than panpsychism) agree that most of the universe does not have conscious experience, so any worth possessed by most of nature does not supervene on consciousness or mentality in the way previous chapters argued it did for humans, and as it was argued above to do for higher animals.

The most elaborate version, the one farthest from the reductivist view of materialism, is the Neoplatonism of Pseudo-Dionysius. He presents a vision of the universe according to which the First Principle, or God, necessarily overflows with love into a creative act which results in a universe of cascading levels, the higher levels being a "celestial hierarchy" of angel-like beings and the lowest levels, farthest from God, constituting the world we see around us. As Umberto Eco explains in his book on Aquinas's aesthetics:

> Ch IV of Dionysius's *The Divine Names* ... presents the universe as a cascade of beauties springing forth from the First Principle, a dazzling radiance of sensuous splendours which diversify in all created being:

> 'That, beautiful beyond being, is said to be Beauty – for
>   It gives beauty from itself in a manner appropriate to each
>   It causes the consonance and splendour of all
>   It flashes forth upon all, after the manner of light, the
> beauty producing gifts of its flowing ray
>   It calls all to itself, when it is called beauty.'[31]

Modern environmental philosophy may not accept the existence of any First Principle and would regard the levels of Pseudo-Dionysius's hierarchy above the natural order as unpopulated. But its picture of the populated lower levels is much the same as his – it finds the splendor of nature, as the pantheist finds God, "more in the waterfall or the rainforest than in the car park and the gasworks"[32] because there really is an order of goodness in which stones and carparks are at the bottom and waterfalls and rainforests at much higher levels.

The doctrine of the Great Chain of Being goes naturally with that of the convertibility of good and being – that every entity is good just in virtue of being the kind of thing it is (of course, some kinds being better than others). That initially seems an unlikely thesis; surely the point of "good" is precisely to contrast with "bad" and there are plenty of things bad in themselves. What is good about the mosquito, or for that matter, mere atoms?

It is certainly defensible that every existing thing is good, to some minimal degree[33] even "stones, though in dignity of nature inferior unto plants."[34] Creating a universe with just atoms and stones may be better than nothing. But it might seem still hardly worth the effort. The main issue for the doctrine of the convertibility of being and good lies in those beings that we take to be bad ones.

The meaning of the doctrine can be appreciated by looking closely at the Monty Python parody of the Anglican hymn "All Things Bright and Beautiful." The well-known hymn, an expression of a Christian version of the goodness of all God's creation, begins:

> All things bright and beautiful,
> All creatures great and small,
> All things wise and wonderful,
> The Lord God made them all.

Monty Python's parody does convict the original of a certain selection bias in the evidence chosen by the hymnist:

> All things dull and ugly,
> All creatures short and squat,
> All things rude and nasty,
> The Lord God made the lot
>
> Each little snake that poisons,
> Each little wasp that stings,
> He made their brutish venom,
> He made their horrid wings.
>
> All things sick and cancerous,
> All evil great and small,
> All things foul and dangerous,
> The Lord God made them all.

That works well as humor, and it does remind us of why we call certain things bad. It is less successful as an attempt to represent the good and evil in creation as symmetrical. "Short and squat" is not a description of badness but an expression of supercilious human perspective. The original "creatures great and small" is more generous in its inclusiveness and its recognition that size is not a morally relevant property. The horridness of wasp wings, too, is a human perspective, not an inherent property of wasps. On the other hand, what makes the sick, cancerous, poisonous, and dangerous things bad is solely their threats to beings that have considerable inherent worth. What is bad about a poison is not anything inherent to it but its deleterious effect on something higher than it in the Chain of Being.[35] The original hymn is philosophically superior in calling attention to the perfections of things that register on our aesthetic sensibility; the parody is parasitic on that.

If "the environment" sometimes seems too large and diffuse an entity to evoke our admiration, we can more easily appreciate the ecosystem of interdependent organs that so intimately underpins our own existence, the human body. Conceived in abstraction from, and simply as infrastructure for, the rational person that inhabits it, the human body as rendered intelligible (in different ways) by Leonardo da Vinci's art and by medical science is a beautiful piece of machinery. It may be said of all nature, but more obviously of an animal body, that "nature, in the sense relevant to moral reflection, is intelligible in its operations, and this intelligibility in turn reflects the goodness as well as the inherent reasonableness of the variety of forms of created existence which go to make up the world."[36]

Artifacts like paintings and steam engines, which some regard as the primary bearers of aesthetic worth (rather than natural objects) are more complex, but bear thinking about for what they show about nature. They are fashioned with a view to the perceptions they cause (for example, a canvas with oils designed to look like a landscape), thus made so as to stimulate senses which are themselves designed (or "designed") to be attuned to nature. They are created with an intention to convey messages or to perform tasks (in the case of machinery); and they refer to the genre and tradition they are in.[37] They are special also in that they express the genius of the artist or craftsman (so that replacing an artwork with a copy breaks the connection to the artist), and our interaction, therefore, involves duties to the artist's legacy.

The aesthetics of artworks is thus more complicated than the aesthetics of nature, and shows up by contrast the simplicity of direct appreciation of natural beauty. And appreciation of artworks is a transferable skill. A landscape artist or sketcher of the nude, as well as a medical illustrator, can teach us how to see nature aesthetically, and see its worth truly.

BASES OF WORTH OF NON-SENTIENT BEINGS

If non-sentient beings like insects, ecosystems, animal bodies, and artworks do have some sort of worth, the metaphysical basis of it must be quite different from that of sentient beings. They have none of the (semblance of) bases like consciousness, rationality, emotional life, individuality, that sentient animals do.

Indeed, the bearers of that kind of worth need not be individual substances at all. Humans and animals, as argued above, are individuals that have worth and have it in virtue of inherent properties of those individuals. For the human and higher animal parts of the world, an Aristotelian (or "Linnean") metaphysics holds: The world is uniquely divided into things, and the things are uniquely classified into species. The rest of the world is not always like that. Apart from stuffs, like water and space, there are entities like sponges and corals, which are to slightly different degrees somewhere between individual things and systems. In such cases there is no significant distinction between things forming a system and parts forming a thing. Rainforests, ecosystems, crystals, galaxies, landscapes, symphonies, and the like have significant structure that does not belong to their parts, parts which may or may not be correctly regarded as individual "things." Even trees, which are normally classified as discrete individuals in discrete species, are more like communities of root, xylem, phloem, and leaf cells; at least they are much more decentralized than animals with a central nervous system giving "orders." For things/stuffs that lack the unified minds of higher animals and humans, unity or non-unity lacks moral significance. An ecosystem can have whatever good it does have without being a thing. Or a landscape. Dietrich von Hildebrand writes:

> The ascent in the individualization from a piece of matter to an organism, and further, in an incomparable manner, to the human person, is of a quite different kind from the ascent from a mere slice of nature to the unity of a landscape in the narrower sense of the word. This individual unity of the landscape is of a purely aesthetic nature and certainly does not make it an ontological individual. Unlike the ontological individuality, it is not clearly demarcated from that which surrounds it. It is not a substance, and is indeed even further removed from substantial individuality than a work of art.[38]

So if biodiversity, for example, is taken to have an absolute and not merely instrumental value, if "richness and diversity of lifeforms are values in themselves,"[39] as deep ecologists (and a large proportion of the general public[40]) hold, it must apply to a system, not any individual organism. Kinds must have worth that is not the sum of the worth of the individual members, so that the extinction of a species is a different kind of evil from the sum of the deaths of individual members.[41] There is no metaphysical objection to that. It is perfectly possible for the kind of worth to which the aesthetic sense is attuned.

If we accept that systems can be the bearers of aesthetic worth, it remains to ask what properties of systems, or parted wholes, could be the bases of that worth. What properties can systems have, on which "aesthetic" worth can supervene?

The classic statement of the bases of aesthetic worth, that of Aquinas, is relevant, although as it stands, it is more adapted to the beauty of individual things. He writes:

> Three things are necessary for beauty: first, integrity or perfection, for things that are lacking in something are for this reason ugly; also due proportion or consonance; and again, clarity, for we call things beautiful when they are brightly colored.[42]

Those properties are all, on Aquinas's view, inherent in the things themselves and not at all in the eye of the beholder.

Of these, "proportion or consonance" is relational and so particularly applicable to systems. A proportion must be *between* different entities in a system, such as musical notes or areas in a natural or painted landscape. The complexity, symmetry, and similar properties (according to one list, "complexity, stability, diversity, connectedness, variety, subtlety, intricacy, ingenuity in some suitably non-intentional sense, fragility, harmony"[43]) that are normally praised as the good-making features of ecosystems or landscapes are the same kind of properties as Aquinas's "proportion or consonance." It is not just any sort of complexity that contributes to aesthetic worth – not, for example, the complexity of a random string of digits. Instead, "in the despoliation of the natural environment what is bad-making is the destruction of an entity which exhibits a complex structural harmony and its replacement by a comparatively unstructured heap lacking the relevant excellences."[44]

Those are strictly mathematical properties – concerned with the same and the different, ratios, symmetry, equality of parts. They are the same kind of thing as the mathematical ratios that Plato said stood behind and explained heard harmonies and that were for him the model of the Good.[45] They are not easily measurable or reducible to algorithmic description – there is, for example, no known way of measuring the complexity that arises in the question "Could an entity as complex as the human body have arisen from a random search process in only 4 billion years?" – while algorithms can write symphonies but not very good ones. Nevertheless they are objective mathematical properties of systems that are parts of the natural world. They are accessible to the aesthetic sense which is thus, as often noted, useful as a guide to truth in physics.[46]

Whether Aquinas's other suggested bases of beauty, integrity and brightness of color, are applicable to systems is not easy to say. The answer is for present purposes not crucial though interesting. "Integrity," or freedom from defect, is most naturally a property of an individual that has a form that it "ought to realize," for example, a human lacks something if he/she is missing a limb or is impaired in rationality.[47] An ecosystem does not have a perfection like that, even though some ecosystems may be richer than others. It is arguable that color is a secondary quality and the physical bases of it such as light wavelength are insufficient for beauty. Perhaps an array of sense-data has a beauty that is objective but additional to that of the physical things seen. We need not decide those questions.

WEIGHING "AESTHETIC" AGAINST SENTIENT WORTH?

As with possible conflicts between the survival of humans and animals, it is possible to raise trolley- or lifeboat-style cases where the survival of humans or sentient animals conflicts with the survival (or one might better say preservation) of an inanimate system of some aesthetic worth. Again, the point is not the resolution of any such dilemmas but their bringing into focus that there is something to compare.

Some writers on the problem of evil, for example, have suggested that there might be a conflict between (objective) aesthetic and strictly moral requirements in God's creation of the world. For example, a justifiable preference for simple and hence aesthetically better laws of nature could result in evil consequences for humans subject to those laws.[48] Do "the actual sufferings of beasts constitute a graver defect in a world than does massive irregularity"?[49] That is hard to say, but the possibility of such a conflict from a God's-eye perspective is intelligible.

Human ethics normally requires preferring moral considerations to aesthetic ones; for example, one does not usually risk lives to save artworks. Though one might do so voluntarily. Many have admired the director of antiquities at Palmyra, Khaled al-Asaad, who was beheaded by ISIS in 2015 after refusing to reveal the location of treasures in his care.[50] Threatened environmental vandalism of a similar scale might attract heroic resistance. Indeed, killings of environmental activists in a number of countries are frequent.[51] One would, though, balk at advising or ordering anyone to put their life at risk for the sake of an inanimate object.

Resolvable or not, such cases usefully highlight the existence of two very dissimilar kinds of worth and the possibility in principle of conflict between them, and the possible existence of cases demanding a balance between them.

SUPERIOR BEINGS

As far as we know, there are no beings superior to humans, except possibly God. But something is gained by thinking about the possibility. Previous centuries did that by believing in angels, which they thought filled up some of the yawning gap in the Great Chain of Being between humans and God. Our age is more inclined to speculate about extraterrestrials or future artificial intelligences, or beings that may be produced by the continuation of evolution, in the style of Teilhard de Chardin. Others look forward to enhancing human beings into a morally superior species.

If such beings do come to exist, they will no doubt write books (or upload thoughts to their common mental workspace, whatever that may be) on their own worth and whether humans have some degree of it and hence some moral rights. Will they regard it as permissible to eat or experiment on humans, or see it as an act of mercy to put down such a defective species, no doubt more humanely than humans did the Neanderthals?

While it is valuable to consider what it would be like not to be the lords of creation, discussion is premature because it has not proved possible to explain convincingly what a significantly different superior species would be like.[52] It is easy to imagine various cognitive, health, and perhaps moral enhancements to humanity, but those are only extensions of the efforts currently made by the education and health systems to improve humans. They do not create a different kind of being. If we review the bases of worth suggested in the previous chapter – capacity for rationality, consciousness, emotions, and the like – then we can imagine any of those marginally improved, but it is hard to find conceptual space for something completely different.[53] Perhaps the most radical change that is readily conceivable is disembodiment, but as we saw in considering the contribution of the physical to the worth of persons, even that is comparatively marginal from an ethical point of view.

It is certainly likely that we will soon create freestanding artificial intelligences, perhaps in the form of soft-skinned robots with AI-powered voice recognition and response. On present scientific theory, they will not have any consciousness, though they will confuse us by appearing to behave like those beings to which we are wired to attribute minds. We do not know how to give them any consciousness, rational will, understanding, or emotions whatsoever, let alone more of those qualities than ourselves. It is conceivable that we should give them a neurology from which consciousness and its accompaniments might emerge, but we know so little about the parallel biological case of embryo brains that we have no purchase on the question.

Speculations on the worth of beings superior to humans are, therefore, at present entertaining but premature.

GOD

A serious discussion of the worth of God is not attempted here. Some but not all religions maintain that God is morally good – that is the thesis which gives rise to the problem of evil. That is not the same question as whether God is a being of surpassing moral worth (a worth that would be retained if, *per impossibile*, he behaved badly).

Christian thought sometimes distinguishes between the "communicable" and "incommunicable" attributes of God. The communicable ones are those that can be shared with humans (or at least some analogue of them can be shared). They include intelligence, goodness, will, and power. The incommunicable attributes are ones which can belong only to God and are negations of creaturely imperfections. They include self-existence, infinity, immensity, and eternity.[54] It will be seen that the communicable attributes closely resemble those human attributes that were argued to be the bases of human worth in the previous chapter. Indeed, all of those – rationality, consciousness, a self unified yet capable of diversity, a rational will, emotions such as love, and individuality – could be attributed to God at least in some analogical fashion. They are so attributed to the personal God of Christianity (and to some extent to the somewhat less personal God of Islam[55]). If God does have those properties, a surpassing worth will supervene on them.

A personal God is not the only possibility. The wide spectrum of pantheisms – views like the Stoic philosophy of Nature, Plotinus's Neoplatonism, Spinoza's pantheism, Absolute Idealism, the Confucian concept of the Mandate of Heaven, and some forms of contemporary deep ecology – model the divine (or Nature) more on the lines of the "aesthetic" worth of non-sentient nature as described above. Such an entity can have intrinsic worth, but as argued above, a quite different kind from a personal consciousness. It can require something from persons, but is hardly the kind of thing to itself care about persons.

WHAT NEXT?

Once we have a solid sense of the absolute worth of persons (and a perhaps less solid sense of the worth of other entities), there are two directions to move in order to widen our understanding of what that implies. The first direction is forward – what does the worth of persons mean when applied to questions about what we ought to do, and how do we know about it? How, that is, does obligation arise from the worth of persons, how do we know what to do from knowing the worth of persons, and how do we know the worth of persons in the first place? Those questions will be addressed in the next two chapters.

The second direction is back – what kind of universe could support such an absolute worth? What, minimally, must the universe be like metaphysically in order not to undermine absolute worth? This is important not only because we want to know what the objectivity of ethics tells us about the universe in general, but because some leading views on the question, such as strict atheistic materialism, threaten to undermine ethics. The appeal of objectivist ethical theories like Kantian, natural law, and worth of persons approaches to ethics is often (like, say, Platonism in the philosophy of mathematics) dismissed as incompatible with deeply held philosophical views about the nature of the universe, such as naturalism. An objectivist philosophy of ethics cannot be self-contained but must be situated in some cosmology. What is the truth? That will have to be the subject of a separate inquiry, but the Epilogue of this book outlines what has to be done.

CHAPTER EIGHT

The Source of Obligation

❖

Moral obligation, action, right and wrong, have been left as late as possible, unlike in most other approaches to ethics. It is time for an explanation of where they come from.

As we saw in Chapter 5, Hume's talk of an is-ought gap, though pointing to a genuine problem, threatened to conflate several different gaps. Three gaps need discussion:

- The natural properties-worth gap (argued in Chapter 5 to be bridged by the notion of supervenience)

- The worth-obligation gap

- The obligation-motivation gap

Besides those, there is the gap between what one ought to do and what one knows one ought to do; epistemology will be treated in the next chapter. And, of course, there is the all-important gap between what one knows one ought to do, and perhaps wishes to do, and what one actually does; but that is a matter more for one's conscience, confessor, and psychiatrist than for a philosophical adviser.

THE WORTH-OBLIGATION GAP

According to the approach of earlier chapters, worth is an intrinsic property of certain entities, such as humans. Moral obligation is quite another kind of thing. It is a relation between an actor and a potential action (or attitude) of that actor. The worth of humans is a (moral) fact about them, but my obligation to assist or respect them is a relation of me to them. If intrinsic worth is somehow to give rise to moral obligation, some substantial story needs to be told to fill the gap between worth and obligation.

As error theorists point out, there is something mysterious about how facts – any sort of facts – could have or imply "requiredness." "The problem ... is precisely to explain how there can be facts that *in themselves*, i.e. irrespectively of the desires, aims, or roles of human beings and other agents, require, or *count in favour of*, certain forms of behaviour."[1] That applies as much to facts about ethical worth as it does to non-moral scientific facts. True, facts about worth have a better initial prospect of explaining obligation than scientific facts do, as they are at least ethical, but it is still not obvious what the connection is between worth and anything to do with action and obligation. There is a substantial gap to cross.

The gap is highlighted by the fact that it is possible, though for obvious reasons rare, to have an ethical theory with worth of some kind but without obligation. John Mackie's teacher, John Anderson, proposed an ethical theory with objective good (for example, criticism is objectively good) but with no obligations to action. He dismissed the idea that obligation could flow from goodness as a "relativist confusion." He argued:

> The notion of that which is unconditionally binding on me falls with every other notion of "that whose nature it is to have a certain relation," viz. in that it treats a relation as if it

were a quality. And if it is argued that the consideration [on which it is binding] in question is goodness, that it is my duty to promote what is good, the answer is that the assertion that certain actions promote good still gives no meaning to the contention that it is "my duty" to perform them.[2]

He is right to the extent that obligation is a relation that is not simply part of or logically implied by the goodness of entities.

G. E. Moore, too, called attention to the logical gap between intrinsic worth and reasons for action:

> If what Mr Frankena means to assert is that the propositional function '*x* is intrinsically good' may be identical with the function 'the fact that an action which you can do would produce *x* is *some* reason for supposing that you ought to do that action' then ... there is a two-way necessary connection between these functions.... But ... Is it not possible to *think* that a thing is intrinsically good without thinking that the fact that an action within our power would produce it would be a reason for supposing that we ought to do that action? It certainly seems as if we can.[3]

So Aquinas is right in saying that a faculty or operation of "synderesis" is needed to understand the connection. In a later idiom, the connection of worth to obligation is synthetic a priori (necessary but not conceptual).[4] When Aquinas says that the first principle is "the good is to be followed and evil avoided," it is true that his concept of good is, as described in Chapter 3, more like Aristotle's "the good for man" than absolute worth. But the point remains valid, that some necessary but not analytic connection needs to be made from "the good," in either sense, to the obligatoriness of action.

The nature of this "worth-obligation" or "good-right" gap has troubled later ethical thinkers, too, and the issue has surfaced in many forms. In recent analytic moral philosophy, the question has generated a debate about "internalism versus externalism": whether something's being good necessarily supplies a reason to act. (Reasons) internalism "claims that it is *a priori* that the recognition of moral facts itself necessarily provides the agent with reason to perform the moral action."[5] (Though sometimes the debate about internalism concerns the gap between recognition of goodness and a *psychological* motive to act, on which more below.)

Yet at the same time the connection between worth and obligatoriness is experienced by normally functioning humans as immediate and obvious; and as Moore puts it, "a two-way necessary connection." If I see someone fall in the river and there is no one else to rescue them, my recognition of the impending harm to them generates an obligation on me to help them (if I can) and I should be happy to shoulder the burden (and feel no need for or benefit from a command to fill the gap). What could there be to deliberate about ethically, given the immediate need and my ability to do something about it?

Kant writes as if there is nothing to deliberate about: "Suppose there were something *whose existence in itself* had an absolute worth, something that, as *end in itself*, could be a ground of determinate laws [of action] …"[6] "Having absolute worth" is one (inherent) thing, being an end and grounding laws is another (relational) thing, but Kant's speaking as if they are obviously equivalent is testament to the felt close connection between the two.

Nevertheless, there is something to explain, if not deliberate about. Just as with visual perception there is no felt deliberation but there is something to explain as to how perception (in here) causes knowledge of seen things (out there).

So what exactly is needed to fill the gap between worth and obligation?

It will help to consider a parallel case which, though not exactly clear, lacks the special difficulties of the moral case. It is the same parallel case that helped understand the supervenience of worth on natural qualities, namely, the parallel with logical reasons for belief. There is another kind of "should," the ought of logic. Why should one believe a proposition that is implied by (or highly probable given) one's total evidence? (Here we are not concerned with the "ethics of belief" – such questions as whether one morally ought not to believe in the absence of sufficient evidence – but with the question of what logic is good for, as regards belief.) There is a gap to be filled: Implication and probability do not just mean something to do with belief. On the contrary, they are relations "out there" (in the objective world of logic, whatever that is). Implication is a property of (a set of) propositions, whereas logical requiredness, if one may call it that, is a relation of a person (with a current set of beliefs) to a potential new belief. Why does p's implying q, my knowing that, and my belief that p, require me as a matter of rationality to believe q? How do facts in the logical world support or imply oughts about my belief-relation to propositions?

The answer is not an instrumental one, as if I will be advantaged if I believe what is implied by my current beliefs because I will believe more true propositions and hence increase my Darwinian fitness. That may be so, but the question here is a prior one, which would not be changed if it turned out that the world were an inherently Stalinist one in which believing the truth would be counterproductive. Euclid's alleged remark to a beginning student in geometry who asked what he would gain from learning it, "Let him be given a three-obol piece, since he must make gain out of what he learns,"[7] illustrates the point. Even in the absence of any use for geometry, the question remains why one's belief in the axioms and the axioms' implying the theorems means that one is logically required to believe the theorems. It is a question about the relation between logical relations among propositions and the right ordering of human beliefs.

The essential answer to the question "Why believe what is implied by or made probable by one's evidence" is just "Because it is implied or probable." Why not believe that the earth is flat? Because the evidence is against it. That is the complete justification and nothing can add to it.[8] A statement like "You should always believe what you have good evidence for" adds generality but not further explanation.

It is similar with worth and its relation to moral obligation. If someone falls in the river near me, it is my responsibility to help him if he appears to need it. That is just because he is another human being in extreme need and I have the ability to save him. His right to be saved and my duty to save him follow from his need and my ability. I may be excused if I don't see him, or if I can't swim, or if there is someone nearby with a better chance of saving him who is willing to try. Those considerations are relevant because they concern the causal connections between myself and saving the victim. But I am not excused on the basis of my not having been elected to the office of lifesaver, or by my having other things I would prefer to be doing, or by my being of a different race from the victim. A prospective injury which I could easily prevent is a harm to something of great worth. If I don't act, I have (partially) caused that harm. It directly imposes on me a moral obligation to prevent it, and nothing can add to that – not any advantage to me, or sympathy with the victim, or enhancement of my virtue, or command of God or human law, or theory about rationality or universalizability.

Perhaps the answer – and the impossibility of adding anything further to bridge the gap – is even clearer in a case of a required refraining from action. Why should I not vandalize a precious artwork, or why should I not shoot the last dodo for fun? Those entities are valuable, so their destruction is absolutely speaking a loss. That and that alone explains why it is wrong for me to destroy them. My remorse, if I did those things and regretted them, would be solely for the loss I had caused.

Wolterstorff writes of the "Ur-principle, one should never treat anything as of less worth than it is ... the requiredness constitutive of obligation is what respect for worth requires. If respect for your worth requires that I treat you in such-and-such a way, then I have an obligation toward you to treat you that way."[9] Worth begets an obligation to respect and act, and nothing further can fill the gap.

THE OBLIGATION-MOTIVATION GAP

The worth-obligation gap is not to be confused with the much-discussed obligation-motivation gap. That is a gap, too, but a different one.

Moral motivation as such is outside the scope of the present work, but it is important to explain the separation between the objective ethics defended here and questions of motivation, since many ethical theories believe in a close connection or even identity between the moral and what motivates. That is true both of an extreme Platonism as portrayed by Mackie, in which the ethical Forms once understood motivate necessarily,[10] and non-cognitivist theories which identify the moral with what motivates, as if to call something good is just to cheer for it.[11] Others have argued for "motivational judgment internalism," the thesis that a judgment that some action is good necessarily provides some motive for doing it, on the ground that it best explains the reliable connection between moral beliefs and commitments to the resulting actions.[12]

It is not true, however, that moral belief and motives are reliably connected in that way. In the virtuous, they are, but that took work in training virtue and the reliability of the (contingent) connection is what makes them virtuous. Whole industries are premised on the general unreliability of many people's moral motivation, including the police, security, surveillance, compliance, investigative journalism, and possibly schoolteaching. And it is not just a theoretical "amoralist" who fails to transmute moral judgement into motivation.[13] "We" may be virtuous but the Devil and those who follow in his path are not. He knows what is good, which is precisely what motivates him to destroy it. At a more mundane level, it is the same with vandalism and cruelty.[14] Vandals and bullies do not pursue a lesser good in place of a greater, in the way that a glutton arguably does; they take what is bad directly as a goal. There is no point vandalizing something of no worth – the better it is, the more vandalism aims to disfigure it. When Milton has Satan say, "Evil, be thou my good,"[15] he does not mean that Satan mistakes evil for some kind of good. Satan is clear-eyed, and intends evil directly. So do all too many people, too much of the time.

So there is no close conceptual connection between obligation and motivation, or even a necessary psychological or practical one. Obligation ought to motivate, but does so only for the virtuous, in the same way that proofs in mathematics cause belief in their conclusions only for those who understand them.

DEDUCING OBLIGATIONS FROM THE WORTH OF PERSONS

If it is accepted that the worth of persons can have implications for obligation, it remains to inquire about two things. Is "implication" to be understood in a strict sense in the way that Euclid's axioms imply geometrical theorems, or should it mean something looser? And do we need any other premises than the (equal) worth of persons to deduce the various obligations of morality?

The answers to be defended are: First, a Euclidean model is correct; and second, the worth of persons is sufficient by itself to imply some important rules of morality, but not all – for some rules, we need some extra axioms about the nature of humans (or in the case of dealings with non-human entities, about their nature). But those axioms are facts about the bases of the worth of persons (and other entities), such as rationality.

Even ethical theorists who have generally approved of the Kantian thesis that respect for persons is the crucial foundational idea have often thought a Euclidean model rather over-strict and beneath the dignity of ethics. Allen Wood writes from a Kantian perspective:

> Moral rules or duties can be *derived* from the first principle [of respect for persons], but not if our only concept of "derivation" is a rigorous deductive procedure. Instead, we should think of the relation between the two more as interpretive or hermeneutical in character. Rules or duties result when the basic value and fundamental principle are *interpreted* in light of a set of general empirical facts about the human condition and human nature, perhaps also as modified by cultural or historical conditions.[16]

But that fails to show why ethics differs from geometry, as the same can be said about applying geometry to real space. Euclid's axioms do not tell you how far it is to the shops without some further empirical facts being taken into account. If facts about human nature are needed to deduce some moral rules (which they are, as argued below), then why are they not just further axioms (or in mathematical language "initial conditions")? That is a suggestion easier to understand than the vaguer "interpreted in the light of."

A model of strict deduction may be attributable to Jesus and thus is ingrained in the Christian tradition. Jesus may not have been familiar with the work of Euclid, but when he says, "All the law and the prophets hang on these two commandments" (Matthew 22:40) (namely, love God and love your neighbor), his words "hang on" are most easily understood as really asserting a logical deduction as from axioms to theorems.

To progress with this question, it would be natural to lay down some axioms, and a fair suite of test cases of accepted moral rules, and see if the rules can be deduced from the axioms.

Let us ask first what the implications are of a single axiom of "respect for persons." Once done, it remains to be seen what obligations might be left over and hence require further axioms.

As persons have worth, they should be respected. Respect just is the recognition of worth, acted on. It has been argued that the notion of respect is too imprecise to make it clear what exactly follows from it,[17] but it is in truth a very strong axiom, especially with equality of worth. Respecting persons in virtue of the worth they have puts many constraints, at the very least, on what can be done to them.

Kant means that one should treat humans as ends because they actually are ends, that is, have intrinsic worth, so the principle already involves a deduction of obligation from worth. As he puts it, humans' *"existence in itself had an absolute worth*, something that, *as end in itself*, could be a ground of determinate laws."[18] So how determinate can the laws arising from worth be?

Non-killing is an obvious deduction. If something is of worth, destroying it (without some strong countervailing reason) must be wrong. There is no need to "interpret in the light of" anything. Harm is evil in itself, in virtue of the worth of the thing harmed, so deliberate harm is wrong. A prohibition on wanton destruction – of humans, races, human opportunities and possessions, animals, environments – comprises a substantial and demanding portion of ethics. It follows with full deductive strictness from the worth of the objects of potential destruction.

Equally obvious is the duty to save something from destruction if feasible. No interpretation or adversion to empirical facts is needed to deduce a duty to save something of worth, or in case of forced choice and other things being equal, a duty to save something of more worth (say a person) over something of less worth (say a dog), or to save six persons over five.

How to proceed further is successfully shown in Robert Audi's project to deduce W. D. Ross's principles of *prima facie* duty from Kant's principle that one should act to treat humanity as an end, not a means.[19] Ross maintained that there were five basic duties: a duty of fidelity, a duty of reparation, a duty of gratitude, a duty of non-maleficence, and a duty of beneficence. The duties of non-maleficence and beneficence arc in effect those just discussed of not harming and of saving from harm a being of worth, so it is clear why the obligation arises deductively from worth. The other three duties are not so clear, but by way of example, we explain below the duty of fidelity to one's word, or truth telling.

One does not necessarily expect from a deductive model the resolution of dilemmas, since those are about balancing the weight of competing claims. The claims themselves should be deducible from the worth (and nature) of persons, but their relative weight may not be. There may be an objectively right answer, but judgment is needed. We will look later at the issue of conflict and balancing of ethical reasons.

ARISTOTELIAN-THOMIST NATURAL LAW ETHICS

Harm is a simple case when it comes to moral obligation and its relation to worth. If something is of worth, harm to it is obviously bad and it is easy to understand why a *prima facie* obligation arises to refrain from causing, to avoid, or to prevent the harm. Other cases of obligation are not so easy. Explaining a right to education, for example, requires either some kind of moral obligation other than preventing harm, or some kind of non-obvious argument as to why failing to provide education should count as a form of harm.

The solution lies in what was said in Chapter 6 about the properties of humans that constitute or form the basis of their worth. Actions that have a causal effect on any of those properties can affect worth and hence give rise to moral obligation (and *mutatis mutandis,*

non-actions). So the worth of persons does strictly imply all obligations, but only after taking into account extra premises. Those premises are, however, not extra factual premises, nor are they extra ethical
premises. They are unfoldings of what the worth of persons supervenes on.

That is the essential idea – though not expressed in quite that
way – of natural law ethics in the tradition of Aquinas. Thomist ethics does not resemble at a foundational level the worth-of-persons
perspective defended here. It regards ethics as fundamentally about
right action or "practical reason" and seeks self-evident principles of
action that promote, in Aristotelian fashion, the *felicitas* and *beatitudo*
(happiness and flourishing) of humans.[20] Its failure to ground those
principles further in the worth of persons or any equivalent has
meant that recent attempts by Catholic thinkers such as Pope John
Paul II to see the "dignity of the human person" as central to ethics
have been hard to relate to the thought of Thomas Aquinas.[21] Nevertheless, the suggested self-evident principles of practical reason are
said to be implied by human nature. In accordance with the doctrine
of the convertibility of being and good (discussed in the last chapter),
genuinely natural inclinations of human nature can be counted as
good and following those inclinations ("for instance, to shun ignorance, to avoid offending those among whom one has to live, and
other such things" in Aquinas's words) can be taken to be a correct
course for practical reason.

Therefore, the present project of extracting principles of obligation from the grounds of worth such as rationality can be expected to
produce a natural law ethics along the lines of the traditional Thomist
one, even if it need not agree with it in detail. That is particularly so
with regard to the consequences of rationality, which is the central
feature of humanity in both worth-based and Aristotelian philosophies. Thus in Thomism, the good of knowledge and the desirability
of pursuing it is one of the basic self-evident truths of practical

reason.[22] In a worth-of-persons perspective, rationality is an important feature that is constitutive of worth (solely constitutive, on some views, but in any case central). Therefore, intellectual activity is a human perfection – it is just the exercise of rationality. Therefore, education (in intellectual matters, and whatever else constitutes rationality, such as prudence) is a right, and failure to be educated is a harm and thus a violation of that right (in the normal circumstance where education is available). Because rationality necessarily gives rise to worth, preserving and enhancing it by education is necessarily a good thing, and hence providing education is a duty for those so situated as to be able to effect it, such as parents, teachers, and those who direct state expenditure. As Mary Wollstonecraft said of the neglect of women's education, "Their first duty is to themselves as rational creatures."[23]

An assault on the person that prevents or impedes the development of rationality from the start, such as drinking in pregnancy that causes fetal alcohol syndrome, is a direct harm. Lesser and later actions that may impede rationality in various ways, such as child labor and narrow schooling in fundamentalist madrassahs, also violate a child's right to education. Those can be correctly called harms, in that they damage the normal development of rationality. Conversely, inspiring teachers are rightly praised for eliciting a higher degree of learning in their pupils than would have been possible without their efforts.

Since aspects of the human person other than rationality strictly so called also contribute to human worth, education has to be appropriately broad. In the words of the Universal Declaration of Human Rights, "Education shall be directed to the full development of the human personality."[24] The emotional aspects of persons must be correctly developed, as the emotions are a deep aspect of personality and, as argued above, one of the bases of worth. It is for psychiatry, supplementing common sense and literary understandings of human nature, to establish the needs of child development for a loving family upbringing, for sexual morality, for training in right actions, and so on.

The essentially social nature of humans has many implications for natural law ethics. The commandments "Honor thy father and thy mother" and "Thou shalt not covet thy neighbor's wife" are relevant only in a social context, and the reasons for them are obvious in that context. Developing such matters would take us too far afield.

Finally, the inclusion of the uniqueness or individuality of humans among the bases of worth explains why a worth-of-persons ethic is not straightforwardly utilitarian or consequentialist. If persons are of equal worth and with equal claims, why not add up worth across humans and maximize it, as a way to determine what action is right? In fact, in cases where the individuality of humans has to be relegated to the background, such as a general deciding between military strategies or in health care or philanthropic allocation, that is the correct approach and the recommendations arising from the worth of persons will resemble those of utilitarianism (a utilitarianism that truly counts people as equal). But in more normal interpersonal relations, humans are respected and loved as individuals. Individuals are not treated as interchangeable as in consequentialism but action is attuned to the personal good of each known person.[25] One can agree that, at least often, "the moral task is not to generate action based on universal and impartial principles but to attend and respond to particular persons,"[26] because of the individuality of persons.

Rather than examine the full range of ethical questions, we take two case studies to show exactly how obligation arises from worth when there is no direct harm involved.

EXAMPLE: WHY IS LYING WRONG?

The case of lying is significant for several reasons. It is not a case of direct and obvious harm, at least in many cases, so the obligation not to lie is not explained straightforwardly in terms of worth in the way that the obligation not to injure is.[27] Further, some explanation is needed of both the strong feeling of moralists like Kant and Aquinas that lying is impermissible in principle, and of the general view that there can be in rare cases good and morally required deceptions. And the most prominent explanations in recent moral philosophy of why lying is wrong appear to miss some of the point. The lack of a worth-of-persons perspective has led to analyses of lying being morally thin and out of contact with the direct revulsion we feel for it. Thus it is a useful case study as a template for how a worth-of-persons perspective explains what more usual theories fail to explain adequately.

Korsgaard suggests three reasons which could be advanced to explain why lying is wrong.[28] First, intuitionists such as W. D. Ross may say it is just wrong for no further reasons (which would have the disadvantage of giving no method of balancing its badness against other reasons, in cases where lying might arguably be required). Second, consequentialist reasons could be given, relying on the harm that typically arises for the one deceived and on the consequences of the degrading of trust generally. Third, Kantians object to the violation of the autonomy of those lied to, which improperly takes away their control over their own lives and decisions and so manipulates them.[29]

Those are all substantial reasons and a worth-of-persons perspective can approve of them. Certainly the human harm arising from lies is substantial and the manipulation of people by lying is an affront to their dignity. But those reasons completely omit something more immediate, the common revulsion against deliberate falsehood as such which is developed by the Aristotelian-Thomist natural law perspective. Aristotle writes that "falsehood is in itself mean and culpable, and truth noble and worthy of praise." He continues, "For the man who loves truth, and is truthful where nothing is at stake, will still more be truthful where something is at stake; he will avoid falsehood as something base, seeing that he avoided it even for its own sake."[30] That is not about either consequences or autonomy.

As they stand, Aristotle's remarks might be about ungrounded intuitions (concerning meanness and nobility), but his thoughts are given a further grounding by Aquinas. The reason why lying is mean is the nature of words. "As words are naturally signs of intellectual acts, it is unnatural and undue for anyone to signify by words something that is not in his mind. Hence the Philosopher says (*Ethic.* iv, 7) that 'lying is in itself evil and to be shunned, while truthfulness is good and worthy of praise.'"[31] The *Catholic Encyclopedia* adds: "Man has the power as a reasonable and social being of manifesting his thoughts to his fellow man. Right order demands that in doing this he should be truthful. . . . Truth is primarily a self-regarding virtue: it is something which man owes to his own rational nature, and no-one who has any regard for his own dignity and self-respect will be guilty of the turpitude of a lie."[32]

That is a classic natural law argument from the purpose of something, the kind of argument sometimes caricatured as "If God had meant us to fly, he would have given us wings." Examining this case will establish whether there is anything in appeals to nature in ethics and how they fit with a worth-of-persons perspective.

We will find ourselves more in sympathy with these thoughts if we recall that language production is done by the whole cognitive and speech system – the mind that knows the truth and decides to utter either the truth or its opposite. Surely there is something to be said for the idea that the point of the cognitive system is be aligned with the truth, as far as possible, and hence that making it serve falsehood is a perversion that is unworthy of its dignity and its role in human life? We are inclined to think of people jailed for fraud,

"You're only on the planet once, what are you doing wasting your life and your intelligence deceiving people?" If we are forced to lie, as in the classic case of misleading a would-be murderer on the location of a knife, that is the right thing to do, certainly – anything else would be collaborating with an assault on a person. But it still does a kind of violence to the cognitive system – indeed, the point of the example is the need for a very serious reason to overcome the natural orientation of the system to the truth. Cognition is integral to being human, not just a tool in the service of consequences or autonomy, which is why the notions of perversion and violence apply.

Rationality is part of what constitutes human worth. Its exercise, which includes finding the truth, is therefore a perfection of human worth. As humans are social beings, the communication of discovered truth is also a perfection of human worth – it is part of communal rationality. So deliberately doing the opposite is a degradation of human nature and is morally revolting. That is so prior to and irrespective of any harms or violations of autonomy that may or may not ensue.

The inherent badness of lying, based on the human significance of rationality, will weigh heavily in the balance when the question arises whether lying may sometimes be justified by good consequences. Trivial deceits like April Fool's Day jokes and inflated advertising claims degrade the commons of trust and will not be justified. But lying may be justified sometimes, since consequences such as deaths or injuries are also based on the worth of persons.

But typically, lying is justified, when it is justified, not simply by the goodness or badness of the consequences but by the actions of the person being deceived placing himself outside the circle of those who deserve the truth. Donagan writes, "Even for a good end, it is impermissible for anybody, in conditions of free communication between responsible persons, to express an opinion he does not hold."[33] But not all communication is free and between responsible persons, and when it is not, the reasons for communicating only the truth do not apply, or apply less.

That explains the unqualified moral admiration normally felt for good deceptions. Examples include probably the largest deception ever, the massive Allied operation in 1944 to convince the Germans that the D-Day invasion would not take place in Normandy,[34] and the Sokal hoax.[35] In those cases, the people deceived well deserved to be deceived and did not deserve any respect; the deceit played an important role in their justified downfall. The case is obvious with the Nazi regime, whose own "Big Lie" was an instrument of extreme evils. In the Sokal case, the institutionalized contempt for truth that went under the name of postmodernism and threatened the existence of humanities faculties in academia deserved exposure by a hoax. Sokal made the punishment fit the crime.

EXAMPLE: "ONE'S OWN PERFECTION"

Some ethicists maintain that one cannot strictly have a duty to oneself, but a worth-of-persons perspective suggests that our own worth equals that of others and hence generates similar obligations: "Insofar as this impersonal point of view requires us to consider ourselves as merely one individual among others, we appear nonetheless obligated to treat ourselves too as an object of our moral concern."[36] Some of the wisest lay particular emphasis on one's duty of self-perfection and avoidance of abasing oneself. Even when not a strict duty, it is praiseworthy to take one's talents and "make the most of them."

In one of the best-known – and most criticized – passages of the *Nicomachean Ethics*, Aristotle asks what is the "function" of man. He concludes that it is not life (which is shared with plants) nor the "life of perception" (which is shared by animals), but what is unique to humans, the exercise of rationality. There have been many complaints that humans do not have a function, or something they are for, as if they are like tools. But Aristotle does not mean "function" in quite that way.[37] He compares man and his "function" not to a flute but to a flute player. A flute is for something, but the flute player (or human *qua* flute player) is not for something else; the playing of the flute is an exercise of a perfection or excellence of the player. There is only a point to a flute player if the flute is played well, and if it is, the playing is the point (or "function") of the exercise. In a Thomist gloss, "What is sought as good is taken to be perfective of the agent."[38] The exercise of rationality, Aristotle says, is the overall point of being human as such, and in exercising it well, one is fully human and achieves a moral perfection. One can say that one has a duty to oneself to exercise rationality to the extent of one's ability. Or equally, one can say it is a moral waste and crying shame not to.

Jesus, too, commands the development of potential in his parable of the talents, a story not closely related to everything else he says.[39] A master goes on a long journey, leaving with one servant five talents, with another two talents, with a third one talent, "according to their abilities." The first two employ their talents profitably and double their money; the third buries his talent to keep it safe. On his return the master praises the two "good and faithful servants" but casts the last "into the outer darkness, where there will be weeping and gnashing of teeth." In the parable, "talent" means a sum of money but it is traditionally interpreted as symbolic of all of God's gifts, talents in the ordinary sense. The message of the parable has been absorbed deeply in Western Christian thought and practice.[40] Margaret Thatcher, certainly a high achiever in a traditionally Western style, said:

> Remember the "Parable of the Talents" in the New Testament? Christ exhorts us to be the best we can be by developing our skills and abilities, by succeeding in all our tasks and endeavors. What better description can there be of capitalism?

> In creating new products, new services, and new jobs, we cre-
> ate a vibrant community of work. And that community of work
> serves as the basis of peace and good will among all men.[41]

Whether capitalism is the ideal system to "unleash talent" is an economic question that can be debated, but the moral ideal is a sound one.

Kant, too, defends a duty to one's own perfection, including to
develop one's natural and moral talents and to avoid self-deception.[42]
A main duty to oneself is to judge oneself in conscience.[43] The connection is obvious between Kant's views on this matter and his commitment to the absolute inner dignity of persons "above any price."

That self-development is a duty (and not just an interest or an ideal
that would be a nice enhancement) is clear from its possible conflict
with duties to others. A classic example is of an unmarried and dutiful
daughter whose development of an outstanding artistic gift would
conflict with a requirement to look after her aged parents. The conflict is a genuine moral one, and only duties can conflict with duties.[44]

The importance of *moral* self-development is illustrated by a story
told by Iris Murdoch for another purpose. A mother-in-law at first
dislikes her daughter-in-law while giving no outward hint of it. But
over time, by giving "careful and just attention" to her, she comes to
see that the daughter-in-law is "not vulgar but refreshingly simple,
not undignified but spontaneous ... and so on."[45] Murdoch's point is
that the mother-in-law has engaged in moral activity even though it
has no outward manifestation (contrary to views that morality is all
about right action). That is correct, but it is only correct because the
moral activity the mother-in-law engages in is moral self-development (in this case, through working to overcome her prejudices and
see her daughter-in-law more clearly and justly).

It would be going too far to maintain, as the Absolute Idealists
did, that self-realization is the sole point of right action.[46] But F. H.
Bradley was surely correct to say that "it is no human ideal to live 'the

life of an oyster'"[47] and von Humboldt to see an important human ideal in "the highest and most harmonious development of his powers to a complete and consistent whole."[48]

Those of us whose good fortune has afforded the opportunity to develop our talents are grateful. We are thus able to recognize the tragedy of what might have been otherwise – how grave are the impediments to human development that others have encountered. Non-natural "enemies of promise" include narrow education, child labor, the communication of low expectations, discrimination such as racism, long confinement in refugee camps, fetal alcohol syndrome. Those assaults on human potential are among the most direct and worst offenses against the worth of persons. Early extreme poverty or sexual abuse steals childhoods and stunts lives, by replacing normal development with uncontrollable anxieties.

Correlatively, if developing one's talents is a duty, deliberately failing to do so is a serious fault and a violation of duties to oneself. Suicide, to take the extreme case, is a direct assault on oneself, at least when there is no urgent reason for it such as a painful terminal illness. It involves, as Kant puts it, a blamable self-contempt.[49] At a lower level, Kant adds, one can act against one's duties to oneself by "self-stupefaction through food and drink."[50]

CONFLICT AND BALANCING OF ETHICAL REASONS

It has been argued so far that all the well-known duties and moral rules follow deductively from the worth of persons. It has not been argued that when dutics conflict, the correct resolution of the dilemma also follows deductively from the worth of persons. That is a separate and more difficult question. Even such an apparently straightforward thesis as that a commitment to life should take priority since life is a precondition for any other moral possibility is not obvious – many have found inspiration in the slogan "liberty or death," and not obviously wrongly.

Much of the vast normative ethics industry concerns casuistry, that is, how to reach decisions when reasons conflict – dilemmas of consequences versus rules, trolley problems, conflicting interests, and opposing virtues. As this is a work on the foundations of ethics rather than normative decision-making, we will not follow in those winding and difficult paths. But some account is called for of how the need for such complex balancing arises from such a simple foundation as the worth of persons. If the worth of persons is meant as a single foundation for ethics, how can there be conflicts at all? And what exactly are the diverse grounds that give rise to the moral demands that conflict with one another?

Let us consider one possible classification of the different sources of ethical obligation, at a level more complex than simply the worth of persons. Garrett Cullity suggests three such sources, intended to cover the full range of ethical obligations. The first is welfare or beneficence, giving rise to a "morality of concern." The second is a "morality of respect," arising from the demands of autonomy or rights. The third is a "morality of cooperation," how one ought to behave in shared projects, such as honoring contracts and promises.[51] Plainly there can be conflict between the moral demands from these three different directions – for example, an intervention on someone's behalf that is suggested by a morality of concern might be considered overly paternalist when autonomy is taken into account. Sound judgment is needed to discover where the balance lies and it is not the role of foundational ethical theory to supply a general recipe for resolving the conflict. "Balancing" is not just a metaphor. As with the balancing of conflicting evidence by a jury, it involves quantitative (no doubt imprecise) strengths which pull in different directions and have a resultant when all are taken into account.[52] As Kant puts it, "grounds of obligation" can clash, but then the stronger one prevails so that there can be no literal conflict of (final, tout court) obligations.[53] Or as Audi puts it, "Final duty is a contextual matter determined by the overall composition of moral forces."[54]

The differing sources arise because the basic worth of persons is, as we saw in Chapter 6, constituted by several different aspects of the human person. The "morality of concern" deals especially with harm, or threats to either survival or the more basic human goods like health. The morality of autonomy involves respect for another person as a rational actor with a life plan. The morality of cooperation concerns the necessarily social aspect of human life. Those all attend to parts of the essential complexity of what gives humans worth. But to different parts, giving rise to the potential for conflict.

For the same reasons, a worth-of-persons ethics is not clearly consequentialist, or deontological, or based on autonomy, or on natural law. Because of the way humans are – the way their worth is based on the various properties laid out earlier, consequences, rules, autonomy, and human nature are all morally important, and considerations can arise from them that potentially conflict with one another. Survival is crucial to a thing of worth, so health care ought to be given, but autonomy is important because one basis of worth is the rational will, so consent for medical treatment is important. If a patient refuses treatment which would benefit them, conflict is inevitable. So even though the worth of persons is a single foundation, its implications are pluralist when it comes to principles.

Even less should one expect deduction from worth to resolve the ever-present allocation dilemmas, of so many useful things one could do and so little time and energy; or the dilemma of Sartre's student as to whether he should join the Free French or stay and look after his aged mother. Sartre complains (not necessarily fairly to Kant):

> The Kantian ethic says, Never regard another as a means, but always as an end. Very well; if I remain with my mother, I shall

be regarding her as the end and not as a means: but by the same token I am in danger of treating as means those who are fighting on my behalf; and the converse is also true, that if I go to the aid of the combatants I shall be treating them as the end at the risk of treating my mother as a means.[55]

First principles and their logical consequences are not for that. You might as well complain that Euclid's theorems on the incommensurability of the diagonal are no use for measuring fields after the Nile flood. They do not address that problem, even though measurement should conform to geometrical principles. Computational casuistics[56] is one thing, foundation of ethics another. That is not to say there is no right and objective answer to such conflicts. There are stronger and weaker conflicting moral reasons for actions, just as there are stronger and weaker probabilistic reasons for and against scientific theories. Judgment is needed to strike the balance.

CONCLUSION

In the end, the reason why ethics, in the sense of obligation, should depend on the worth of persons is simple: If persons were worthless, what they did or what was done to them would be of no moral significance. Actions would not matter, so ethics would be contentless. Given that they are of worth, it follows that what happens to them matters, so actions affecting them are subject to moral evaluation. Worth generates obligations.

CHAPTER NINE

How Do We Know?

How could we come to know the worth of persons?

We could proceed in one of two ways. The first alternative would be to consider and adapt reasonable suggestions that have been made about ways of knowing objective moral facts in general. Possibilities include:

- A priori intuition, as of basic mathematical truths

- Moral perception

- Emotional reactions such as empathy and gut feelings on witnessing atrocities

- Moral development by understanding injustice to ourselves and applying a symmetry argument

- Love as revelatory of the dignity of others

- A transcendental argument that anything capable of understanding worth must itself be valuable

- Divine revelation that all humans are made "in the image and likeness of God"

The second alternative would be to proceed along the path outlined in previous chapters for the metaphysics of worth: explain knowledge of the "sub-moral" bases like rationality and individuality, then of the supervenience of worth on them. If we were optimistic, we might hope that pursuing both paths would lead to their meeting in the middle.

In fact, they do. A careful examination of how those various suggested modes of moral knowledge work will show that they reveal worth via supplying knowledge of one or more of the bases of worth (except possibly in the case of divine revelation, which we leave aside). Given the diversity of bases of worth, it is not surprising that there should be different modes of knowing them – that, for example, knowing rationality requires a different approach from knowing emotions or individuality.

However, that will still need explanation of how to know the supervenience of moral worth on natural properties. That will require separate treatment.

ALLEGED IMPOSSIBILITY OF MORAL EPISTEMOLOGY

Before beginning, however, we will learn something about moral epistemology by looking at arguments that it is impossible – arguments that are close to common philosophical sentiments that alleged moral facts of any kind would be somehow too "queer" and unscientific to permit knowledge of themselves. Dworkin raises the problem:

> The ordinary view holds that people do not become aware of moral facts the way they become aware of physical facts. Physical facts impinge on human minds: we perceive them, or we perceive evidence for them. Cosmologists take the observations of their huge radio telescopes to have been caused by

ancient emissions from the edges of the universe; cardiologists take the shape of electrocardiogram printouts to be caused by a beating heart. But the ordinary view insists that moral facts cannot create any impression of themselves in human minds: Moral judgment is not a matter of perception the way color judgment is. How then can we be "in touch with" moral truth?[1]

Richard Garner writes, more fully endorsing the argument:

> If moral disagreement is disagreement about properties that are really there, then we do need to say something about them and about our apprehension of them. We learned our colour words in front of observable coloured objects, and properties like yellow are integrated into a network of beliefs about the relation of colour to light, paint, perception, physiology, prisms, and photography. Intrinsic values and moral obligations don't fit into any system like this. We have no duty receptors or instruments to detect the presence of trace amounts of intrinsic value.[2]

Those are epistemological versions of Mackie's ontological "queerness" argument. To recall, what was wrong with that argument was that there is nothing queer about the bases of worth, such as rationality, nor about the notion of supervenience. Both are familiar in areas unconnected with ethics. The same considerations apply to the epistemological version. The ways we know ethically are, in principle, the ways we know in (some) non-ethical areas.

In particular, the parallel between mathematics and ethics shows how ethical knowledge is possible in principle without the need for "duty receptors." I can perceive a heap of shoes, but it needs an intellectual operation to distinguish the set of shoes in the heap from the set of pairs of shoes – if I count the shoes, I get one answer; if I count the pairs of shoes, I get a different answer. I don't have instruments to detect the presence of trace amounts of twoness; instead I count, intellectually, different sets which are present in the same physical heap of shoes.

Nor does the validity of modus ponens cause knowledge of the validity of modus ponens; it is not the sort of thing able to act physically. "It won't in general be the case that the subject-matter of what you know *a priori* ... causes you to know that thing."[3] Mathematical and logical knowledge arises from thinking about things (to speak as minimally as possible), not from the recordings of senses or instruments. So does other a priori knowledge, such as moral knowledge – if we can explain how it actually happens.

KNOWING THE BASES OF WORTH

Let us recall the list of properties argued in Chapter 6 to be the bases of worth, the properties of humans on which worth supervenes: rationality, consciousness, the unified self, the diversified self, the rational will with freedom, love and the emotions, individuality. They are natural in the sense of not being explicitly ethical. The ethical supervenes on them, rather than being identical with them. But they are not exactly scientific properties like mass, length, and charge either. The "detectors" of those properties cannot be purchased from a supplier of lab equipment but are more intimately related to how it is to be human. To understand what it is like to be another human, with a unique life history and experience, point of view and emotions, requires a kind of imaginative sympathy that can be objectively right or wrong but which contrasts with the method of the natural sciences.

Rationality and consciousness are easy. At least knowing one's own is. "I think, therefore I am rational" and "I think, therefore I am conscious" are as incontrovertible as "I think, therefore I am," and for the same reason. If you are reading this book (which you are), you are rational – if you weren't rational, you couldn't read it. Scientific activities may not directly detect rationality, but they instantiate rationality (or they would not be scientific). The scientific world picture cannot excise knowledge of rationality without sawing off the branch it is sitting on.

In principle, to know rationality and consciousness as such, it would be sufficient to know one example, oneself. But, in fact, knowledge of the rationality and consciousness of others is possible, though harder work. (Non-autistic) three-year-olds successfully develop a "theory of other minds"[4] and human communication depends on success being the norm when inferring how other humans are thinking. Our "rationality detectors" are just our comparison of the conclusions drawn by others with those drawn by our own rationality, which we intuit. Animals, highly cognitive as they are in a way, cannot do that.

The difference between scientific knowledge and the "human knowledge" of the sort that detects rationality (and the other bases of worth) is evident in the Turing test. We could be confronted by a computer system that appears to mimic rationality – and seventy years after Turing's suggestion, we often are confronted with voice recognition systems whose automated responses imitate human ones eerily well. From a third-person scientific point of view, a human and such a computer system are the same – they produce identical observable behavior. But we know that in a voice recognition system, there is "no one home"; we are experiencing only the remote trace effects of the programmer's rationality. We know to attribute rationality, the rationality that we experience in ourselves, only to other humans.

As has been widely discussed, that makes the social sciences methodologically different from the natural sciences, more hermeneutic and needing an operation of Verstehen to understand what actors are doing. Although it is possible to have purely naturalist investigations in the social sciences, for example, predicting the number of suicides next year from the number this year, there cannot be much progress in economics or anthropology without understanding why people buy things or conduct ceremonies.[5] People's exercise of their rational will is the proximate cause of the phenomena investigated in the social sciences, so leaving it out would result in sciences impoverished in the same way as behaviorist psychology.

The rational will – one's own and others' – ought to be as accessible as rationality and consciousness, and in the same way. We experience it from the inside when deliberating, and can attribute it to other minds as part of understanding what those are like. The only problematic aspect is that knowledge of the rational will appears to imply knowledge of free will, which many have thought conflicts with science. David Oderberg suggests this reasoning in support of concluding that the will is free:

> Having a reason for doing X requires reasoning about the doing of X in a way in which that reason figures; but reasoning about the doing of X amounts to reasoning about whether to do X; and reasoning about whether to do X implies the possibility of not doing X ...; but the possibility of not doing X means that one is free not to do X; so one must have free will.[6]

According to views that science implies determinism, reasoning about whether to do X does not imply the possibility of not doing X, but only the *apparent* possibility of not doing X; the reasoning does not play a causal role in the decision but only appears to.

At present, the question is not so much whether determinism is true, but whether if it were, it would undermine the knowledge of the rational will in the sense in which it is a basis of worth. It seems that it would do so only to a degree. If our sense of ourselves as deliberating and making decisions turned out to be an illusion and we were wholly the puppets of neural or Freudian forces, that would be tragic.

But the reason it would be tragic, in a Sisyphean way, as opposed to not worth worrying about, is that the observed structure of rational deliberation and action partly makes us human, not just the (hopefully free) effects of that via action. We know immediately the structure of rational deliberation, the essence of that basis of worth, and would continue to do so even if it proved to be controlled by outside forces.

We could continue in similar vein by looking at the knowledge of our own emotional structure, love, unity, diversity, and individuality. But we may learn more with a change of pace, considering next existing investigations on ways of knowing some of the bases of worth of (mostly) others.

JUSTICE, SYMPATHY, AND SYMMETRY

We could become aware of our own worth, perhaps initially by being loved and then aided by challenges to it such as injustice toward ourselves. We could then apply a symmetry argument to conclude that other people have the same worth, since there is no relevant difference between them and us. As the book of Exodus commands, "You shall not wrong a sojourner or oppress him, for you were sojourners in the land of Egypt."[7] Or we could have a natural direct sympathy with others that convinced us of their worth as a precondition of our sympathy having meaning.

Studies of child moral development suggest that both of these routes to moral knowledge are taken by normal children. But it is also possible that both can fail.

The first way was emphasized by Piaget's classic work on the sense of justice in children aged about five to seven years. (As Dickens says, "In the little world in which children have their existence ... there is nothing so finely perceived and so finely felt, as injustice."[8]) Children (at least those living in an appropriately supportive culture) are able to develop concepts of fairness, by recognizing that other minds are not relevantly morally different to their own, when it comes to getting what they deserve.[9] Piaget describes how very young children believe that what is right is simply what is forbidden by adult authority. But at a later stage they develop a sense of fairness based on a sense of equality – initially a rather simplistic one:

> Some children are playing ball in a courtyard. When the ball goes out of bounds and rolls down the road one of the boys goes of his own free will to fetch it several times. After that he is the only one they ask to go and fetch it. What do you think of that?
>
> Wal (6) 'It isn't fair. – Why? – Because another boy should go.'
>
> Schma (7) 'It's not fair, because they should have asked the others, and each in turn.'

But the simple "same for each" standard of equality soon comes to have added to it a capacity to take into account differences in the individuals, which may require differences in how they are treated in order to make the treatment fair.

> Two boys were running races. One was big, the other small. Should they both have started from the same place, or should the little one have started nearer?
>
> Bri (6) 'The little boy must have a start because the big boy can run faster than the little one.'

The adaptation to differing circumstances is not a qualification of the principle of equality, but an implication of it – "purely equalitarian justice is tempered by considerations of equity."[10] But both the initial pure equality stance and its adaptation involve a recognition of symmetry of worth, of respect due.

But there is a prior problem. To apply a symmetry argument, and conclude that other people have worth and deserve respect because oneself does, one must first know one's own worth to be positive. That does not just happen automatically, and it can fail to happen. It happens naturally, but not infallibly. One can learn that injustice to oneself is only what is to be expected. We will consider the possibility of self-hate in a later section.

Later research on the moral development of infants has tended to show that what Piaget was looking at was already a considerably developed stage, and there are more basic underpinnings of ethical concern visible at ages as far back as one or two. Those earlier stages do not involve just acceptance of parental rules, as Piaget thought, but a clear feeling of natural sympathy for others.[11] Infant development is relevant not just for the sake of empirical evidence, but because it demonstrates possibility – if infants can learn something (whether about ethics or anything else) from a standing start, knowledge of it must be possible with the resources of infants. Alison Gopnik summarizes the findings:

> Piaget thought that children didn't have genuine moral knowledge because he thought that they couldn't take the perspective of others, infer intentions, and follow abstract rules.
>
> Modern science shows that just isn't true. Literally from the time they're born children are empathic. They identify with other people and recognize that their own feelings are shared by others. In fact, they literally take on the feelings of others. One-year-olds understand the difference between intentional and unintentional actions, and behave in genuinely altruistic ways. Three-year-olds have already developed a basic ethic of care and compassion.[12]

Humans are rational animals, and that goes for human infants, too.

EMOTIONS AND EMPATHY

The babies are right. Empathy is at the bottom of ethics, and it is a form of ethical knowledge.

Many ethical writers, for example in the tradition of Brentano and Scheler, have urged that ethics based on pure reason is missing something and that emotions are essential to supplement it, arguing that emotions are a correct response to value.[13] But being a correct response to known value is not the same as being a mode of knowledge of value in the first place. The question is how in the present realist theory of worth, empathy, understood as attunement to the emotions of others, can be a form or source of knowledge.

The reason empathy can be a form of *knowledge* is that the emotional structure of persons is part of the bases of worth, as argued in Chapter 6. Empathy is an awareness of – by sharing in – some aspect of that emotional structure of another person. It is by "catching" some degree of someone else's feeling that we know it. To this kind of knowledge especially applies Aristotle's gnomic saying about knowledge, "The soul is in a way all things."[14] In empathy, our soul is (to a degree) in the very same state as that of the person who is its object. Thus via emotional attunement we come to know one of the bases of someone else's worth, and so have moral knowledge (unless, as we will discuss later, some defect such as psychopathy prevents us knowing the supervenience of worth on its base).

Our immediate emotional reaction to the famous pictures of the survivors of the Holocaust death camps is, therefore, a direct perception that what happened to those people was a terrible evil. Someone who does not have an immediate reaction of horror to photographs of the death camps lacks a necessary insight into the worth of persons. In another example, Raimond Gaita asks us to imagine a tutorial in which one of its members had been a victim of a terrible evil of which all the other members were aware. What if the tutor asked the class to consider whether our sense of the terribleness of evil were not an illusion? "Everyone would be outraged if their tutor were not serious and struck by unbelieving horror if he was."[15] The tutor's suggestion of moral skepticism, Gaita suggests, is not only an obvious falsehood, but an evil act against the victim of evil. The class's insight involves both a symmetry, in putting themselves in the place of the victim, and an emotional understanding (up to a point, as far as imagination permits) of what it would be like to undergo the experience. The worth of the victim becomes evident in understanding their suffering, which makes plain how their worth stands as a moral limit to what may be done to them.

It would not be helpful to try to recast that reaction as a deliverance of "reason," if reason is a term designed to contrast with "emotion." Gaita rightly complains of "a distinction between reason and emotion that distorts our understanding of one of the most important facts about the ethical – that we often learn by being moved by what others say or do."[16] Our ability to acquire moral knowledge by immediate emotional empathy with other humans is why serious novels can deepen our moral understanding – for example, when Pasternak in *Doctor Zhivago* has the fully developed character of Lara disappear into the Gulag, it is the empathy the reader has developed with the character that points up the moral horror of a political system that treats people as anonymous vermin. A fundamental demand of humans to be recognized as human by others is one of the "needs of the soul," in Simone Weil's words[17]; it is prior (in knowledge) to any speculations about what features of human nature may generate it, or any identification of rights. And without at least some of that initial emotional attunement to the irreducible worth of humans, there can be no meaning to discussions of human nature or rights.

Other emotions with a prospect of delivering moral insights include grief, admiration for someone who acts better than one could hope to do oneself, awe, joy, gratitude, guilt and remorse, and the emotion called in the Old Testament "fear of the Lord" (which is said to be the "beginning of wisdom"[18]). Indignation is a possibility, but as evident on social media, as likely to deliver moral vanity as moral insight.

LOVE

Again, it is a familiar idea that love is some use in being ethical – in philosophy, the idea is most associated with Iris Murdoch – but in the present theory, what use is it, and how can it be a form of or cause of ethical *knowledge*? If love is to be a source of knowledge, it must be explained how it is not only a sound response to recognized worth, but prior to that somehow a means of knowing that worth.

Let us recall, from Chapter 4, Raimond Gaita's story of working in a psychiatric ward with very severely mentally ill patients, ones with few human reactions or human lives as normally understood. He admired those psychiatrists who nevertheless treated them as human beings with dignity. Then:

> One day a nun came into the ward.... everything in her demeanour towards them – the way she spoke to them, her facial expressions, the inflexions of her body – contrasted and showed up the behaviour of those noble psychiatrists. She showed that they were, despite their best efforts, condescending, as I too had been. She thereby revealed that such patients were, as the psychiatrists and I had sincerely and generously professed, the equals of those who wanted to help them; but she also revealed that in our hearts we did not believe this.... her behaviour was striking not for the virtues it expressed, or even for the good it achieved, but for its power to reveal the full humanity of those whose affliction had made their

humanity invisible. Love is the name we give to such behaviour.[19]

Maternal love for a new baby is also a paradigm of "revealing the full humanity" of an entity that is exhibiting only a narrow range of human behavior.

Love is not just an emotion but an action (so it makes sense to command it, as Jesus says). Before any physical action on behalf of its object, it requires a mental action, attention. The role of attention is familiar in perceptual knowledge, too, in the contrast between listening and hearing, or looking and seeing (as in the proverb "None so blind as those who will not see"). The activity of attention (looking or listening attention, or loving attention, as the case may be) directs the mind toward some reality that can be known.

So what does love attend to, and respond to? It would be pointless or delusional without value to respond to (even God's gratuitous love, which is directed to species that are worth loving). It is on the lookout for anything good in the object of love, so is keen to recognize any of the bases of worth (and in the case of Gaita's nun, to grieve at their loss of expression). Love delights in any perfection of the beloved, any progress toward being more fully human, any toddler's first steps or first words.

Iris Murdoch speaks of love as a form of perception, but emphasizes that it is an active or attending rather than a passive form, and needs further (internal) action to keep honest: "Great art teaches us how real things can be looked at and loved without being seized and used, without being appropriated into the greedy organism of the self. This exercise of *detachment* is difficult and valuable whether the thing contemplated is a human being or the root of a tree."[20] The attention that embodies love, she says, is strictly objective and fairminded: In cases of difficult decisions about people, such as whether a married couple should stay together for the sake of the children,

"The love which brings the right answer is an exercise of justice and realism and really *looking*."[21]

David Velleman, too, says, "Love is rather an appreciative response to the perception of that value. And I mean 'perception' literally: the people we love are the ones whom we succeed in perceiving as persons, within some of the human organisms milling about us."[22] It is true that a basic recognition of others as persons may engender an attitude that is correct but much less than love, namely respect. But that is on the way. "I regard respect and love as the required minimum and optional maximum responses to one and the same value.... Love, like respect, is the heart's response to the realization that it is not alone."[23] Where respect recognizes the rational and the rational will, love recognizes a more complete humanity.

There is one potential problem for regarding love as a source of knowledge. Surely love is of an individual person while recognition of value is of repeatable properties? If love were a response to some value-giving property of a person, would we not love all twins or clones of someone we came to love, or feel obliged to love those with qualities resembling those we do love? But it will be remembered that one of the bases of worth, as argued in Chapter 6, was individuality itself. That is one of the things – perhaps the principal thing – that love responds to. Dietrich von Hildebrand writes:

> The idea of participating in some value-in-general makes no sense here. The beauty of the individual person as a whole, or, as we could say, of the unique unrepeatable idea of God embodied in this person, is after all no general value type, but already as a quality it is something entirely individual and unique.[24]

"Love is not love which alters when it alteration finds"[25] because its object is an individual, not the qualities of an individual.

Self-love is as much a perception of reality as love of others is. The command to "love your neighbor as yourself" presumes you do love yourself, which is the normal case but is not a given. It must come from somewhere. "We can love ourselves only if we have first been loved by someone else.... If an individual is to accept himself, someone must say to him: 'It is good that you exist' – must say it, not with words, but with that act of the entire being that we call love."[26] Being loved at the beginning of life is necessary for recognizing one's own worth, as studied in John Bowlby's *Attachment* and subsequent work.[27] That was particularly evident in the study of the large number of Romanian orphans consigned by the Ceaușescu regime to orphanages that provided only basic food with no love or personal attention. Assigned randomly after the fall of the regime to foster carers or further orphanage life, those given proper human care slowly improved, though not to the level of normal children with parents.[28]

Even independent adults with normally robust self-esteem can appreciate and benefit from a reminder of their self-worth by way of one-off loving behaviors, such as gratuitous thanks or pleasantness from a receptionist "above and beyond the call of duty." To have one's self-worth mirrored is a reminder of a truth which, under stress, can be doubted.

Like any form of knowledge, love can make mistakes. But it can also, as Brentano says, have self-evidence of the sort found in mathematical or logical judgments. It is self-evident that the love of persons is justified but the love of money as such is not.[29] Everyone can see what is ridiculous in Donald Duck's Uncle Scrooge experiencing the height of pleasure in splashing around in his Money Bin.

It is true that one can rightly be said to love objects that are not persons or any kind of substances – to love knowledge, justice, art, the tradition of one's community, universal law, a good will, or some other perfection. Those are, however, possible objects of love only because of their intimate connection with the bases of the worth of persons – knowledge, for example, because of its being an exercise and perfection of rationality. A love of freedom, for example, is a commitment to the importance of the rational will. That is even so with something as apparently impersonal as universal law in the Kantian sense: "Reverence for the law, which has struck so many as making Kantian ethics impersonal, is in fact an attitude toward the person, since the law that commands respect is the ideal of a rational will, which lies at the heart of personhood."[30] Love of those objects, like love of persons, involves an honest attentiveness to them and so is a partial cause of knowledge of them.

UNITY, DIVERSITY, AND INDIVIDUALITY OF THE SELF: THE NOVEL AS KNOWLEDGE

The more complex bases of the worth of persons, as argued in Chapter 6, include the unity in diversity of the self; the diversity and complexity of the self, despite its unity; and the individuality of persons, with their unique histories and life plans. Being complex, they need a complex way of knowing that reveals the full roundedness of persons. That is what serious novels are for; though, of course, reading novels just extends what the reader knows from attending to persons in real life. The best novels provide a moral education (to those rightly disposed by their charitably curious attitude to real life). And that does not just mean instruction in right and wrong. It means a broadening of understanding of the human bases of right and wrong.

That is perfectly exemplified in the perfect novel, *Pride and Prejudice*. It acts as a moral education for the reader, by portraying the moral education (mostly self-education) of the main characters, Elizabeth and Darcy. It is told from the point of view of Elizabeth, who is a virtuous, intelligent, and fully realized character – as we first meet her, "a lively, playful disposition, which delighted in anything ridiculous"[31] – but, as it turns out, with certain blind spots related to pride (in her own judgment) and prejudice (against the apparently arrogant Mr. Darcy). Her sense of self-unity is strong, but she has a capacious and diverse mind with interests in all the doings and characters of the people around her. In the pivotal chapter of the novel, after rejecting Darcy's rather inept proposal with a torrent of accusations against him, she receives his letter explaining himself. A careful reading makes it clear that he is in the right and she must rethink her view of herself and her hasty judgments about him.

"How despicably I have acted!" she cried; "I, who have prided myself on my discernment! I, who have valued myself on my abilities! ... Till this moment I never knew myself."[32] What she comes to know are the unique features of her individuality, such as how her prejudice contrasts with the "generous candour" of her also virtuous but less lively and demonstrative sister. In following these developments, the reader gains an education in the moral possibilities of variety of character and their development by interaction with one another.

Jane Austen has the genius to portray vice as revolting (as with Lydia and Wickham). She distinguishes vice from culpable cognitive limitations, or foolishness, which she subjects to ridicule (as with Mrs. Bennet, Mr. Collins, Lady Catherine, and Mary). Vice is a defect of the rational will, but foolishness is a defect more of rationality – a culpable one in virtue of not having developed one's wisdom. Those minor characters are not drawn as whole people but are more ciphers for defects, in the sense that we hear little of them except for their defects (and their actions that advance the plot). A novel could be written from the point of view of any one of them, but might be less interesting. The strictly partial views of them provided in the novel point up by contrast the virtues of the main characters, who, as literary critics put it, "matter" and whom "we care about" – the "we" positing an omniscient (morally) objective observer.[33]

A literary approach is not the only possible one to knowledge of the unity, diversity, and individuality of persons. As we saw in Chapter 6, psychology and psychiatry have something valuable to say about the structure of personality. But for knowledge of the individuality of persons, especially, the novel's focus on particularity is essential, and can only be matched by real-life experience (for those with good skills in understanding other people's minds) and perhaps autobiographies (at least, the honest ones).

KNOWING THE SUPERVENIENCE OF WORTH
ON NATURAL PROPERTIES

While such methods, adapted in their various ways to the different bases of worth, show good promise of some kind of direct knowledge of the worth of persons via knowledge of the bases of worth, they are not very helpful with explaining the supervenience of moral worth on natural human properties.

Normally, no further step is needed. Once we know rationality, emotions, the uniqueness of (actual, individual) persons, it "goes without saying" that we have understood their worth. Given the intimacy of the supervenience relation, something would be wrong if the step was not made.[34] Still, in principle it might not be. It is possible that in one form of psychopathy, the connection might not be made – that someone could understand perfectly well other people's rationality, hopes, and decisions, and take that as an opportunity to manipulate them through not attributing any moral worth to them. If psychopaths, in fact, "fail to pass through a crucial moral developmental stage in early childhood" and thus are "incapable of forming genuine moral concepts and so lack the essential prerequisites of moral life," as some research holds,[35] then they can be taken to have a defect in knowing the supervenience of worth, the genuinely moral, on the bases such as rationality, which they (unlike the seriously autistic) do understand. That is not the only possible view of the still poorly understood moral deficits of psychopathy – which can include cognitive deficits concerning others' emotions, as well as possibly a deliberately chosen path of viciousness. But it is sufficient to show how some gap could in principle open between knowledge of the bases such as rationality and knowledge of the worth that supervenes on them.

The literature on supervenience, for all its strength on the metaphysical side, is thin on epistemology. How can relations of supervenience be known? Let us return to the simplest examples, especially the one that was argued to be the closest parallel of the ethical case, the supervenience of the rationality of belief on logical relations. How, exactly, do we know that if our evidence implies a proposition, it is reasonable – we logically ought – to believe it? Logical relations are one thing, our beliefs another: How do we know the connection? It is certainly possible, indeed only too common, to have a kind of "logical psychopathy" that believes things on the basis of blind faith or wishful thinking or righteous indignation instead of logical relations. It is not just the Red Queen who has believed as many as six impossible things before breakfast.[36] So there is something nontrivial to be known.

How then do we know that, if I know p and know that p implies q, then I ought to, or would be well advised to, believe q? (In general, how do we know that logical relations are normative for belief?) It is not a matter of observation, and any further reasoning for it would be circular.[37] We are reduced to invoking "intuition" or understanding.

The understanding is a very direct mode of knowing. It is most familiar in mathematics and logic, where its direct deliverances (such as understanding why $2 + 3 = 3 + 2$, or why "the set of points equidistant from one point" defines a circle, or why affirming the consequent is invalid) form the basic truths of those disciplines.[38] That is true in philosophy, too, where, it is said, understanding the point of the Euthyphro dilemma is a reliable sign of basic philosophical ability. Speculations on the origin of that faculty, whether via a Darwinian fairytale or invocation of divine illumination or some other hypothesis, are beside the point even if true.

Similarly we can only refer to the understanding for our knowledge of other cases of supervenience. The singleton set {x} is not the same thing as x, but supervenes on x. Once we understand what sets are, we know that; there is nothing further that can be added. And again with the supervenience of worth on bases such as rationality, consciousness, unity, and individuality. Once we understand those properties – which we do by having or being them – we understand why they raise us "above the beasts of the field," not to mention stones; that is, why the destruction of something with those qualities is a tragic loss, absolutely speaking. That is, we understand the supervenience of worth on those properties.

It is still possible to wonder if one could, whether rationally or not, recognize one's own consciousness, rationality, rational will, unity, and individuality, and still fail to take the extra step of concluding to one's own worth. That brings us to the question of self-respect, made so much of by Kant. To fail to deduce one's worth from normal recognition of one's human properties would be exactly to lack self-respect. Since lack of self-respect is sometimes observed, some inquiry is needed into its rationality and causes.

Kant says that lack of self-respect, a failure to think or act as if one does have worth, leads to servility. He has in mind regarding oneself as a slave to one's passions, a mere thing, as much as servility in the more usual sense of abasing oneself as a tool of supposedly superior persons.[39] He says also that one has a *duty* of self-respect, implying that a failure is not merely a cognitive but a moral defect, either deliberate (as in the case of flattery) or by self-deception.[40]

But here we are concerned more with the cognitive than the moral aspects of self-respect. Commentators have criticized Kant for failing to take note of non-culpable failures of self-respect caused by the deception of others, such as being continually told one is scum.[41]

That is a familiar phenomenon in families and groups and between classes and races, where a claim of superiority on the part of one is internalized by the person(s) told they are inferior.

Within such cases it is desirable to distinguish between beliefs of relative and of absolute inferiority. If a humble villager prays, "God bless the squire and his relations, and keep us in our proper stations," but deals on a basis of equality with the fellow villagers he sees every day, his assumption of relative inferiority to the distant gentry may not have a serious effect on his self-respect. It is still epistemologically unsound because it is based on no morally relevant differences. However, it is much more serious when someone becomes really convinced of his or her own absolute worthlessness. The possibility of self-hate is a disturbing one, but sometimes realized. The outsider, who can see no morally relevant difference between himself and the self-hater, normally seeks some psychiatric cause for the self-hate, such as trauma in early childhood. The causation of later self-harm by childhood trauma and early disturbances of attachment is among the best-known and most solidly established facts of modern psychiatry.[42] As usual in epistemology, believing the truth is what is expected by default, even though belief has causes. It is when the normal ways of knowing go wrong that extra causes are invoked to explain the error.

"I am worthless" can be believed, but only in error.

So it is certainly possible to recognize one's own consciousness, rationality, rational will, unity, and individuality, and still fail to take the extra step of concluding to one's worth; that is, to fail to recognize the supervenience of worth on the base properties. But it cannot be done rationally. If one does that, some cause of the error, such as trauma, is to be invoked. The supervenience of worth on rationality, consciousness, and its other bases is, like any supervenience, obvious to a well-disposed mind that understands the question.

A TRANSCENDENTAL ARGUMENT TO WORTH?

A certain kind of transcendental argument has become familiar in ethical theory, to the effect that agency requires some perception of oneself as having value. Eating cake has no point for the cake, or in itself as an event in the abstract, but only as a benefit for the agent eating it. So a presupposition of such an action is that the agent thinks the benefit to itself is worthwhile or has some point. To do so, the agent must attribute some value to itself, in order for acts for its benefit to have point.[43]

Such a line of argument is unlikely to reach convincingly any conclusion that there is genuine ethical worth of the kind defended here. If agents do see themselves as having value, the most elegant and minimal hypothesis to explain that would be that evolution has implanted in them a rosy glow of self-esteem to keep them motivated to survive until reproduction. It would be as if the gods had mercifully granted Sisyphus the illusion that stone rolling was a good in itself. But those perceptions contain no self-justification.

The argument is nevertheless suggestive in showing that an assumption of the worth of persons is not easy to eliminate from ethics. It confirms the reasoning of Chapter 1, that to speak morally about actions cashes out in notions of worth and makes no sense without it.

To make progress toward genuine knowledge of worth, we would need an argument to cross the gap from perception or ascription of value to actual value; an argument that "I value, therefore I am valuable."

An argument of that sort seems to have some initial prospect of success. The activity of valuing is possible only for a certain sort of entity. Inquiring into what sort of entity can understand the notion of valuing could in principle reveal that that entity must itself have (intrinsic) value. By way of comparison, the argument "I attribute consciousness to other humans, therefore I am conscious" appears to be sound, since only a conscious being could understand what it is to attribute consciousness to another being.

Intuitively, being able to attribute worth does seem to require in the attributer a breadth of moral understanding that is itself sufficient to underpin worth. Human beings have characteristic emotions of awe and wonder, senses of moral worth and aesthetic profundity, recognition of others as centers of ethical standing. They have a sense of meaning and purpose, and an intuition that there is something larger than themselves. No matter how much findings about the world "out there" (say the discovery that it was just atoms and void) were to undercut those intuitions, surely those abilities themselves constitute the person as a remarkable – morally remarkable – entity, whose own worth cannot be denied?

However, it is possible to be more precise with the argument, by looking at the knowledge of the various bases of worth and what they presuppose. As just observed, to attribute consciousness to anything, it is necessary to be conscious oneself (to even understand what it means to attribute consciousness). If it is accepted, as argued before, that consciousness is one of the bases on which worth supervenes, then an entity's ability to attribute consciousness (to another or even oneself) must presuppose consciousness in the entity and hence (in principle, even if not explicitly) the worth that supervenes on it.

It is the same with all the other bases of worth argued for in Chapter 6. Being able to attribute them to any entity – which from common experience we can – implies possessing them ourselves, and hence possessing the worth that supervenes on them. Barring any cognitive defect standing in the way of recognizing the supervenience, knowledge of human worth should arise naturally from the attributions of the bases of worth.

Take, for example, the rational will. To attribute a rational will to another person (or by mistake, to a robot), seeing them as a unified center of free decisions made for reasons, it is necessary to be such a center oneself. One would have no idea what it is to attribute free agency (even apparently free agency), unless one had one's own experience of it. So attributing free agency, which we do continually in dealing with people, implies our possession of free agency, and hence of the worth that so intimately supervenes on it. Similarly with the unity and diversity of consciousness, the emotional structure of humans, and individuality. To understand what it is to attribute those, one must have them, and to a considerable degree. Otherwise the attribution is a mere form of words.

(It is not quite so obvious with love. Could one attribute love to others while lacking it completely oneself? It may be theoretically possible but it is not so easy. C. S. Lewis imagines the devils' research department applying ever bigger grants to devise ever more complex hypotheses to find out what humans' love is really for. "Success is hourly expected."[44] They cannot recognize love because they have none. The normal case, at least, is that one understands love by having it, as with the other basic human properties.)

Plainly those attributions of the bases of human worth are very different from the attribution of length and electrical charge, or other physical properties. Those are measured in physical things by well-understood scientific procedures. To measure the charge of an electron, there is no need to know what it is like to be an electron.

We may conclude then that a transcendental argument to human worth is successful: We know the bases of worth in virtue of possessing them, and barring any cognitive defect, we can conclude to the worth that supervenes on them.

WHY SO MUCH ERROR IN ETHICS?

Ethical epistemology will not be complete without some theory of error in ethics. If the worth of persons is so obvious, and is the foundation of ethics, why is there so much disagreement in ethics? Should ethics not be like that other abstract discipline, mathematics, where agreement is legendary? How could societies have accepted something so obviously and directly contrary to the worth of persons as slavery?

That does need some explanations or, it might be more honest to say, excuses.

It has been commonly argued that widespread moral disagreement (between individuals or tribes) is itself a reason to believe there is no fact of the matter as to whether ethical statements are true; that argument was orthodoxy in anthropology for much of the twentieth century.[45] That is not in itself convincing because disagreement is typical in philosophical questions, without anyone taking that as a reason to believe there are no right answers. Either the mind is identical to the brain or it isn't, but disagreement on that question is endemic and ongoing. It is easy to have a "theory of error" to explain why there is so much disagreement about the philosophy of mind: The question is hard (or perhaps, human cognition is not well adapted to the question so it is hard for humans).

In looking for a theory of error for ethical propositions, it is useful to divide the problem in two different ways. First, there is disagreement about particular moral issues versus disagreement about foundations. Second, there are intellectual versus moral reasons for making mistakes.

Given the complexity of human social life, it is hardly surprising that there would be many reasonable disagreements about the rightness of particular courses of action, even if there were agreement on the foundations (say, if it was agreed that the worth of persons was the correct foundation). Dilemmas are genuine, arising from how the worth of persons plays out through different aspects of the human person (for example, paternalism versus autonomy, both based in respect for the person dealt with but in virtue of different aspects). The rightness of some actions really is relative to tribal custom, since the social meaning of the action could be rude in one tradition but normal in another. Consequences can be hard to calculate – even strict utilitarians, who in principle converted ethical decisions into mathematics, failed to achieve certainty in their recommendations; indeed, everyone complains that one of the difficulties of utilitarianism is its uncertainty in calculating the net effects of actions. Education or indoctrination is important in creating errors, since it is part of human nature to assume that "the way we do things around here" is the natural way to do it. With a lot to take into account and with bounded time and rationality, people just make mistakes, as they do playing lightning chess.

Those are examples of intellectual obstacles to reaching agreement on particular ethical decisions, but there is no shortage of moral and emotional pressures as well. Self-deceit, rationalization, and choosing the most favorable or nearest moral and legal advice are phenomena too familiar to need describing. So is a natural emotional commitment to those close at hand, which can lead to favoring their interests excessively. Those causes of error are found in mathematics, too – if rarely in pure mathematics, frequently in accountancy, where instances of "creative accounting" continually appear in the courts and professional bodies keep trying to raise standards to suppress them.

Those obstacles to reaching the truth are easy to understand (if not easy to avoid). They are not reasons for thinking there is no fact of the matter to reach.

That leaves to be explained how it is possible to go wrong with something as simple and straightforward as the worth of persons, and even with the less basic but still simple enough equality of the worth of persons. According to what has been said above, the worth of persons supervenes, and obviously supervenes, on properties that every normally functioning human knows that they and other humans possess, such as rationality, emotional structure, and individuality. If people did not assume other people had those properties, they would not be able to hold conversations with them. So how is it possible to end up thinking that an obvious gross violation of the worth of persons, such as slavery, is morally acceptable?

Again, it is useful to divide the causes of error into intellectual (including social) and moral ones. The moral ones are obvious. Plainly anyone (or any class, race, or caste) benefiting from slavery, bullying, fraud, or any other practice that violates the worth of persons has a powerful motive for rationalizing those practices, so it will not be surprising to find "justifications" generated; or more likely, assumptions not questioned. The remaining question is whether there are some not specifically moral, "natural" tendencies in human thinking that might obscure the worth of persons and suggest that I or "we" are superior to "them," so that "their" interests can be disregarded.

The obvious suggestion is that the evolved mental habits needed to socially bond with one's tribe have an almost inevitable tendency to define tribal membership by contrast with other tribes' non-membership. If we are "we," then others are "they" and are "constructed as other." Although it is not inevitable that "they" should be considered lesser or alien beings, there is always the danger that our positive view of "us" results in a negative view of "them," especially if we have not met them because they live over the hill, or if they behave, look, or dress differently.

That kind of theory is not purely speculative, because it is observed in infant moral development. Three-year-olds assort people into "us" and "them" groups based on many characteristics – language, gender, hair color, color of T-shirt – and find their own group preferable. Family loyalty especially is strong. That occurs simultaneously with the development of empathy, which can in principle extend to anyone.[46]

So there is something natural about both universal human sympathy and discriminating between humans based on group membership. Social pressure can reinforce one or the other tendency. It needs effort to increase the circle of concern to all people, while balancing that with family, group, and role responsibilities. Given the subtleties, it is surely not surprising that errors concerning the equality of persons have been common. When it comes to an inexcusable error like approving slavery or not caring about cruelty to the animals we eat, we should be shocked, but not surprised.

EPILOGUE

What Kind of Universe?

❖

T HE ACCOUNT OF ethical foundations given here is a metaphysics-
heavy one. The worth of persons, and the bases for it such as rationality and individuality, were argued to be metaphysically weightier
than ordinary scientific properties. As a result, there is an elephant in
the room. What sort of universe is compatible with such a rich metaphysics? Without at least a sketch of an answer to that question, a
theory of the foundations of ethics will "hang in the air." It will seem
to require unexamined assumptions offstage, and to be undermined
if those assumptions are false. Similarly, if one were writing on philosophy of mind and defended Cartesian dualism, it would be necessary to call attention to its incompatibility with some theories of the
universe, such as atheist materialism.

It is a very large task to examine theories of the universe and the
place of ethical foundations in them. That cannot be attempted here
but only promised for the future. But it is possible to sketch what the
question is, so as to lay out what has to be attempted.

Prima facie, the realist theory of the worth of persons sketched
here is not compatible with the two clearest and most extreme cosmological theories – strictly materialist atheism and personal theism
with a divine command theory of ethics. A strict materialism, as
opposed to a softer "naturalism" of some sort, regards humans as the
same sort of entities as lifeless galaxies, just collocations of atoms. If
that were so, Mackie would be right. There is no conceptual space for

such a scientifically "queer" property as intrinsic worth to settle on, arise from, or be reducible to physical properties. In such a universe, the death of a human is as little a tragedy as the explosion of a lifeless galaxy, because the sort of entities that cease to be are the same in each case.

At the other extreme is personal theism with a divine command theory of ethics that includes, as is traditional, the "discretion thesis" or "theological voluntarism": that God can command anything to be right or wrong.[1] That is also incompatible with a realist ethics based on the worth of persons, according to which murder must be wrong because it is the deliberate destruction of a being of worth. God or anyone else cannot make it otherwise by commanding anything. Command has no purchase on what is necessarily true.

It is not easy to determine the compatibility of a realist theory of the worth of persons with the rest of the spectrum of cosmological views, from a softer naturalism through pantheism to a personal theism constrained by moral truths. For one thing, that spectrum has not been laid out with any clarity, and those particular views within it that have been developed clearly have often not attended centrally to their position on the foundations of ethics.

Pantheisms, for example, which at first glance look hospitable to some kind of naturally occurring and metaphysically robust absolute worth,[2] in practice have not been very successful at supporting the irreducible worth of humans. A wide range of views like the Stoic philosophy of Nature, Plotinus's Neoplatonism, Spinoza's pantheism, the Absolute Idealism beloved of the late Victorians, some forms of contemporary deep ecology, and the Confucian concept of the Mandate of Heaven see the universe as having semidivine properties and a degree of genuine moral quality. In recent times, views of the same general type have been revived in books such as Thomas Nagel's *Mind and Cosmos*, Ronald Dworkin's *Religion Without God*, and Antony Flew's *There Is a God*, which deny personal theism but argue that mental, ethical, and aesthetic features of the universe point to some non-materialist view of the universe as a whole. However, their position really is *pan*theism – it is the whole that has value, and that can be at the expense of the (human) parts. That is most evident in the more extreme forms of deep ecology that regard humans as a pest whose extinction would be a net gain for the ecosystem, but the tendency is inherent in the pantheist focus on the cosmos, not on the worth inherent to persons.[3] If we are "all part of some greater whole," we may not matter much in the big picture, either as a species or, even more, individually.

Two positions on the spectrum of cosmological views appear to have a better prospect of compatibility with an absolute worth of persons.

The first is the not very clearly recognized position, between atheist materialism and pantheism, that could be called "emergentism"[4] (after its subthesis of the same name, which is well known in the philosophy of mind). According to that thesis, materialist atheism used to be true and still is true of most of the universe. But in one small corner of one galaxy, a series of unlikely but chance events took place, and it was revealed that the properties of matter contained the potentiality to produce entities of a semidivine though limited nature – human consciousnesses with powers of reason and with objective moral worth, capable of understanding such concepts as worth, reason, and divinity. They are entities of an entirely different kind from those admitted by materialist atheism. They "emerged" in the same sense as biological properties emerged from physical ones or social properties arose from mental ones. The emergence is necessary in the sense that the potentialities are inherent and the higher properties must arise if the conditions for them happen to come into being. The emergence is recapitulated in every human birth, when an embryo grows according to biological laws and a new individual consciousness and rational will reliably emerge from it unless some biological cause prevents it.

The second cosmological view that seems likely to be compatible with the natural worth of persons is a constrained personal theism. It chooses the horn of the Euthyphro dilemma according to which God approves of something because it is good rather than it being good because God approves of it. If right and wrong arise necessarily from the worth of persons, God cannot intervene in that necessary connection, any more than he can make 7 + 5 add up to anything other than 12.

That threatens to make the God hypothesis a spare wheel in ethical theory. If the foundations of ethics and the deductions from them are set in (logical) stone, what role could God have? That is contrary to the view of the Abrahamic religions that God and ethics are somehow closely connected.

God, in that theory, does have some possible roles in ethics, but they are not foundational. One is epistemological: God could reveal (and according to Judaic tradition has revealed) that humans are "made in the image of God" and thus of transcendent worth. That is not an idea that occurred to Greek and other ethical traditions. The moral worlds of the *Iliad* or *Njáls Saga* are not ones where "we" agree on the equality of persons or the wrongness of lying or the desirability of world peace. Since the assumptions of modern Western ethical theory about the equality of persons and human rights descend from the Judeo-Christian tradition's views on that point, that revelation or alleged revelation has proved to have point. Some have thought also that revealed divine rewards and punishments might help everyone behave better.

Another role for God in ethics is to confer being on humans and their environment (perhaps even being obliged to create the best of all possible environments, as Leibniz thought).[5] Though the worth of persons is necessary, if there are persons, the existence of any is not. If there is anything to the cosmological argument for God's existence, God is needed to create contingent beings. Another role is to be, in some sense, the source of good. Perhaps it is not only humans who are in God's image, but, as pseudo-Dionysius thought (described in Chapter 7), all worldly goodness is an overflowing of and partial reflection of the divine goodness. A similar theory has been held by some recent Christian ethical philosophers, who advance a divine command theory without the discretion thesis: They argue that God commands the good necessarily, in accordance with his own essentially good nature (so that right and wrong arise from the divine nature but not the divine will).[6] They are more divine resemblance theorists than divine command ones.

These considerations, it is evident, take us far from ethical theory itself. That is why a separate study is needed on the interaction of ethics and cosmology.

SELECT BIBLIOGRAPHY

This is not in any sense a complete bibliography of foundations of ethics or of works referred to. It lists just those books and articles that have proved especially valuable for forming the point of view of this book.

Audi, Robert (2004), *The Good in the Right: A Theory of Intuition and Intrinsic Value* (Princeton University Press, Princeton).

Donagan, Alan (1977), *The Theory of Morality* (University of Chicago Press, Chicago).

Downie, Robert S., and Elizabeth Telfer (1970), *Respect for Persons: A Philosophical Analysis of the Moral, Political and Religious Idea of the Supreme Worth of the Individual Person* (Schocken Books, New York).

Franklin, James (1998), Accountancy as computational casuistics, *Business and Professional Ethics Journal* 17 (4), 31–37.

——— (2004), On the parallel between mathematics and morals, *Philosophy* 79, 97–119.

——— (2012), Global justice: an anti-collectivist and pro-causal ethic, *Solidarity: The Journal of Catholic Social Thought and Secular Ethics,* 2 (1).

——— (2021), 'Let no-one ignorant of geometry...': mathematical parallels for understanding the objectivity of ethics, *Journal of Value Inquiry,* online first, doi: 10.1007/s10790-021-09831-z.

Gaita, Raimond (2005), *Good and Evil: An Absolute Conception,* 2nd ed. (Routledge, London).

Garthoff, Jon (2015), The priority and posteriority of right, *Theoria* 81 (2015), 222–48.

Hampton, Jean (2007), *The Intrinsic Worth of Persons: Contractarianism in Moral and Political Philosophy,* ed. Daniel Farnham (Cambridge University Press, Cambridge).

Kant, Immanuel (1785), *Groundwork of the Metaphysics of Morals.*

——— (1797/1996), *The Metaphysics of Morals,* trans. M. Gregor (Cambridge University Press, Cambridge).

Macdonald, Paul A. (2018), Grounding human dignity and rights: A Thomistic response to Wolterstorff, *Thomist* 82, 1–35.

May, William E. (1976), What makes a human being to be a being of moral worth? *Thomist* 40, 416–43.

Moore, G. E. (1903), *Principia Ethica* (Cambridge University Press, Cambridge).

Ross, W. D. (1930), *The Right and the Good* (Oxford University Press, Oxford).

Sulmasy, Daniel P. (2007), Human dignity and human worth, in J. Malpas and N. Lickiss, eds., *Perspectives on Human Dignity: A Conversation* (Springer, Dordrecht), 9–18.

Vlastos, Gregory (1962), Justice and equality, in R. B. Brandt, ed., *Social Justice* (Prentice Hall, Englewood Cliffs NJ), 31–72.

Voh́anka, Vlastimil (2017), The nature and uniqueness of material value-ethics clarified, *Ethical Perspectives* 24, 225–58.

Von Hildebrand, Dietrich (1953), *Christian Ethics* (D. McKay, New York).

Wolterstorff, Nicholas (2008), *Justice: Rights and Wrongs* (Princeton University Press, Princeton).

Wood, Allen (2008), *Kantian Ethics* (Cambridge University Press, New York).

ACKNOWLEDGMENT

I am very grateful to Damian Grace for his careful reading of and valuable comments on the entire book.

NOTES

CHAPTER ONE

1. Contrary to Peter Singer, Introduction, in Peter Singer, ed., *Ethics* (Oxford University Press, Oxford, 1994), 3–13, at 3: "Ethics is about how we ought to live. What makes an action the right, rather than the wrong, thing to do? What should our goals be?"; one supporter of the present thesis is G.E.Moore, Preface, *Principia Ethica* (Cambridge University Press, Cambridge, 1903), on which more is presented below.

2. Raimond Gaita, *Good and Evil: An Absolute Conception*, 2nd ed. (Routledge, Abingdon, 2004), 315.

3. Roy Holland, Absolute ethics, mathematics and the impossibility of politics, in *Against Empiricism* (Blackwell, Oxford, 1980), 126–42, at 129.

4. Jeanette Kennett, Autism, empathy and moral agency, *Philosophical Quarterly* 52 (2002), 340–57; Timothy Krahn and Andrew Fenton, Autism, empathy and questions of moral agency, *Journal for the Theory of Social Behaviour* 39 (2009), 145–66.

5. Luke 10: 25–37.

6. Hannah Arendt, *The Origins of Totalitarianism* (Meridian Books, New York, 1962), 458–59.

7. Ibid., 452.

8. Ibid., 447, 451.

9. Ibid., 445; discussion in George Kateb, Existential values in Arendt's treatment of evil and morality, *Social Research* 74 (2007), 811–54.

10. George Kateb, *Human Dignity* (Belknap Press, Cambridge, MA, 2011), Chap. 2.

11. Patricia E. Roy, A choice between evils: The Chinese and the construction of the Canadian Pacific Railway in British Columbia, in Hugh A. Dempsey, ed., *The CPR West: The Iron Road and the Making of a Nation* (Douglas and MacIntyre, Vancouver, 1984), 13–34.

12. Peter W. Bartrip and Sandra B. Burman, *The Wounded Soldiers of Industry: Industrial Compensation Policy, 1833–1897* (Clarendon, Oxford, 1983); Robert Asher, Experience counts: British workers, accident prevention and compensation, and the origins of the welfare state, *Journal of Policy History* 15 (2003), 359–88.

13. This distinction made in Govert den Hartogh, Is human dignity the ground of human rights? in M. Düwell et al., eds., *Cambridge Handbook of Human Dignity* (Cambridge University Press, Cambridge, 2014), 200–7; discussion also in Jeremy Waldron, Dignity and rank, in J. Waldron and M. Dan-Cohen, eds.,

Dignity, Rank and Rights (Oxford University Press, Oxford, 2012), 13–36; Daniel P. Sulmasy, Human dignity and human worth, in J. Malpas and N. Lickiss, eds., *Perspectives on Human Dignity: A Conversation* (Springer, Dordrecht, 2007), 9–18; the German literature on bioethics connects dignity and "Menschenwürde," e.g. Lennart Nordenfelt and Andrew Edgar, The four notions of dignity, *Quality in Ageing and Older Adults* 6 (2005), 17–21.

14. Thomas E. Hill, Servility and self-respect, *Monist* 57 (1973), 87–104.

15. Paul Benson, Free agency and self-worth, *Journal of Philosophy* 91 (1994), 650–68.

16. The relation is presupposition, in the language of Robert S. Downie and Elizabeth Telfer, *Respect for Persons* (Allen and Unwin, London, 1971), Chap. 2.

17. Alan Donagan, *The Theory of Morality* (Chicago University Press, Chicago, 1977), 65–66; similar in Neil Brown, *The Worth of Persons* (Catholic Institute of Sydney, Sydney, 1983).

18. Allen W. Wood, *Kantian Ethics* (Cambridge University Press, Cambridge, 2007), 43–54.

19. Bernard Gert, *Morality: Its Nature and Justification* (Oxford University Press, New York, 2005), 14.

20. Gert himself does not emphasize this, preferring to define harms in terms of irrationality, *Morality,* 92.

21. Sam Harris, *The Moral Landscape: How Science Can Determine Human Values* (Transworld, London, 2010), 11, 15, 197. Harris's claim that "well-being" is a scientific concept is argued against later. Similar ideas are found in Erik J. Wielenberg, *Value and Virtue in a Godless Universe* (Cambridge University Press, New York, 2005), which founds ethics on the self-evidence of such propositions as "pain is bad."

22. We follow here the realist interpretation of Kant's ethics of Allen Wood, *Kant's Ethical Thought* (Cambridge University Press, New York, 1999), e.g. 157–58.

23. Kant, *The Metaphysics of Morals*, 6:435, trans. M. Gregor (Cambridge University Press, Cambridge, 1991), 186.

24. G. E. Moore, Preface, *Principia Ethica*.

CHAPTER TWO

1. Tony Judt, *Postwar: A History of Europe Since 1945* (Heinemann, London, 2005), 501–3.

2. For example, Hualing Fu and Richard Cullen, Weiquan (rights protection) lawyering in an authoritarian state: building a culture of public-interest lawyering, *China Journal* 59 (2008), 11–27; the Western nature of rights discussed in Jack Donnelly, Human rights and human dignity: an analytic critique of non-Western conceptions of human rights, *American Political Science Review* 76 (1982), 303–16.

3. Universal Declaration of Human Rights, Art. 1.

4. Sun Pinghua, Pengchun Chang's contributions to the drafting of the UDHR, *Journal of Civil and Legal Sciences* 5 (2016), 209–18.

5. Nicholas Wolterstorff and Terence Cuneo, *Understanding Liberal Democracy: Essays in political philosophy* (Oxford University Press, Oxford, 2012), 182.

6. Helsinki Accords, 1975, Art. 7.

7. Gregory Vlastos, Justice and equality, in J. Waldron, ed., *Theories of Rights* (Oxford University Press, Oxford, 1984), 41–76, at 55.

8. Jean Hampton, in Jeffrie C. Murphy and Jean Hampton, *Forgiveness and Mercy* (Cambridge University Press, Cambridge, 1988), 43–44.

9. Ronald Dworkin, *Justice for Hedgehogs* (Harvard University Press, Cambridge, MA, 2011), 335.

10. James Griffin, *On Human Rights* (Oxford University Press, Oxford, 2008), 92.

11. Mary Ann Glendon, *Rights Talk: The Impoverishment of Political Discourse* (Free Press, New York, 1991).

12. Simone Weil, Human personality, in G.A. Panichas, ed., *The Simone Weil Reader* (McKay, New York, 1977), 325.

13. Stanley Hauerwas, On the "right" to be tribal, *Christian Scholars Review* 16 (1987), 238–41.

14. Nicholas Wolterstorff, *Justice: Rights and Wrongs* (Princeton University Press, Princeton, 2008), 7

15. Ibid., 9.

16. For example, Louis P. Pojman, Are human rights based on equal human worth? *Philosophy and Phenomenological Research* 52 (1992), 605–22.

17. Kant, *Metaphysics of Morals*, 6:385, trans. M. Gregor (Cambridge University Press, Cambridge, 1991), 150.

18. Argued in G.E.M. Anscombe, Modern moral philosophy, *Philosophy* 33 (1958), 1–19; discussion in M. Homiak, Moral character, *Stanford Encyclopedia of Philosophy* 2003/2015, https://plato.stanford.edu/entries/moral-character/.

19. For example, Rosalind Hursthouse, Virtue ethics, *Stanford Encyclopedia of Philosophy*, 2003/2016, http://plato.stanford.edu/entries/ethics-virtue/.

20. James Martineau, *Types of Ethical Theory*, 2nd ed. (Oxford, 1886), 1.

21. Gary Watson, On the primacy of character, in O. Flanagan and A. O. Rorty, eds., *Identity, Character and Morality: Essays in Moral Psychology* (MIT Press, Cambridge, MA, 1993), 449–83, at 459.

22. Nicholas Wolterstorff, *Justice: Rights and Wrongs* (Princeton University Press, Princeton, 2008), 290.

23. Rosalind Hursthouse, *On Virtue Ethics* (Oxford University Press, Oxford, 1999), 167; similar to Thomas Aquinas, *Summa Theologiae* I–II, Q. 55, Art. 4.

24. Alasdair MacIntyre, *After Virtue: A Study in Moral Theory*, 3rd ed. (University of Notre Dame Press, Notre Dame, IN, 2007), Chap. 14.

25. Philippians 4:8.

26. Martin Heidegger, Letter on humanism, in D. F. Krell, ed., *Basic Writings*, 2nd ed. (Routledge, London, 1993), 251 (265 of http://pacificinstitute.org/pdf/ Letter_on_%20Humanism.pdf).

27. Giancarlo Marchetti and Sarin Marchetti, Behind and beyond the fact/value dichotomy, in G. Marchetti and S. Marchetti, eds., *Facts and Values: The Ethics and Metaphysics of Normativity* (Routledge, New York, 2017), Introduction.

28. Annette C. Baier, The need for more than justice, *Canadian Journal of Philosophy* 17 (supplementary) (1987), 41–56.

29. Joan C. Tronto, *Moral Boundaries: A Political Argument for an Ethic of Care* (Routledge, New York, 1993), 133.

30. John Christman, Autonomy in moral and political philosophy, *Stanford Encyclopedia of Philosophy*, 2003/2020, https://plato.stanford.edu/entries/autonomy-moral/.

31. John Stuart Mill, *On Liberty*, Chap. 1.

32. R. S. Downie and Elizabeth Telfer, *Respect for Persons* (Allen and Unwin, London, 1969), 39.

33. J. David Velleman, A right of self-termination? *Ethics* 109 (1999), 606–28.

34. Peter Singer, *Practical Ethics*, 2nd ed. (Cambridge University Press, Cambridge, 1993), 21.

35. H. J. McCloskey, An examination of restricted utilitarianism, *Philosophical Review* 66 (1957), 466–85.

36. J. J. C. Smart, in J. J. C. Smart and B. Williams, *Utilitarianism: For and Against* (Cambridge University Press, Cambridge, 1973), 71.

37. William Farr Church, *Richelieu and Reason of State* (Princeton University Press, Princeton, 1973), 168–70, 263–66; Michael Walzer, Political action: the problem of dirty hands, *Philosophy and Public Affairs* 2 (1973), 160–80.

38. Daniel Statman, Supreme emergencies revisited, *Ethics* 117 (2006), 58–79.

39. Raimond Gaita, *Thinking About Torture* (Routledge, London, 2007).

40. James Franklin, Evidence gained from torture: wishful thinking, checkability and extreme circumstances, *Cardozo Journal of International and Comparative Law* 17 (2009), 281–90.

CHAPTER THREE

1. Gilbert Harman, *The Nature of Morality: An Introduction to Ethics* (Oxford University Press, New York, 1977), 94.

2. Edward O. Wilson, *Sociobiology: The New Synthesis* (Belknap Press, Cambridge, MA, 1975), 3; at more length in E. O. Wilson and M. Ruse, Moral philosophy as applied science, *Philosophy* 61 (1986), 173–92, discussion in William Fitz-Patrick, Morality and evolutionary biology, *Stanford Encyclopedia of Philosophy*, 2008/2014.

3. James Franklin, Stove's discovery of the worst argument in the world, *Philosophy* 77 (2002), 615–24.

4. D. C. Stove, *Scientific Irrationalism: Origins of a Postmodern Cult* (Transaction, New Brunswick, NJ, 2001), 181.

5. Tatiana Zerjal et al., The genetic legacy of the Mongols, *American Journal of Human Genetics* 72 (2003), 717–21; the Darwinian naturalness of the human desire to dominate and control admitted in Larry Arnhart, *Darwinian Natural Right: The Biological Ethics of Human Nature* (SUNY Press, Albany, 1998), 29–36 and argued for in Randy Thornhill and Craig T. Palmer, *A Natural History of Rape: Biological Bases of Sexual Coercion* (MIT Press, Cambridge, MA, 2000).

6. J. P. Rushton, Ethnic nationalism, evolutionary psychology and Genetic Similarity Theory, *Nations and Nationalism* 11 (2015), 489–507.

7. C. Stephen Evans, *Natural Signs and Knowledge of God: A New Look at Theistic Arguments* (Oxford University Press, Oxford, 2010), 119–20.

8. Annette C. Baier, What do women want in a moral theory? *Noûs* 19 (1985), 53–63, at 62.

9. Bernard Williams, Evolution, ethics and the representation problem (1983), repr. in B. Williams, *Making Sense of Humanity* (Cambridge University Press, Cambridge, 1995) at 110.

10. Sharon Street, A Darwinian dilemma for realist theories of value, *Philosophical Studies* 127 (2006), 109–66, developed by Guy Kahane, Evolutionary debunking arguments, *Nous* 45 (2011), 103–25, and Richard Joyce, Ethics and evolution, in Hugh LaFollette and Ingmar Persson, eds., *The Blackwell Guide to Ethical Theory,* 2nd ed. (Blackwell, Malden, MA, 2013), 123–47.

11. See David Enoch, *Taking Morality Seriously: A Defense of Robust Realism* (Oxford University Press, Oxford, 2011), especially 163–77.

12. Calvinist version in Richard J. Mouw, *The God Who Commands: A Study in Divine Command Ethics* (University of Notre Dame Press, Notre Dame, IN, 1990); Islamic developments in Mariam al-Attar, *Islamic Ethics: Divine Command Theory in Arabo-Islamic Thought* (Routledge, New York, 2010).

13. Discussion in Mark Murphy, Theological voluntarism, *Stanford Encyclopedia of Philosophy,* 2012, Sect. 3.2.

14. Discussion on the necessary limitations to omnipotence in Peter Geach, Omnipotence, *Philosophy* 48 (1973), 7–20.

15. Jean-Paul Sartre, Existentialism and humanism (1946), https://www.marxists.org/reference/archive/sartre/works/exist/sartre.htm.

16. Kant, *Groundwork for the Metaphysics of Morals*, Sect. 2.

17. David Baggett and Jerry L. Walls, *Good God: The Theistic Foundations of Morality* (Oxford University Press, Oxford, 2011), Chap. 7; C. Stephen Evans, *God and Moral Obligation* (Oxford University Press, Oxford, 2013), Chap. 2.

18. Hume, *Treatise*, III.i.1, similar in *Enquiry Concerning the Principles of Morals*, I.

19. Roger Teichmann, *Nature, Reason, and the Good Life: Ethics for Human Beings* (Oxford University Press, Oxford, 2011), 1.

20. Ibid., 3–4.

21. Plato, *Republic*, 527a–b.

22. Kurt Baier, *The Moral Point of View: A Rational Basis of Ethics* (Cornell University Press, Ithaca, 1958), 314.

23. Michael Smith, *The Moral Problem* (Blackwell, Oxford, 1994), 182.

24. Ibid., 184.

25. Charles Larmore, *Morality and Metaphysics* (Cambridge University Press, Cambridge, 2021), 39.

26. Donald C. Williams, The meaning of "good," *Philosophical Review* 46 (1937), 414–23.

27. Aquinas's eudaimonism explained in Scott MacDonald, Egoistic rationalism: Aquinas' basis for Christian morality, in M. D. Beaty, ed., *Christian Theism and the Problems of Philosophy* (University of Notre Dame Press, Notre Dame, 1990), 327–54; a full treatment in Jean Porter, *Nature as Reason: A Thomistic Theory of the Natural Law* (Eerdmans, Grand Rapids, MI, 2005).

28. David S. Oderberg, *Moral Theory: A Non-Consequentialist Approach* (Blackwell, Oxford, 2000), 35.

29. Aquinas, *Summa Theologiae* I–II, Q. 94, Art. 2.

30. Dietrich von Hildebrand, *Christian Ethics* (D. McKay, New York, 1953), 50–51; aspects of Aquinas, but not this particular one, defended in M. Waldstein, Dietrich von Hildebrand and St Thomas Aquinas on goodness and happiness, *Nova et Vetera*, English ed., 1 (2) (2003), 403–64, https://www.scribd.com/doc/50609890/Waldstein-Michael-Dietrich-von-Hildebrand-and-St-Thomas-Aquinas-on-Goodness-and-Happiness, and discussed in Martin Cajthaml, Von Hildebrand's conception of value, *Studia Neoaristotelica* 15 (2018), 95–130, Sect. 3.

31. Roy Holland, Is goodness a mystery?, in *Against Empiricism* (Blackwell, Oxford, 1980), 92–109, at 99–100.

32. Philippa Foot, *Natural Goodness* (Clarendon Press, Oxford, 2001), 15.

33. John F. Post, Naturalism, reduction and normativity: pressing from below, *Philosophy and Phenomenological Research* 73 (2006), 1–27; more fully in John F. Post, *From Nature to Norm: An Essay in the Metaphysics of Morals* (BookSurge, Charleston SC, 2008).

34. G. E. M. Anscombe, Modern moral philosophy, reprinted in *The Collected Philosophical Papers of G. E. M. Anscombe,* Vol. 3: *Ethics, Religion, and Politics* (Blackwell, Oxford, 1981), 26–42, at 26.

35. Mark Murphy, *Natural Law and Practical Rationality* (Cambridge University Press, Cambridge, 2001), 203, explained in C. Stephen Evans, *God and Moral Obligation,* 72.

36. Nicholas Wolterstorff, *Justice: Rights and Wrongs* (Princeton University Press, Princeton, 2008), 389.

37. Derek Parfit, *On What Matters* (Oxford University Press, Oxford, 2011), Vol. 1, 222.

38. Ibid., Vol. 2, 145.

39. Raimond Gaita, *Good and Evil: An Absolute Conception,* 2nd ed. (Routledge, London, 2014), xxi.

CHAPTER FOUR

1. Usually stated in terms of the supervenience of right action on states of affairs as in Tristram McPherson, Supervenience in ethics, *Stanford Encyclopedia of Philosophy,* 2015, https://plato.stanford.edu/entries/supervenience-ethics/, but equally applicable to the worth of substances.
2. J. F. Post, Objective value, realism, and the end of metaphysics, *Journal of Speculative Philosophy* 4 (2) (1990) 146–60, at 159.
3. Kenneth Harris, *Attlee* (Weidenfeld and Nicholson, London, 1995), 563–64.
4. Raimond Gaita, *A Common Humanity: Thinking About Love & Truth & Justice* (Text, Melbourne, 1999), 21, 20; discussion in Sarah Bachelard, *Resurrection and Moral Imagination* (Routledge, London, 2017), 15–18.
5. Ibid, 285.
6. Raimond Gaita, *Good and Evil: An Absolute Conception,* 2nd ed. (Routledge, London, 2014), 269–70.
7. Nicholas Wolterstorff, *Justice: Rights and Wrongs* (Princeton University Press, Princeton, 2008), 319–20; some argument against in Roger Fjellstrom, A sketch of equal human value, *SATS: Northern European Journal of Philosophy* 8 (2007), 97–112.
8. Nicholas Wolterstorff and Terence Cuneo, *Understanding Liberal Democracy: Essays in Political Philosophy* (Oxford University Press, Oxford, 2012), 182.
9. John Rawls, *A Theory of Justice,* 2nd ed. (Harvard University Press, Cambridge, MA, 1999), 79; a Thomist commentary with resemblances to the present one in Michael Pakaluk, The Dignity of the Human Person in the Philosophy of John Rawls, Conference on "The Philosophical Foundations of Human Dignity," Washington DC, 8 Mar 2007, http://michaelpakaluk.files.wordpress.com/2012/02/the-dignity-of-the-human-person-in-the-philosophy-of-john-rawls.pdf.
10. Rawls, *Theory of Justice,* 386; similar comments apply to Korsgaard's "description under which you value yourself and find your life to be worth living": Christine Korsgaard, *The Sources of Normativity* (Cambridge University Press, Cambridge, 1996), 102.
11. Michael J. Sandel, *Liberalism and the Limits of Justice,* 2nd ed. (Cambridge University Press, Cambridge, 1998), 14.
12. Ronald Dworkin, Justice and rights, in *Taking Rights Seriously* (Harvard University Press, Cambridge, MA, 1977), 182; hints of agreement from Rawls himself in *Theory of Justice,* 442–43, 447.
13. John Rawls, Justice as fairness: political not metaphysical, *Philosophy & Public Affairs* 14 (3) (1985), 223–51 at 230–31.

14. Ibid., at 240. (Rawls then says that the metaphysical differences between Leibniz, Kant, etc., are not relevant, which is true, but what they have in common is what is important.)

15. Rawls, *Theory of Justice*, 442.

16. Ronald Dworkin, The original position, *University of Chicago Law Review* 40 (1973), 500–33, at 527.

17. Ronald Dworkin, *Justice for Hedgehogs* (Belknap Press, Cambridge, MA, 2011), 26.

18. Richard Rorty, Human rights, rationality and sentimentality, in *Truth and Progress: Philosophical Papers* (Cambridge University Press, Cambridge, 1998), 167–85; Wolterstorff, *Justice*, 320–21.

19. Jürgen Habermas, Themes in postmetaphysical thinking, in *Postmetaphysical Thinking: Philosophical Essays* (MIT Press, Cambridge, MA, 1996), 28–53.

20. G. Grisez, J. Boyle, and J. Finnis, Practical principles, moral truth, and ultimate ends, *American Journal of Jurisprudence* 32 (1987), 99–151, at 102.

21. Wolterstorff and Cuneo, *Understanding Liberal Democracy*, 186–88.

22. Thomas Christiano, Rationality, equal status and egalitarianism, in U. Steinhoff, ed., *Do All Persons Have Equal Moral Worth?: On "Basic Equality" and Equal Respect and Concern* (Oxford University Press, New York, 2014), Chap. 4; argued at length in Bernard Williams, The idea of equality, in P. Laslett and W. G. Runciman, eds., *Philosophy, Politics and Society,* Series II (Blackwell, Oxford, 1962), 110–31; Ian Carter, Respect and the basis of equality, *Ethics* 121 (2011), 538–71, Sect. II.

23. Héctor Wittwer, The irrelevance of the concept of worth to the debate between egalitarianism and non-egalitarianism, in U. Steinhoff, ed., *Do All Persons Have Equal Moral Worth?*, Chap. 5.

24. Jeremy Waldron, *One Another's Equals: The Basis of Human Equality* (Harvard University Press, Cambridge, MA, 2017), 48.

25. Charles Larmore, *Morality and Metaphysics* (Cambridge University Press, Cambridge, 2021), 41.

26. Plato, *Menexenus* 239a; J. M. Kelly, *A Short History of Western Legal Theory* (Clarendon, Oxford, 1992), 29–30, 104–5, 146–48.

27. Amartya Sen, *Inequality Reexamined* (Clarendon, Oxford, 1992), Chap. 1.

28. Wolterstorff, *Justice,* 331.

29. Ibid., 329–33.

30. Discussion in Agnieszka Jaworska and Julie Tannenbaum, The grounds of moral status, *Stanford Encyclopedia of Philosophy* 2013/2018, https://plato.stanford.edu/entries/grounds-moral-status/, Sect. 5.4.

31. Wolterstorff and Cuneo, *Understanding Liberal Democracy,* 188.

32. Similar argument in Paul A. Macdonald, Grounding human dignity and rights: A Thomistic response to Wolterstorff, *Thomist* 82 (2018), 1–35, Sect. 2.

33. In Thomist language, they "lack the use of reason accidentally, i.e. through

some impediment in a bodily organ" (Aquinas, *Summa Theologiae* III, Q. 68, Art. 12, ad 2); discussion in Xavier Symons, Love to the very end: a theology of dementia, *Church Life Journal*, 3 Dec 2021.

34. Wolterstorff and Cuneo, *Understanding Liberal Democracy*, 192.

35. C. F. Cranor, On respecting human beings as persons, *Journal of Value Inquiry* 17 (1983), 103–17; or "dignity of the human" versus "dignity of the person," in the language of Gilbert Meilaender, *Neither Beast Nor God: The Dignity of the Human Person* (Encounter Books, New York, 2009).

36. Gaita, *Good and Evil,* xiii–xiv; similar ideas in Gregory Vlastos, Justice and equality, in R. B. Brandt, ed., *Social Justice* (Prentice Hall, Englewood Cliffs, NJ, 1962), 31–72.

37. Elizabeth Anderson, *Value in Ethics and Economics* (Harvard University Press, Cambridge, MA, 1993), 26, 20.

38. Ben Bradley, Two concepts of intrinsic value, *Ethical Theory and Moral Practice* 9 (2006), 111–30, at 122.

39. Fred Feldman, *Utilitarianism, Hedonism and Desert* (Cambridge University Press, Cambridge, 1997), 163.

40. William E. May, What makes a human being to be a being of moral worth? *Thomist* 40 (1976), 416–43.

41. Wolterstorff, *Justice,* Chap. 6; something similar defended more explicitly in Robert Audi, *Moral Knowledge and Ethical Character* (Oxford University Press, New York, 1997), Chap. 11.

42. G. E. Moore, *Principia Ethica* (Cambridge University Press, Cambridge, 1903), §113.

43. Noah M. Lemos, *Intrinsic Value: Concept and Warrant* (Cambridge University Press, Cambridge, 1994), 28, also argued in Zimmerman, *The Nature of Intrinsic Value*, Chap. 3.

44. Jonathan Schaffer, Metaphysics of causation, *Stanford Encyclopedia of Philosophy,* 2003/2016, Sect. 1.

45. Peter Singer, *Practical Ethics*, 3rd ed. (Cambridge University Press, Cambridge, 2011), 20.

46. Ibid., 163–65; Tatjana Višak, Do utilitarians need to accept the replaceability argument?, in T. Višak and R. Garner, ed., *The Ethics of Killing Animals* (Oxford University Press, Oxford, 2015), Chap. 7.

47. Rawls, *Theory of Justice*, 140.

48. Discussion in Dennis McKerlie, Egalitarianism and the separateness of persons, *Canadian Journal of Philosophy* 18 (1988), 205–66.

49. J. David Velleman, Love as a moral emotion, *Ethics* 109 (1999), 338–74.

50. Complained of and references given in Zimmerman, *The Nature of Intrinsic Value,* 33.

51. Richard Rorty, Human rights, rationality and sentimentality, in *Truth and Progress: Philosophical Papers* (Cambridge University Press, New York, 1998),

167–85; a similar theory of social conferral in L. Nandi Theunissen, *The Value of Humanity* (Oxford University Press, Oxford, 2020).

52. Wolterstorff, *Justice*, Chap. 16.

53. Wolterstorff and Cuneo, *Understanding Liberal Democracy*, 199.

54. Similar argument in Macdonald, Grounding human dignity and rights, Sect. 3, and in Jordan Wessling, A dilemma for Wolterstorff's theistic grounding of human dignity and rights, *International Journal for Philosophy of Religion* 76 (2014), 277–95.

55. Except in the marginally canonical Sirach 3:13 and possibly in the stories of the Annunciation and Visitation, Luke 1:35 and 1:41.

CHAPTER FIVE

1. Jonathan Dancy, Should we pass the buck? *Royal Institute of Philosophy Supplement* 47 (2000), 159–73, at 164, similar in T. M. Scanlon, *What We Owe to Each Other* (Harvard University Press, Cambridge, MA, 1998), 95–100.

2. Frank Jackson, *From Metaphysics to Ethics: A Defence of Conceptual Analysis* (Clarendon Press, Oxford, 1998), 127.

3. G. E. Moore, *Principia Ethica* (Cambridge University Press, Cambridge, 1903), §10.

4. Anna Wierzbicka, *Semantics: Primes and Universals* (Oxford University Press, Oxford, 1996), 51–54.

5. Scott MacDonald, Introduction: the relation between being and goodness, in Scott MacDonald, ed., *Being and Goodness: The concept of the Good in Metaphysics and Philosophical Theology* (Cornell University Press, Ithaca, NY, 1991), 1–28.

6. Scott A. Davison, *On the Intrinsic Value of Everything* (Continuum, London, 2012).

7. John F. Crosby, Doubts about the privation theory that will not go away: Response to Patrick Lee, *American Catholic Philosophical Quarterly* 81 (2007), 489–505, at 492.

8. Dietrich von Hildebrand, *Ethics* (Franciscan Herald Press, Chicago, 1972), 186, discussed by Crosby.

9. For example, Thomas Aquinas, *Quaestiones disputatae de potentia dei*, Q. 1, Art. 1.

10. Ricki Bliss and Kelly Trogdon, Metaphysical grounding, *Stanford Encyclopedia of Philosophy*, 2014.

11. Tristram McPherson, Supervenience in ethics, *Stanford Encyclopedia of Philosophy*, 2015.

12. G. E. Moore, The conception of intrinsic value, in G. E. Moore, *Philosophical Studies* (1922), 253–275, http://www.ditext.com/moore/intrinsic.html.

13. Frank Jackson, *From Metaphysics to Ethics*, 118.

14. Classically in Donald Davidson, *Essays on Actions and Events* (Clarendon, Oxford, 1980), 214.

15. Discussion in Gideon Rosen, Metaphysical dependence, in B. Hale and A. Hoffmann, eds, *Modality: Metaphysics, Logic, and Epistemology* (Oxford University Press, Oxford, 2010), 109–35.

16. Paul Audi, Grounding: towards a theory of the in-virtue-of relation, *Journal of Philosophy* 109 (2012), 685–711.

17. Pekka Väyrynen, Grounding and normative explanation, *Proceedings of the Aristotelian Society Supplementary Volume* 87 (2013), 155–78.

18. Terence Cuneo, *The Normative Web* (Oxford University Press, Oxford, 2007), 6; other versions in Richard Rowland, Moral error theory and the argument from epistemic reasons, *Journal of Ethics and Social Philosophy* 7 (1) (2012); Conor McHugh, Jonathan Way, and Daniel Whiting, eds, *Normativity: Epistemic and practical* (Oxford University Press, Oxford, 2018), Introduction.

19. Ibid., 54.

20. Ibid., Chap. 3.

21. T. M. Scanlon, *Being Realistic About Reasons* (Oxford University Press, Oxford, 2014), 2.

22. Owen Griffiths and A.C. Paseau, Isomorphism invariance and overgeneration, *Bulletin of Symbolic Logic* 22 (2016), 482–503; Mario Gómez-Torrente, Logical truth, *Stanford Encyclopedia of Philosophy* 2006/2018, https://plato.stanford.edu/entries/logical-truth/; Jeremiah Joven Joaquin and James Franklin, A causal-mentalist view of propositions, *Organon F* 29 (2022), 47–77; Charles Larmore, *Morality and Metaphysics* (Cambridge University Press, Cambridge, 2021), 36–38.

23. Cynthia A. Stark, The rationality of valuing oneself: A critique of Kant on self-respect, *Journal of the History of Philosophy* 35 (1997), 65–82, at 79, based on Charles Landesman, Against respect for persons, *Tulane Studies in Philosophy* 31 (1982), 31–43.

24. Arthur O. Lovejoy, *The Great Chain of Being: A Study in the History of an Idea* (Harvard University Press, Cambridge, MA, 1936)

25. Magdalena Holy-Luczaj, Heidegger's support for deep ecology reexamined once again: Ontological egalitarianism, or farewell to the Great Chain of Being, *Ethics and the Environment* 20 (2015), 45–66.

26. David Hume, *Treatise of Human Nature*, Book III, Sect. i.

27. Charles Pigden, Hume on *is* and *ought*: logic, promises and the Duke of Wellington, in P. Russell, ed., *The Oxford Handbook of Hume* (Oxford University Press, Oxford, 2016), Chap. 20.

28. Julian Dodd and Suzanne Stern-Gillet, The is/ought gap, the fact/value distinction and the naturalistic fallacy, *Dialogue* (Canada) 34 (1995), 727–45.

29. G. E. Moore, *Principia Ethica,* Sect. 13; discussion in Matthew Lutz and James Lenman, Moral naturalism, *Stanford Encyclopedia of Philosophy,* 2006/2018, https://plato.stanford.edu/entries/naturalism-moral/, Sect. 2.

30. G. E. Moore, The refutation of idealism, 1903; discussion in Mark Shroeder,

Realism and reduction: the quest for robustness, *Philosophers' Imprint* 5 (1) (2005), 1–18.

31. John Mackie, *Ethics: Inventing Right and Wrong* (Harmondsworth, 1977), 38.

32. John Mackie, A refutation of morals, *Australasian Journal of Philosophy* 24 (1946), 77–90.

33. Mackie, *Ethics*, 44; defended in Richard T. Garner, On the genuine queerness of moral properties and facts, *Australasian Journal of Philosophy*, 68 (1990), 137–46.

34. Richard Joyce, The error in "The error in the error theory," *Australasian Journal of Philosophy* 89 (2011), 519–34, at 525.

35. D. O. Brink, Moral realism and the skeptical arguments from disagreement and queerness, *Australasian Journal of Philosophy* 62 (1984), 111–25, Sect. 4; Ramon Das, Why companions in guilt arguments still work: reply to Cowie, *Philosophical Quarterly* 66 (2016), 152–60, with further references; review in Christopher Cowie, Companions in guilt arguments, *Philosophy Compass* 13 (11) (2018) e12528.

CHAPTER SIX

1. Robert Audi, *The Good in the Right: A Theory of Intuition and Intrinsic Value* (Princeton University Press, Princeton, 2004), 157.

2. Shakespeare, *Hamlet*, Act II, Scene 2.

3. David G. Kirchhoffer, Personhood and human dignity, in J. Ozolins and J. Grainger, eds., *Foundations of Healthcare Ethics: Theory to Practice* (Cambridge University Press, Port Melbourne, 2015), 51–69.

4. Augustine, *De Genesi ad litteram*, Book 6, Chap. 12, quoted in Thomas Aquinas *Summa Theologiae* I, Q. 93, Art. 2; discussion in Christian Tornau, Saint Augustine, *Stanford Encyclopedia of Philosophy* (2019), Sect. 6.2. But Aquinas includes love, in a Trinitarian image.

5. Boethius, *Liber de persona et duabus naturis contra Eutychen et Nestorium*, Chap. 2.

6. Kant, *Groundwork for the Metaphysics of Morals*, 4:428–49.

7. John Finnis, *Aquinas: Moral, Political, and Legal Theory* (Oxford University Press, New York, 1998), 179.

8. Alan Donagan, *The Theory of Morality*, 235; objections in Raimond Gaita, *Good and Evil: An Absolute Conception*, 2nd ed. (Routledge, Abingdon, 2004), 267.

9. Catherine Legg and James Franklin, Perceiving necessity, *Pacific Philosophical Quarterly* 98 (2017), 320–43.

10. Gideon Lewis-Kraus, The great A. I. awakening, *New York Times*, 14 Dec 2016, www.nytimes.com/2016/12/14/magazine/the-great-ai-awakening.html.

11. Linda Zagzebski, Recovering understanding, in M. Steup, ed., *Knowledge, Truth and Duty: Essays on Epistemic Justification, Responsibility and Virtue* (Oxford University Press, New York, 2001), 235–58; Stephen Grimm, The value of understanding, *Philosophy Compass* 7 (2012), 103–17.

12. Zdzislaw Kuksewicz, The potential and the agent intellect, Chap. 29 of *The*

Cambridge History of Later Medieval Philosophy, ed. N. Kretzmann et al., Cambridge, 1988.

13. Robert Pasnau, Divine illumination, *Stanford Encyclopedia of Philosophy*, revised 2006, http://plato.stanford.edu/entries/illumination/.

14. Aristotle, *Nicomachean Ethics*, Book 10, 7–8; later developments in Rik van Nieuwenhove, Contemplation, intellectus and simplex intuitus in Aquinas, *American Catholic Philosophical Quarterly* 91 (2017), 199–225.

15. Thomas Aquinas, *Summa Theologiae* I–II, Q. 3, Art. 8.

16. J. David Velleman, Love as a moral emotion, *Ethics* 109 (1999), 338–74, at 365.

17. As argued at length in the aesthetic theories of Aquinas and Kant, e.g. Umberto Eco, *The Aesthetics of Thomas Aquinas*, trans. H. Bredin (Harvard University Press, Cambridge, MA, 1988), Chap. 7.

18. Peter J. Colosi, The uniqueness of persons in the life and thought of Karol Wojtyła/Pope John Paul II, with emphasis on his indebtedness to Max Scheler, in N. M. Billias, A. B. Curry and G. F. McLean, eds., *Karol Wojtyla's Philosophical Legacy* (Council for Research in Values and Philosophy, Washington DC, 2008), Chap. 3, n. 8, http://peterjcolosi.com/wp-content/uploads/2012/02/Colosi-Personal-Uniqueness-Wojtyla-Scheler.pdf.

19. For example, Frank Palmer, *Literature and Moral Understanding: A Philosophical Essay on Ethics, Aesthetics, Education, and Culture* (Clarendon, Oxford, 1992); Martha Nussbaum, *Love's Knowledge: Essays on Philosophy and Literature*, rev. ed. (Oxford University Press, New York, 1992).

20. Peter Forrest, *Intellectual, Humanist and Religious Commitment: Acts of Assent* (Bloomsbury, London, 2019), Sect. 10.3.

21. G. E. Moore, *Principia Ethica* (Cambridge University Press, Cambridge, 1903), Chap. 6, §113; defended at length in Joshua Shepherd, *Consciousness and Moral Status* (Routledge, New York, 2018).

22. W. D. Ross, *The Right and the Good* (Clarendon, Oxford, 1930), 122.

23. Christine M. Korsgaard, Personal identity and the unity of agency: a Kantian response to Parfit, *Philosophy & Public Affairs* 18 (1989), 101–32; more fully in Tim Bayne and David J. Chalmers, What is the unity of consciousness? in A. Cleeremans, ed., *The Unity of Consciousness: Binding, Integration, Dissociation* (Oxford University Press, New York, 2003), 23–58.

24. Louis A. Sass and Josef Parnas, Schizophrenia, consciousness and the self, *Schizophrenia Bulletin* 29 (2003), 427–44.

25. Andrew Brook and Paul Raymont, The unity of consciousness, *Stanford Encyclopedia of Philosophy*, 2001/2017, https://plato.stanford.edu/entries/consciousness-unity/, especially Sect. 2.1.

26. Philip Gerrans and Jeanette Kennett, Neurosentimentalism and moral agency, *Mind* 119 (2010), 585–614; Paul Ricoeur, Narrative identity, *Philosophy Today* 35 (1991), 73–81.

27. David W. Shoemaker, Personal identity and practical concerns, *Mind* 116 (2007), 317–57.

28. Jeanette Kennett and Steve Matthews, The unity and disunity of agency, *Philosophy, Psychiatry, & Psychology* 10 (2003), 305–12; Brook and Raymont, The unity of consciousness, Sect. 4.

29. Alasdair MacIntyre, *After Virtue: A Study in Moral Theory* (University of Notre Dame Press, Notre Dame IN, 1981), 191.

30. Nicholas Wolterstorff, *Justice: Rights and Wrongs* (Princeton University Press, Princeton, 2008), Chap. 6.

31. MacIntyre, *After Virtue*, 199.

32. For example, Shaun Gallagher, *How the Body Shapes the Mind* (Oxford University Press, New York, 2005); Antonio Damasio, *The Feeling of What Happens: Body and Emotion in the Making of Consciousness* (Harcourt, San Diego, 2000); Andy Clark, *Supersizing the Mind: Embodiment, Action and Cognitive Extension* (Oxford University Press, New York, 2011).

33. J. J. Macintosh, Perception and imagination in Descartes, Boyle and Hooke, *Canadian Journal of Philosophy* 13 (1983), 327–52.

34. Edmund Husserl, *Ideas: General Introduction to Pure Phenomenology*, trans. W. R. Boyce Gibson (Routledge, London, 2012), 101.

35. For example, Allen R. McConnell, Christina M. Brown, and Tonya M. Shoda, The social cognition of the self, in D. E. Carlson, ed., *The Oxford Handbook of Social Cognition* (Oxford University Press, Oxford, 2013), Chap. 24.

36. We do not accept transcendental arguments attributed to Kant to the effect that action necessarily requires valuing the actor in him/herself, for reasons explained in Donald H. Regan, The value of rational nature, *Ethics* 112 (2002), 267–91.

37. John Stuart Mill, *On Liberty* (Collins, London, 1962, 187), Chap. 3.

38. Robert S. Downie and Elizabeth Telfer, *Respect for Persons* (Allen and Unwin, London, 1971), 20

39. Discussion in James Griffin, *On Human Rights* (Oxford University Press, Oxford, 2008), Chap. 8.

40. F. H. Bradley, *Ethical Studies* (Henry S. King, London, 1876, repr. Cambridge University Press, Cambridge, 2012), 14.

41. Bradley, *Ethical Studies*, 19; discussion in Robert Kane, *The Significance of Free Will* (Oxford University Press, New York, 1998), 86; also Randolph Clarke, *Libertarian Accounts of Free Will* (Oxford University Press, New York 2003), 5–7.

42. Kane, *Significance of Free Will*, 79.

43. Kant, *Foundations of the Metaphysics of Morals*, trans. L. W. Beck (Bobbs-Merrill, Indianapolis, 1959), 52; Kane, *Significance of Free Will*, 87.

44. Iris Murdoch, The sublime and the good, in P. Conradi, ed., *Existentialists and Mystics: Writings on Philosophy and Literature* (Penguin, New York, 1997), 205–20, at 215.

45. 1 Corinthians 13:2.

46. Jeanette Kennett, Autism, empathy and moral agency, *Philosophical Quarterly* 52 (2002), 340–57.

47. John Bowlby, *Attachment* (*Attachment and Loss*, Vol. 1) (Basic Books, New York, 1969), Part III.

48. Michael Stocker, *Valuing Emotions* (Cambridge University Press, New York, 1996), Chap. 10.

49. Stocker, *Valuing Emotions,* 1–2.

50. Ibid., 186.

51. Mette Lebech, Edith Stein's philosophy of education, in *The Structure of the Human Person*, in *REA, Religion, Education & the Arts*, Issue V: The Philosophy of Education, ed. I. Leask, 2005, 55–70, (http://eprints.maynoothuniversity.ie/3009/), Sect. 3.

52. Surveys in C. Dubray, Faculties of the soul, *Catholic Encyclopedia* (Appleton, New York, 1909), Vol. 5, http://www.newadvent.org/cathen/05749a.htm; Hendrik Lorenz, Ancient theories of soul, *Stanford Encyclopedia of Philosophy,* 2002/2009, http://plato.stanford.edu/entries/ancient-soul/.

53. http://nccc.georgetown.edu/body_mind_spirit/resources.html.

54. Nicholas Wolterstorff and Terence Cuneo, *Understanding Liberal Democracy: Essays in political philosophy* (Oxford University Press, Oxford, 2012), 218–20.

55. Thomas Aquinas, *De principiis naturae*, §10.

56. Robin S. Dillon, Respect, *Stanford Encyclopedia of Philosophy*, 2003/2018, https://plato.stanford.edu/entries/respect/.

57. Hannah Arendt, *The Human Condition*, 2nd ed. (University of Chicago Press, Chicago, 1958), 242.

58. Erich Auerbach, Odysseus's scar, *Mimesis: The Representation of Reality in Western Literature*, 50th anniv. ed. (Princeton University Press, Princeton, 2003), Chap. 1, http://www.westmont.edu/~fisk/articles/odysseusscar.html.

59. Boris Pasternak, *Doctor Zhivago,* Part 15, Chap. 17.

60. Hannah Arendt, *Origins*, 1962, 453–54.

61. Similar ideas of Max Scheler discussed in Joshua Miller, Scheler on the two-fold source of personal uniqueness, *American Catholic Philosophical Quarterly* 79 (2005), 163–81.

62. In A. Kerrigan, ed., J. L. Borges, *Ficciones* (Grove Press, New York, 1962), 45–55.

63. Colosi, The uniqueness of persons in the life and thought of Karol Wojtyła, at 69.

64. William Butler Yeats, "For Anne Gregory"; comments in Velleman, Love as a moral emotion.

65. Bennett Helm, Love, *Stanford Encyclopedia of Philosophy,* 2005/2017, https://plato.stanford.edu/entries/love/, Sect. 6.

66. Discussed in Gregory Vlastos, Justice and equality, in R. B. Brandt, ed., *Social Justice* (Prentice Hall, Englewood Cliffs, NJ, 1962), 31–72, at 44.

67. Kant, *Groundwork of the Metaphysics of Morals,* 4:434; discussion in Velleman, Love, at 364–65.

68. Alasdair MacIntyre, *After Virtue*, Chap. 15, 192.

69. For example, Cicero, *De officiis*, Book I, Chap. 110.

70. Marya Schechtman, *The Constitution of Selves* (Cornell University Press, Ithaca, 1996), 93.

71. Emphasized by Max Scheler: Joshua Miller, Scheler on the twofold source of personal uniqueness, *American Catholic Philosophical Quarterly* 79 (2005), 163–81, at 164.

72. *Babylonian Talmud*, Sanhedrin 37a.

73. History in Colin Morris, *The Discovery of the Individual, 1050–1200* (S.P.C.K., London, 1972); and throughout Auerbach's *Mimesis*; C. W. Bynum, Did the twelfth century discover the individual? *Journal of Ecclesiastical History* 31 (1980), 1–17.

74. Catherine Peters, quoted in Susan Tridgell, *Understanding Our Selves: The Dangerous Art of Biography* (Peter Lang, Bern, 2004), 111.

75. O. Carter Snead, *What It Means to Be Human: The Case for the Body in Public Bioethics* (Harvard University Press, Harvard, 2020), 5, 3.

76. James C. Anderson, Species equality and the foundations of moral theory, *Environmental Values* 2 (1993), 347–65.

CHAPTER SEVEN

1. For example, Louis Lombardi, Inherent worth, respect and rights, *Environmental Ethics* 5 (1983), 257–70; Paul W. Taylor, *Respect for Nature* (Princeton University Press, Princeton, 1986).

2. Aquinas, *Disputed Questions on Truth*, Q. 24, Art. 2; discussion in Hilary Yancey, Frontiers of analogous justice: a Thomistic approach to Martha Nussbaum's justice for animals, *Proceedings of the American Catholic Philosophical Association* 91 (2017), 201–10.

3. Peter van Inwagen, *The Problem of Evil* (Oxford University Press, Oxford, 2006), 126.

4. Clement of Alexandria, *Stromata (Miscellanies)*, Book V, Chap. 14.

5. John Haldane, Rational and other animals, *Royal Institute of Philosophy Supplement* 41 (1996), 17–28.

6. Thomas Aquinas, *Disputed Questions on Truth*, Q. 24, Art. 2.

7. Robert C. Roberts, The sophistication of non-human emotion, in Robert W. Lurz, ed., *The Philosophy of Animal Minds* (Cambridge University Press, Cambridge, 2009), 218–36, at 220.

8. Aquinas, *Disputed Questions on Truth*, Q. 24, Art. 2.

9. Christine M. Korsgaard, *The Sources of Normativity* (Cambridge University Press, Cambridge, 1996), 93.

10. Tom Regan, The case for animal rights, in P. Singer, ed., *In Defence of Animals* (Blackwell, Oxford, 1985), 13–26, at 24, http://www.animal-rights-library. com/texts-m/regan03.htm; further in Christine M. Korsgaard, *Fellow Crea-*

tures: Our Obligations to the Other Animals (Oxford University Press, Oxford, 2018), Chap. 4.

11. Mary Midgley, *Animals and Why They Matter* (University of Georgia Press, Athens, GA, 1983), 14.

12. Jeremy Bentham, *An Introduction to the Principles of Morals and Legislation,* Chap. 17, n. 122.

13. David Oderberg, *Applied Ethics: A Non-consequentialist Approach* (Blackwell, Oxford, 2005), 128.

14. Stephen R. L. Clark, *The Moral Status of Animals* (Clarendon, Oxford, 1977), 30.

15. Humphrey Primatt, in A. Broome, ed., *The Duty of Humanity to Inferior Creatures, Deduced from Reason and Scripture* (London, 1831), 22.

16. Porphyry, *On Abstinence* 3.20.1.

17. Elizabeth Harman, The moral significance of animal pain and animal death, in T. L. Beauchamp and R. L. Frey, eds., *The Oxford Handbook on Ethics and Animals* (Oxford University Press, New York, 2011), Chap. 26.

18. https://www.bioedge.org/bioethics/peter-singer-disinvited-from-german-philosophy-festival/11491.

19. R. E. Sonnino and R. E. Banks, Ethical issues: Impact of the animal rights movement on surgical research, *Pediatric Surgery International* 11 (1996), 438–43.

20. W. D. Ross, *The Right and the Good* (Clarendon, Oxford, 1930), 140.

21. G. E. Moore, *Principia Ethica* (Cambridge University Press, Cambridge, 1903), 28, 83ff, 188ff.

22. Holmes Rolston III, Are values in nature subjective or objective? *Environmental Ethics* 4 (1982), 125–51, at 145.

23. Review in Chelsea Batavia and Michael Paul Nelson, For goodness sake! What is intrinsic value and why should we care?, *Biological Conservation* 209 (2017), 366–76, especially Sect. 4.2.

24. For example, Bruce Morito, Intrinsic value: a modern albatross for the ecological approach, *Environmental Values* 12 (2003), 317–36; Toby Svoboda, Why there is no evidence for the intrinsic value of non-humans, *Ethics and the Environment* 16 (2011), 25–36; discussion in Katie McShane, Why environmental ethics shouldn't give up on intrinsic value, *Environmental Ethics* 29 (2007), 43–61.

25. Douglas H. Erwin and James W. Valentine, *The Cambrian Explosion: The Reconstruction of Animal Biodiversity* (Roberts & Co, Greenwood Village, CO, 2013).

26. Simon Conway Morris, *The Crucible of Creation: The Burgess Shale and the Rise of Animals* (Oxford University Press, Oxford, 1998).

27. Richard Dawkins, *The God Delusion* (Transworld, London, 2006), 31.

28. Charles Darwin, *On the Origin of Species* (John Murray, London, 1859), 490.

29. Richard Routley, Is there a need for a new, an environmental ethic? *Proceedings of the XVth World Congress of Philosophy* (Sofia Press, Varna, 1973), 205–10;

Singer's opposite conclusion is simply a corollary of his theory that only sentience matters: Peter Singer, Not for humans only, in K. Goodpaster and K. M. Sayre, eds., *Ethics and Problems of the 21st Century* (Notre Dame University Press, Notre Dame, 1979), 191–206, at 203–4.

30. Robert Elliot, Environmental degradation, vandalism and the aesthetic object argument, *Australasian Journal of Philosophy* 67 (1989), 191–204.

31. Umberto Eco, *The Aesthetics of Thomas Aquinas*, trans. H. Bredin (Harvard University Press, Cambridge, MA, 1988), 23–24; a modern version in Gerard Manley Hopkins's poem "God's Grandeur."

32. William Mander, Pantheism, *Stanford Encyclopedia of Philosophy*, 2020.

33. Scott A. Davison, *On the Intrinsic Value of Everything* (Continuum, London, 2012); David S. Oderberg, *The Metaphysics of Good and Evil* (Routledge, London, 2019), Chap. 3.

34. Richard Hooker, *Of the Lawes of Ecclesiastical Politie* (London, 1594), Book I, Chap. vi.

35. A recent development of the evil as privation theory in Oderberg, *Metaphysics of Good and Evil*, Part II.

36. Jean Porter, *Nature as Reason: A Thomistic Theory of the Natural Law* (Eerdmans, Grand Rapids, Mich, 2005), 57.

37. Discussion in Andrew Brennan, The moral standing of natural objects, *Environmental Ethics* 6 (1984), 35–56, Sect. III.

38. Dietrich von Hildebrand, *Aesthetics* (Hildebrand Project, Steubenville, OH, 2016), Vol. I, 309–10.

39. Arne Naess, *Ecology, Community and Lifestyle: Outline of an Ecosophy*, trans. and ed. D. Rothenberg (Cambridge University Press, Cambridge, 1989), 29; similar in Holmes Rolston III, Biodiversity, in D. Jamieson, ed., *A Companion to Environmental Philosophy* (Blackwell, Oxford, 2001), Chap. 28.

40. Willett M. Kempton, James S. Boster, and Jennifer A. Hartley, *Environmental Values in American Culture* (MIT Press, Cambridge, MA, 1995).

41. Alastair S. Gunn, Why should we care about rare species? *Environmental Ethics* 2 (1980), 17–37.

42. Aquinas, *Summa Theologiae* I, Q. 39, Art. 8; Eco, *Aesthetics*, 65.

43. Robert Elliot, Environmental degradation, vandalism and the aesthetic object argument, *Australasian Journal of Philosophy* 67 (1989), 191–204, at 193.

44. Ibid., summarizing Stanley Benn.

45. Plato, *Republic* 531; Myles Burnyeat, Plato on why mathematics is good for the soul, *Proceedings of the British Academy* 103 (2000), 1–81, Sect. 10.

46. James W. McAllister, Is beauty a sign of truth in scientific theories? *Scientific American* 86 (2) (Mar–Apr 1998), 174–83.

47. The foundational idea of the scholastic theory of goodness, as developed in Oderberg, *Metaphysics of Good and Evil*, Chap. 1.

48. For example, Peter Forrest, *Developmental Theism: From Pure Will to Unbounded*

Love (Clarendon, Oxford, 2007), Chap. 4; Charles Nussbaum, Aesthetics and the problem of evil, *Metaphilosophy* 34 (2003), 250–83.

49. Peter van Inwagen *The Problem of Evil* (Oxford University Press, Oxford, 2006), 121.

50. Kareem Shaheen and Ian Black, Beheaded Syrian scholar refused to lead Isis to hidden Palmyra antiquities, *The Guardian,* 19 Aug 2015, https://www.the-guardian.com/world/2015/aug/18/isis-beheads-archaeologist-syria.

51. Amy Gunia, 164 environmental activists were killed while protecting their homes last year, watchdog says, *Time,* July 30, 2019, https://time.com/5638438/global-witness-environmental-activists-murdered/.

52. Discussions in Allen Buchanan, Moral status and human enhancement, *Philosophy and Public Affairs* 37 (2009), 346–81; Nick Bostrom and Julian Savulescu, Introduction, in J. Savulescu and N. Bostrom, eds., *Human Enhancement* (Oxford University Press, Oxford, 2009); David Oderberg, Could there be a superhuman species? *Southern Journal of Philosophy* 52 (2014), 206–26.

53. Discussion in James Wilson, Transhumanism and moral equality, *Bioethics* 21 (2007), 419–25; Thomas Douglas, Human enhancement and supra-personal moral status, *Philosophical Studies* 162 (2013), 473–97.

54. Sebastian Rehnman, Theistic metaphysics and biblical exegesis: Francis Turretin on the concept of God, *Religious Studies* 38 (2002), 167–86; J. Fox, Divine Attributes, in *Catholic Encyclopedia* (Appleton, New York, 1907), http://www.newadvent.org/cathen/02062e.htm.

55. Seyyed Hussein Nasr, God, in S. H. Nasr, ed., *Islamic Spirituality: Foundations* (Routledge, Abingdon, 1987), Chap. 16.

CHAPTER EIGHT

1. Jonas Olson, In defence of moral error theory, in M. Brady, ed., *New Waves in Metaethics* (Palgrave Macmillan, Basingstoke, 2010), 7.

2. John Anderson, The meaning of good, *Australasian Journal of Psychology and Philosophy* 20 (1943), 111–40; James Franklin, *Corrupting the Youth: A History of Philosophy in Australia* (Macleay Press, Sydney, 2003), 40–41.

3. G. E. Moore, A reply to my critics, in P. A. Schilpp, ed., *The Philosophy of G. E. Moore* (Tudor, New York, 1942), 151–52; discussion in Jonas Olson, G. E. Moore on goodness and reasons, *Australasian Journal of Philosophy* 84 (2006), 525–34.

4. Thomas Aquinas, *Summa Theologiae* I–II, Q. 94, Art. 2; discussion in Germain Grisez, The first principle of practical reason: a commentary on the *Summa Theologiae* 1–2, Q. 94, Art. 2, *American Journal of Jurisprudence* 10 (1965), 168–201.

5. D. O. Brink, Moral realism and the skeptical arguments from disagreement and queerness, *Australasian Journal of Philosophy* 62 (1984), 111–25.

6. Kant, *Groundwork for the Metaphysics of Morals,* 4:428.

7. Stobaeus, *Florilegium,* in Thomas Heath, *A History of Greek Mathematics,* Vol. 1 (Clarendon, Oxford, 1921), 357.

8. David Stove, Why should probability be the guide of life? in D. W. Livingston and D. T. King, eds., *Hume: A Re-evaluation* (Fordham University Press, New York, 1976), 50–68, reprinted in R. McLaughlin, ed., *What?, Where?, When?, Why?* (Reidel, Dordrecht/Boston, 1982), 27–48.

9. Nicholas Wolterstorff, *Justice: Rights and Wrongs* (Princeton University Press, Princeton, 2008), 372.

10. John Mackie, *Ethics: Inventing Right and Wrong* (Harmondsworth, 1977), 23; an Aristotelian version defended in John McDowell, Virtue and reason, *Monist* 62 (1979), 331–50.

11. Survey in Connie S. Rosati, Moral motivation, *Stanford Encyclopedia of Philosophy,* 2006/2016.

12. Michael Smith, *The Moral Problem* (Blackwell, Oxford, 1994), 72–76; Rosati, Moral motivation, Sect. 3.2.

13. The present considerations avoid some of the issues of the amoralist and "internalism" about moral motivation, surveyed in James Lenman, Moral naturalism, *Stanford Encyclopedia of Philosophy,* 2006, https://plato.stanford.edu/entries/naturalism-moral/, Sect. 3.

14. Discussion in Michael Stocker, Desiring the bad, *Journal of Philosophy* 76 (1979), 738–53. Augustine speaks similarly of his younger self stealing pears only to throw them away, *Confessions,* Book 2, Chap. 6.

15. John Milton, *Paradise Lost,* Book 4, line 110.

16. Allen W. Wood, *Kantian Ethics* (Cambridge University Press, Cambridge, 2008), 60.

17. Argued in William K. Frankena, The ethics of respect for persons, *Philosophical Topics* 14 (1986), 149–67.

18. Kant, *Groundwork for the Metaphysics of Morals,* 4:428.

19. Robert Audi, *The Good in the Right: A Theory of Intuition and Intrinsic Value* (Princeton University Press, Princeton, 2004), Chap. 3.

20. Aquinas, *Summa Theologiae* I–II, Q. 94, Art. 2; John Finnis, Aquinas's moral, political, and legal philosophy, *Stanford Encyclopedia of Philosophy,* 2005/2017, Sect. 2.

21. Some attempt in Jove Jim S. Aguas, The notions of the human person and human dignity in Aquinas and Wojtyla, *Kritike* 3(1) (June 2009), 40–60.

22. John Finnis, *Natural Law and Natural Rights,* 2nd ed. (Oxford University Press, Oxford, 2011), 64–69.

23. Mary Wollstonecraft, *A Vindication of the Rights of Women* (1792), Chap. 9.

24. Universal Declaration of Human Rights, Art. 26.

25. Similar from a Kantian perspective in Robert Audi, *Means, Ends and Persons: The Meaning and Psychological Dimensions of Kant's Humanity Formula* (Oxford University Press, Oxford, 2016), 109–14.

26. Lawrence Blum, Iris Murdoch and the domain of the moral, *Philosophical Studies* 50 (1986), 343–67, at 344, based on Iris Murdoch, *The Sovereignty of Good* (Routledge & Kegan Paul, New York, 1970).

27. An attempt to explain in terms of harm in Alan Donagan, The scholastic theory of moral law in the modern world, in A. Kenny, ed., *Aquinas: A Collection of Critical Essays* (Anchor Books, Garden City, NY, 1969), 325–39.

28. C. Korsgaard, What's wrong with lying?, *Philosophical Inquiry: Classic and Contemporary Readings* (Hackett, 2007), www.people.fas.harvard.edu/~korsgaar/CMK.WWLying.pdf; Sissela Bok, *Lying: Moral Choice in Public and Private Life* (Vintage Books, New York, 1999), Chap. 2 relies mainly on consequences.

29. Argued also in Paul Faulkner, Why is lying wrong? *Philosophy and Phenomenological Research* 75 (2007), 535–57.

30. Aristotle, *Nicomachean Ethics*, Book 4, Chap. 7.

31. Aquinas, *Summa Theologiae* II–II, Q. 110, Art. 3; defended in Christopher O. Tollefsen, *Lying and Christian Ethics* (Cambridge University Press, Cambridge, 2014).

32. *Catholic Encyclopedia,* 1907–12, Lying, http://www.newadvent.org/cathen/09469a.htm.

33. Donagan, *The Theory of Morality,* 89.

34. Anthony Cave Brown, *Bodyguard of Lies* (Harper & Row, New York, 1975); Mary K. Barbier, *D-Day Deception: Operation Fortitude and the Normandy invasion* (Praeger Security International, Westport, CT, 2007).

35. Alan D. Sokal et al., *The Sokal Hoax: The Sham That Shook the Academy* (University of Nebraska Press, Lincoln, 2000).

36. Charles Larmore, *Morality and Metaphysics* (Cambridge University Press, Cambridge, 2021), 52.

37. Argued in Christine M. Korsgaard, *The Constitution of Agency: Essays on Practical Reason and Moral Psychology* (Oxford University Press, Oxford, 2008), Chap. 4; Plato's treatment in *Republic* 601d–e and 353a–e is somewhat cruder.

38. Ralph M. McInerny, *Ethica Thomistica: The Moral Philosophy of Thomas Aquinas,* rev. ed. (Catholic University of America Press, Washington DC, 1997), 13.

39. Matthew 25:14–30; Luke 19:12–27.

40. For example, Milton's sonnet "When I Consider How My Light Is Spent."

41. Margaret Thatcher, The moral foundations of society, *Imprimis* 24 (3) (Mar 1995), https://imprimis.hillsdale.edu/the-moral-foundations-of-society/.

42. Lara Denis, *Moral Self-Regard: Duties to Oneself in Kant's Moral Theory* (Routledge, London, 2015).

43. Kant, *Metaphysics of Morals,* 6:441.

44. Robert S. Downie and Elizabeth Telfer, *Respect for Persons* (Allen and Unwin, London, 1971), 76.

45. Iris Murdoch, *The Sovereignty of Good* (Routledge & Kegan Paul, London, 1970), 17–19.

46. F. H. Bradley, *Ethical Studies: Selected Essays* (Bobbs-Merrill, Indianapolis,

1951), Essay II; David Crossley, Francis Herbert Bradley's moral and political philosophy, *Stanford Encyclopedia of Philosophy*, 2011/2017, https://plato.stanford.edu/entries/bradley-moral-political/.

47. Bradley, *Ethical Studies,* 18.

48. Wilhelm von Humboldt, *The Limits of State Action* (1792), Chap. 2, quoted in J. S. Mill, *On Liberty,* Chap. 3.

49. Kant, *Metaphysics of Morals,* 6:422–23.

50. Ibid., 6:427.

51. Garrett Cullity, Demandingness and arguments from presupposition, in T. Chappell, ed., *The Problem of Moral Demandingness: New Philosophical Essays* (Palgrave Macmillan, Basingstoke, 2009), 8–34, Sect. 1.1.

52. As developed in the "principlist" approach to bioethics: Tom L. Beauchamp and James F. Childress, *Principles of Biomedical Ethics,* 5th ed. (Oxford University Press, New York, 2001), 18–21; Tom Tomlinson, Balancing principles in Beauchamp and Childress, Twentieth World Congress of Philosophy, Boston, 1998, https://www.bu.edu/wcp/Papers/Bioe/BioeToml.htm.

53. Kant, Introduction, *Metaphysics of Morals,* Sect. 3 (6:224).

54. Audi, *The Good in the Right,* 156.

55. J.-P. Sartre, Existentialism is a humanism (1946), in S. Priest, ed., *Jean-Paul Sartre: Basic Writings* (Routledge, London, 2001), 33.

56. James Franklin, Accountancy as computational casuistics, *Business and Professional Ethics Journal* 17 (4) (1998), 31–37.

CHAPTER NINE

1. Ronald Dworkin, *Justice for Hedgehogs* (Harvard University Press, Cambridge, MA, 2010), 29.

2. Richard T. Garner, On the genuine queerness of moral properties and facts, *Australasian Journal of Philosophy* 68 (1990), 137–46, at 141.

3. Colin McGinn, *A priori* and *a posteriori* knowledge, *Proceedings of the Aristotelian Society* 76 (1975–6), 195–208.

4. Review in Virginia Slaughter, Theory of mind in infants and young children: a review, *Australian Psychologist* 50 (2015), 169–72.

5. James Franklin, *What Science Knows: And How It Knows It* (Encounter Books, New York, 2009), Chap. 11; the relevance of classical origins in Dilthey and Weber discussed in Austin Harrington, Dilthey, empathy and Verstehen: A contemporary reappraisal, *European Journal of Social Theory* 4 (2001), 311–29.

6. David S. Oderberg, *Applied Ethics: A Non-consequentialist Approach* (Blackwell, Oxford, 2000), 130; he attributes the basic idea to Anthony Kenny.

7. Exodus 22:21.

8. Charles Dickens, *Great Expectations*, Chap. 8.

9. Jean Piaget et al., *The Moral Judgment of the Child* (London: Routledge & Kegan

Paul, 1932); Ronald Duska and Mariellen Whelan, *Moral Development: A Guide to Piaget and Kohlberg* (New York: Paulist Press, 1975); Charles C. Helwig, Children's conceptions of fair government and freedom of speech, *Child Development* 69 (1998), 518–31; Robert L. Campbell and John Chambers Christopher, Moral development theory: a critique of its Kantian presuppositions, *Developmental Review* 16 (1996), 1–47.

10. Jean Piaget et al., *The Moral Judgment of the Child*, trans. M. Gabain (Free Press, New York, 1965), 309–15.

11. Among many studies a classic is Judith G. Smetana, Preschool children's conceptions of moral and social rules, *Child Development* 52 (1981), 1333–36; reviews of later developments in special issue on "Becoming Moral," *Human Development* 61 (nos. 4–5) (2018).

12. Alison Gopnik, *The Philosophical Baby: What Children's Minds Tell Us About Truth, Love & the Meaning of Life* (Bodley Head, London, 2009), 204.

13. For example, Roderick M. Chisholm, Brentano's theory of correct and incorrect emotion, *Revue Internationale de Philosophie* 20 (1966), 395–415; Jonathan J. Sanford, Affective insight: Scheler on feeling and values, *Proceedings of the American Catholic Philosophical Association* 76 (2002), 165–81; in the analytic tradition, Michael Stocker, How emotions reveal value and help cure the schizophrenia of modern ethical theories, in R. Crisp, ed., *How Should One Live? Essays on the Virtues* (Oxford University Press, Oxford, 1996), Chap. 11.

14. Aristotle, *De Anima* 431b21.

15. Raimond Gaita, *Good and Evil: An Absolute Conception* (Basingstoke: Macmillan, 1991), 319.

16. Raimond Gaita, Reflections on the euthanasia debate, *Eureka Street* 5 (10) (Dec 1995), 22–27.

17. Simone Weil, *The Need for Roots* (Routledge & Kegan Paul, London, 1952), 3.

18. Proverbs 9:10.

19. Raimond Gaita, *A Common Humanity: Thinking About Love & Truth & Justice* (Text, Melbourne, 1999), 20–22; discussion in Elizabeth Drummond Young, Defending Gaita's example of saintly behaviour, *Ethical Theory and Moral Practice* 15 (2012), 191–202.

20. Iris Murdoch, *The Sovereignty of Good* (Routledge, Abingdon, 2014), 64.

21. Ibid., 89; discussion in J. David Velleman, Love as a moral emotion, *Ethics* 109 (1999), 338–74.

22. Daniel Velleman, Beyond price, *Ethics* 118 (2008), 191–212.

23. Velleman, Love as a moral emotion, at 366.

24. Dietrich von Hildebrand, *The Nature of Love*, trans. John F. Crosby (St. Augustine Press, South Bend, IN, 2009), 73; discussion in John F. Crosby, Is love a value-response? Dietrich von Hildebrand in dialogue with John Zizioulas, *International Philosophical Quarterly* 55 (2015), 457–70.

25. Shakespeare, Sonnet 116.

26. Joseph Ratzinger, *Principles of Catholic Theology: Building Stones for a Fundamental Theology* (St. Ignatius Press, San Francisco, 1987), 79–80.

27. John Bowlby, *Attachment and Loss*, Vol. 1: *Attachment* (Hogarth Press, London, 1969), review in Monique Wonderly, Early relationships, pathologies of attachment, and the capacity to love, in A. M. Martin, ed., *Routledge Handbook of Love in Philosophy*, (Routledge, New York, 2019), Chap. 2.

28. Charles A. Nelson, Nathan A. Fox, and Charles H. Zeanah, *Romania's Abandoned Children: Deprivation, Brain Development, and the Struggle for Recovery* (Harvard University Press, Cambridge, MA, 2014).

29. Franz Brentano, *The Origin of the Knowledge of Right and Wrong*, trans. Cecil Hague (A. Constable & Co, London, 1902), Sect. 27.

30. Velleman, Love as a moral emotion.

31. Jane Austen, *Pride and Prejudice*, Chap. 3.

32. Ibid., Chap. 36.

33. Discussion in Christel Fricke, The challenges of *Pride and Prejudice*: Adam Smith and Jane Austen on moral education, *Revue Internationale de Philosophie* 269 (2014), 343–72; Alan H. Goldman, Moral development in *Pride and Prejudice*, in G. L. Hagberg, ed., *Fictional Characters, Real Problems: The Search for Ethical Content in Literature* (Oxford University Press, Oxford, 2016), Chap. 13.

34. A similar point made about moral perception in Robert Audi, *Moral Perception* (Princeton University Press, Princeton, 2013), 60–61.

35. Cordelia Fine and Jeanette Kennett, Mental impairment, moral understanding and criminal responsibility: Psychopathy and the purposes of punishment, *International Journal of Law and Psychiatry* 27 (2004), 425–43.

36. Lewis Carroll, *Through the Looking Glass*, Chap. 5.

37. Susan Haack, The justification of deduction, *Mind* 85 (1976), 112–19.

38. James Franklin, *An Aristotelian Realist Philosophy of Mathematics: Mathematics as the Science of Quantity and Structure* (Palgrave Macmillan, Basingstoke, 2014), Chap. 11.

39. Stephen J. Massey, Kant on self-respect, *Journal of the History of Philosophy* 21 (1983), 57–73.

40. Cynthia A. Stark, The rationality of valuing oneself: A critique of Kant on self-respect, *Journal of the History of Philosophy* 35 (1997), 65–82, at 79, based on Charles Landesman, Against respect for persons, *Tulane Studies in Philosophy* 31 (1982), 31–43.

41. Erica A. Holberg, Kant, oppression, and the possibility of nonculpable failures to respect oneself, *Southern Journal of Philosophy* 55 (2017), 285–305.

42. For example, Bessel A. van der Kolk, J. Christopher Perry, and Judith Lewis Herman, Childhood origins of self-destructive behavior, *American Journal of Psychiatry* 148 (1991), 1665–1671; Sarah E. Romans, Judy L. Martin, Jessie C. Anderson, G. Peter Herbison, and Paul E. Mullen, Sexual abuse in childhood and deliberate self-harm, *American Journal of Psychiatry* 152 (1995), 1336–42;

Nan Hua, Catherine L. Taylor, Jianghong Li, and Rebecca A. Glauert, The impact of child maltreatment on the risk of deliberate self-harm among adolescents: A population-wide cohort study using linked administrative records, *Child Abuse & Neglect* 67 (2017), 322–37.

43. Christine Korsgaard, *The Sources of Normativity* (Cambridge University Press, Cambridge, 1996), 121–22; discussion in Robert Stern, Transcendental arguments, *Stanford Encyclopedia of Philosophy* 2019, Sect. 5.

44. C. S. Lewis, *The Screwtape Letters* (Centenary Press, London, 1942), Chaps. 19, 29.

45. Elvin Hatch, *Culture and Morality: The Relativity of Values in Anthropology* (Columbia University Press, New York, 1983); Francis Snare, The empirical bases of moral skepticism, *American Philosophical Quarterly* 21 (1984), 215–35.

46. Gopnik, *Philosophical Baby*, 216–21; review in Talee Ziv and Mahzarin R. Banaji, Representations of social groups in the early years of life, in S. T. Fiske, C. N. Macrae, eds., *The SAGE Handbook of Social Cognition,* (SAGE, Los Angeles, 2012), Chap. 19.

EPILOGUE

1. Mark Murphy, Theological voluntarism, *Stanford Encyclopedia of Philosophy,* 2002/2019.

2. Michael P. Levine, Pantheism, ethics and ecology, *Environmental Values* 3 (1994), 121–138.

3. William Grey, Anthropocentrism and deep ecology, *Australasian Journal of Philosophy* 71 (1993), 463–75; William Mander, Pantheism, *Stanford Encyclopedia of Philosophy,* 2012/2020, Sect. 13.

4. James Franklin, Emergentism as an option in the philosophy of religion: between materialist atheism and pantheism, *Suri: Journal of the Philosophical Association of the Philippines* 7 (2) (2019), 1–22.

5. James Franklin, The global/local distinction vindicates Leibniz's theodicy, *Theology and Science* 20 (4) (2022), forthcoming.

6. David Baggett and Jerry L. Walls, *Good God: The Theistic Foundations of Morality* (Oxford University Press, New York, 2011); C. Stephen Evans, *God and Moral Obligation* (Oxford University Press, Oxford, 2012).

INDEX